let's form
a great partnership —
we can do *wonders*
together!

*Sam Cappellin*

BEST WISHES!

*Randy Tegarden*

# The CERT® Guide to
# Insider Threats

# The CERT® Guide to Insider Threats

*How to Prevent, Detect, and Respond to*
*Information Technology Crimes*
*(Theft, Sabotage, Fraud)*

Dawn Cappelli
Andrew Moore
Randall Trzeciak

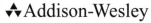
✦ Addison-Wesley

Upper Saddle River, NJ • Boston • Indianapolis • San Francisco
New York • Toronto • Montreal • London • Munich • Paris • Madrid
Capetown • Sydney • Tokyo • Singapore • Mexico City

**Software Engineering Institute** | **Carnegie Mellon**

The SEI Series in Software Engineering

*Cataloging-in-Publication Data is on file with the Library of Congress.*

ISBN-13: 978-0-321-81257-5
ISBN-10:    0-321-81257-3

Text printed in the United States on recycled paper at Courier in Westford, Massachusetts.
First printing, January 2012

*For Fred, Anthony, and Alyssa. You are my life—I love you!*
*—Dawn*

*For those who make my life oh so sweet: Susan, Eric, Susan's amazing family, and my own Mom, Dad, Roger, and Lisa.*
*—Andy*

*For Marianne, Abbie, Nate, and Luke. I am the luckiest person in the world to have such a wonderful family.*
*—Randy*

# Contents

# Preface

A night-shift security guard at a hospital plants **malware**[1] on the hospital's computers. The malware could have brought down the heating, ventilation, and cooling systems and ultimately cost lives. Fortunately, he has posted a video of his crime on YouTube and is caught before carrying out his illicit intent.

A programmer quits his job at a nuclear power plant in the United States and returns to his home country of Iran with simulation software containing schematics and other engineering information for the power plant.

A group of employees at a Department of Motor Vehicles work together to make some extra money by creating driver's licenses for undocumented immigrants and others who could not legally get a license. They are finally arrested after creating a license for an undercover agent who claimed to be on the "No Fly List."

These insider incidents are the types of crimes we will discuss in this book—crimes committed by current or former employees, contractors, or business partners of the victim organization. As you will see, consequences of malicious insider incidents can be substantial, including financial losses, operational impacts, damage to reputation, and harm to individuals. The actions of a single insider have caused damage to organizations ranging from a few lost staff hours to negative publicity and financial damage so extensive that businesses have been forced to lay off employees and even close operations. Furthermore, insider incidents can have repercussions beyond the victim organization, disrupting operations or services critical to a specific sector or creating serious risks to public safety and national security.

---

1. **Malware:** code intended to execute a malicious function; also commonly referred to as **malicious code.** [Note: The first time any word from the Glossary is used in the book it will be printed in boldface.]

We use many actual case examples throughout the book. It is important that you consider each case example by asking yourself the following questions: Could this happen in my organization? Could a night-shift security guard plant malicious code on our computers? Do we have employees, contractors, or business partners who might steal our sensitive information and give it to a competitor or foreign government or organization? Do we have systems that our employees could be paid by outsiders to manipulate?

For most of you, the answer to at least one of those questions will be an unequivocal *yes!* The good news is that after more than ten years of research into these types of crimes, we have developed insights and mitigation strategies that you can put in place in your organization to increase your chances of avoiding or surviving these types of situations.

Insider threats are an intriguing and complex problem. Some assert that they are the most significant threat faced by organizations today. High-profile insider threat cases, such as those conducted by people who stole and passed proprietary and classified information to WikiLeaks, certainly support that assertion, and demonstrate the danger posed by insiders in both government and private industry.[2]

Unfortunately, insider threats cannot be mitigated solely through hardware and software solutions. There is no "silver bullet" for stopping insider threats. Furthermore, malicious insiders go to work every day and bypass both physical and electronic security measures. They have legitimate, authorized access to your most confidential, valuable information and systems, and they can use that legitimate access to perform criminal activity. You have to trust them; it is not practical to watch everything each of your employees does every day. The key to successfully mitigating these threats is to turn those advantages for the malicious insiders into advantages for you. This book will help you to do just that.

In 2001, shortly before September 11, the Secret Service sponsored the Insider Threat Study, a joint project conducted by the Secret Service and the Software Engineering Institute CERT Program at Carnegie Mellon University. We never dreamed when we started that study that it would have such far-reaching impacts, and that we would become so passionate about the subject that we would end up devoting more than a decade (to date!) of our careers to the problem.

---

2. For information regarding the WikiLeaks insider threat cases, see http://en.wikipedia.org/wiki/Wikileaks.

When we started our work on the insider threat problem, very little was known about insider attacks: Who commits them, why do they do it, when and where do they do it, and how do they set up and carry out their crimes? After delving deep into the issue, we are happy to say that we now know the answers to those questions. In addition, we have come a long way in designing mitigation strategies for preventing, detecting, and responding to those threats.

We have the largest collection of detailed insider threat case files that we know of in the world. At the time of this publication, we had more than 700 cases, and that number grows weekly. We've had the opportunity to interview many of the victims of these crimes, giving us a unique chance to find out from supervisors and coworkers how the insider behaved at work, what precipitating events occurred, what technical controls were in place at the time, what policies and procedures were in place but not followed, and so on. We've also had the unique opportunity to actually interview convicted insiders and ask them probing questions about what made them do it, what might have made them change their mind, and what technical measures should have been in place to prevent this from happening.

We have a comprehensive database—the CERT insider threat database— where we track the technical, behavioral, and organizational details of every crime. We have combined our technical expertise in the CERT Insider Threat Center with psychological expertise from federal law enforcement, the U.S. Department of Defense (DOD), and our own independent consultants to ensure that we consider the "big picture" of the problem, not just the technical details. We have created "crime models" or "crime profiles" that describe the patterns in the crimes so that you can recognize an escalating insider threat problem in your own organization. We have created an insider threat lab where we are developing new technical solutions based on our models. We created an insider threat vulnerability assessment based on all of the cases in the CERT database so that you can learn from past mistakes and not suffer the same consequences as previous victim organizations. We publish best practices for mitigating insider threats, hold workshops, and conduct technical exercises for incident responders. Finally, we continue to collect new cases of malicious insider compromises to track the changing face of the threat.

We have been publishing our work for the past ten years; now we've decided that for the tenth anniversary of the start of our work, it is appropriate to pull all of our most current information into a book. This book provides a comprehensive reference for our entire body of knowledge on insider threats.

## Scope of the Book: What Is and Is Not Included

Let's begin by defining what we mean by **malicious insider threats:**

> A malicious insider threat is a current or former employee, contractor, or business partner who has or had authorized access to an organization's network, system, or data and intentionally exceeded or misused that access in a manner that negatively affected the confidentiality, integrity, or availability of the organization's information or information systems.

There are a few important items to note. First of all, malicious insider threats are not only employees.[3] We chose to include contractors in our definition because contractors often are granted authorized access to their clients' information, systems, and networks, and the nontechnical controls for contractors are often much more lax than for employees. Interestingly, we did not include business partners in our original definition of insider threats in 2001. However, over time we found that more and more crimes involved not employees or contractors, but trusted business partners who had authorized access to the organization's systems, networks, or information. We encountered cases involving outsourcing, offshoring, and, more recently, cloud computing. These cases raise complex insider threat risks that should not be overlooked; therefore, we decided to add business partners to our definition.

Second, note that malicious insider attacks do not only come from current employees. In fact, one particular type of crime, insider IT sabotage, is more often committed by former employees than current employees.

Now that we have explained *whom* we will discuss in the book, let's focus on what types of crimes we will examine. Before we describe the types of crimes, it is important that you understand why we categorized them the way we have. Much of the success in our work is due to the identification of patterns found in the insider threat cases. These patterns describe the "story" behind the cases. Who commits these crimes? Why? Are there signs that they might commit a crime beforehand, so-called observable behaviors, in the workplace? When do they do it, where, and do they do it alone or with others?

The important thing to remember is that the patterns are different for each type of crime. There is not one single pattern for insider threats in general.

---

3. Henceforth, for simplicity, reference to insider threats specifically means malicious insider threats unless otherwise specified.

Instead, we have identified three models, or profiles, for insider threats. Those three types of crimes are as follows.

- **IT sabotage:** An insider's use of information technology (IT) to direct specific harm at an organization or an individual.
- **Theft of intellectual property (IP):** An insider's use of IT to steal intellectual property from the organization. This category includes industrial espionage involving insiders.
- **Fraud:** An insider's use of IT for the unauthorized modification, addition, or deletion of an organization's data (not programs or systems) for personal gain, or theft of information that leads to an identity crime (e.g., identity theft, credit card fraud).

Note that this book does not specifically describe **national security espionage** crimes: the act of obtaining, delivering, transmitting, communicating, or receiving information about the national defense with an intent, or reason to believe, that the information may be used to the injury of the United States or to the advantage of any foreign nation. Espionage is a violation of 18 United States Code sections 792–798 and Article 106, Uniform Code of Military Justice.[4] The CERT Insider Threat Center does work in that area, but that research is only available to a limited audience. However, there are many similarities between national security espionage and all three types of crimes: fraud, theft of intellectual property, and IT sabotage. Therefore, we believe there are many lessons to be learned from these insider incidents that can be applied to national security espionage as well.

In addition, this book deals primarily with *malicious* insider threats. We certainly recognize the importance of **unintentional insider threats**— insiders who accidentally affect the confidentiality, availability, or integrity of an organization's information or information systems, possibly by being tricked by an outsider's use of social engineering. However, we only recently began researching those types of threats; intentional attacks have kept us extremely busy for the past ten years! In addition, we believe that many of the mitigation strategies we advocate for malicious insiders could also be effective against unintentional incidents, as well as those perpetrated by outsiders. And finally, it is difficult to gather information regarding unintentional insider threats; because no crime was committed, organizations tend to handle these incidents quietly, internal to the organization, if possible.

---

4. Dictionary of Military and Associated Terms. U.S. Department of Defense, 2005.

Finally, we use many case examples from the CERT database throughout the book. Some of the examples go into greater detail than others; we include only the details that serve to illustrate the point we are making in that part in the book. We also have included a large collection of case examples in Chapter 8, as we believe these will be of great interest to many of you. Again, we stress that you should use that chapter to examine your organization and decide if you need to take any proactive measures to ensure that you do not fall victim to the same types of incidents.

As a matter of policy, we never identify the organizations or insiders involved in our case examples. Some, however, may be apparent to readers, inasmuch as they are drawn from public records, including court documents and newspaper accounts. For examples not in the public domain, we have further masked the targeted organizations to shield their identities.

## Intended Audience

A common misconception is that insider threat risk management is the responsibility of IT and information security staff members alone. Unfortunately, that is one of the biggest reasons that insider attacks continue to occur, repeating the same patterns we have observed in cases since 1996, the earliest cases in the CERT database. IT and information security personnel will benefit from reading this book, as we will suggest new technical controls you can implement using technology you are already using in the workplace. In addition, this book can be used by technical staffs to motivate other stakeholders within their organization, since IT and information security cannot successfully implement an effective insider threat mitigation strategy on their own.

We wrote this book with a diverse audience in mind. The ideal audience includes top management, as their support will be needed to implement the organization-wide insider threat policies, procedures, and technologies we recommend. It is important that *all* managers understand the patterns they need to recognize in their employees, and to advocate up the management chain for support for an insider threat program.

For the same reasons, government leaders will benefit from this book, since they need to support the government-wide insider threat policies, procedures, and technologies we recommend.

Human resources personnel need to understand this book, as they are often the only ones who are aware of indicators of potential increased risk of insider threats in individual employees. Other staff members who should understand this information include security, software engineering, and physical security personnel, as well as data owners. It is also essential to include your general counsel in any discussions about implementing technical and nontechnical controls to combat the insider threat, to ensure compliance with federal, state, and local laws.

In summary, an effective insider threat program requires understanding, collaboration, and buy-in from across your organization.

## Reader Benefits

After reading this book you will realize that the insider threat is real and the consequences of malicious insider activities can be extremely damaging. Real-life case studies will drive home the point that "this could happen to me." Many organizations focus their technical defenses against outsiders attempting to gain unauthorized access. This book emphasizes the need to balance defense against outsider threats with defense against insider threats, understanding that insider attacks can be more damaging than outsider attacks.

After reading this book you also will be able to recognize the high-level patterns in the three primary types of insider threats: IT sabotage, theft of intellectual property, and fraud. In addition, you will understand the details of how insiders commit those crimes. We present concrete defensive countermeasures that will help you to defend against insider attacks. You can compare your own defensive strategies to the controls we propose and determine whether your existing controls are sufficient to prevent, detect, and respond to insider attacks like those presented throughout the book. Once you identify gaps in your defensive posture, you can implement countermeasures we propose to fill those gaps.

## Structure of the Book: Recommendations to Readers

We begin the book in Chapter 1, Overview, by describing the insider threat problem, and raise awareness to the complexity of the problem—tangential issues such as insider threats from trusted business partners, malicious insiders with ties to the Internet underground, and programming techniques used as an insider attack tool. Next, we provide a breakdown of the crimes in the CERT database, followed by an overview of the CERT Insider Threat Center. Because our crime "profiles" or "models" have had such an impact on the understanding of insider threats, we also provide a short section describing why those models are so important. We end with a brief timeline of the evolution of our body of work in the CERT Insider Threat Center.

It is important that you read the first chapter so that you understand the concepts and terminology used throughout the remainder of the book. After that, you can use the book in various ways. If the first chapter has been an eye-opener for you and you are interested in gaining a comprehensive understanding of insider threats, continue reading the book from beginning to end. However, it is not necessary to read the book in that manner; it is designed such that Chapters 2 through 9 and the appendices can be used as stand-alone references.

Chapters 2, 3, and 4 are devoted to the three types of insider threats: insider IT sabotage, theft of intellectual property, and fraud. In each chapter we describe who commits the crime so that you know which positions within your organization pose that particular type of threat. We describe the patterns in how each type of crime evolves over time: What motivates the insider, what behavioral indicators are prevalent, how do they set up and carry out the crime, when do they do it, whether others are involved, and so on. We also suggest mitigation strategies throughout each chapter.

We recommend that everyone reads Chapter 2, Insider IT Sabotage, as that crime has occurred in organizations in every critical infrastructure sector.

Most organizations have some type of intellectual property that must be protected: strategic or business plans, engineering or scientific information, source code, and so on. Therefore, it is important that you read Chapter 3, Insider Theft of Intellectual Property, so that you fully understand who inside your organization poses a threat to that information.

Chapter 4, Insider Fraud, is applicable to you if you have information or systems that your employees could use to make extra money on the side. Credit card information and Personally Identifiable Information (PII) such as Social Security numbers are valuable for committing various types of fraud. However, it is also important that you also consider threats posed by insiders modifying information for financial gain. Do you have systems that outsiders would be willing to pay your employees to manipulate? Or do you have systems that your employees could illicitly use for personal financial gain, perhaps by colluding with other employees? If so, Chapter 4 is applicable to you. Note that Chapter 4 also describes the insider threats in the CERT database involving organized crime, as all of those crimes were fraud.

Chapter 5, Insider Threat Issues in the Software Development Life Cycle, explores said issues. The **Software Development Life Cycle** (SDLC) is synonymous with "software process" as well as "software engineering"; it is a structured methodology used in the development of software products and packages. This methodology is used from the conception phase to the delivery and end of life of a final software product.[5] We explore each phase of the SDLC and the types of insider threats that need to be considered at each phase. In addition, we describe how oversights at various phases have resulted in system vulnerabilities that have enabled insider threats to be carried out later by others, often by end users of the system. If your organization develops software, you should carefully consider the lessons learned in this chapter. It should make you look differently at the entire SDLC: from how to consider potential insider threats in the requirements and design phases, to potential threats posed by developers in the implementation and maintenance phases.

If you are looking for information on mitigation strategies, go to Chapters 6 and 7. You can use Chapter 6, Best Practices for the Prevention and Detection of Insider Threats, to compare best practices for prevention and detection of insider threats to your organization's practices. Many of the best practices were described in previous chapters, but Chapter 6 summarizes all of the suggestions in a stand-alone reference. This chapter is based on our "Common Sense Guide to Prevention and Detection of Insider Threats," for years one of the top downloads on the entire CERT Web site.

If you are in a technical security role and would like more detailed information on new controls you can implement, you should read Chapter 7, Technical Insider Threat Controls. This chapter describes the technical solutions we have developed in the CERT insider threat lab. These technical solutions are based on technologies that you most likely are already using for technical security. We provide new signatures, rules, and configurations for using them for more effective detection of insider threats.

---

5. Whatis.com

Chapter 8, Case Examples, contains a collection of case examples from the CERT database. We provide a summary table at the beginning of the chapter so that you can reference specific cases by type of crime, sector of the organization, and brief summary of the crime. Many people have requested this type of information from us over the years, so we believe this will provide enormous value to many of you. We highly recommend that you review these cases and consider your vulnerability to the same type of malicious actions within your organization. Chapter 8 is also of value to researchers who might want to use case examples for their own research.

Chapter 9, Conclusion and Miscellaneous Issues, contains a final collection of miscellaneous information that didn't fit anywhere else in the book. For example, we provide an analysis of insiders with connections to the Internet underground. We also provide details on insiders who attacked not their own organization, but trusted business partners that had a formal relationship with their employer.

After the chapters, we provide a series of appendices.

Appendix A, Insider Threat Center Products and Services, contains information on products and services provided by the CERT Insider Threat Center, including insider threat assessments, workshops, online exercises, and technical controls. We also discuss sponsored research opportunities for the Insider Threat Center. If you are extremely concerned about insider threats and want immediate assistance from the CERT Program, be sure to read this appendix.

Appendix B, Deeper Dive into the Data, contains interesting data mined from the CERT database.

Appendix C, CyberSecurity Watch Survey, contains data collected from the CyberSecurity Watch Survey, an annual survey we conduct in conjunction with *CSO* Magazine and the Secret Service.[6]

Appendix D, Insider Threat Database Structure, contains the database structure for the CERT database. If you are interested in exactly what kind of data we track for each case, you should read this appendix. Also, we frequently respond to queries to mine the CERT database for interesting data—if you see a field or fields you would like us to explore with you, please contact us. We can be reached via email at insider-threat-feedback@cert.org.

Appendix E, Insider Threat Training Simulation: MERIT *InterActive*, contains detailed information about an interactive virtual simulation we

---

6. Note that in some years Deloitte and Microsoft also participated in the survey.

developed for insider threat training. It is basically a prototype of a video game for insider threat training. What do you need for a successful video game? Good guys playing against the bad guys, complex plots, interesting characters—that's insider threat! We didn't want to distract you with that information in the body of the book, but some of you might find it interesting, so we included it in this appendix. In addition, if you are interested in new and innovative training methods, this appendix should be of interest.

Appendix F, System Dynamics Background, provides background information on **system dynamics**.[7] We provide brief references to system dynamics throughout the book, but it is not necessary that you understand system dynamics when you read the book. Nonetheless, we wanted to provide more in-depth information for those of you who wish to learn more.

Finally, the book concludes with references, a glossary, and a complete index.

Note that the accompanying Web site, www.cert.org/insider_threat, contains our system dynamics models for use by other researchers. It is also updated regularly with new insider threat controls, best practices, and case examples.

In summary, the book is intended to be a reference for many different types of readers. It contains the entire CERT Insider Threat Center body of knowledge on insider threats, and therefore can be used as a reference for raising awareness, informing your risk management processes, designing and implementing new technical and nontechnical controls, and much more.

## About the CERT Program

The CERT Program is part of the Software Engineering Institute (SEI), a federally funded research and development center at Carnegie Mellon University in Pittsburgh. Following the Morris worm incident, which brought 10% of Internet systems to a halt in November 1988, the Defense Advanced Research Projects Agency (DARPA) charged the SEI with setting up a center to coordinate communication among experts during security emergencies and to help prevent future incidents. This center was named the CERT Coordination Center (CERT/CC).

---

7. "System dynamics is a computer-aided approach to policy analysis and design. It applies to dynamic problems arising in complex social, managerial, economic, or ecological systems—literally any dynamic systems characterized by interdependence, mutual interaction, information feedback, and circular causality" (www.systemdynamics.org/what_is_system_dynamics.html).

While we continue to respond to major security incidents and analyze product vulnerabilities, our role has expanded over the years. Along with the rapid increase in the size of the Internet and its use for critical functions, there have been progressive changes in intrusion techniques, increased amounts of damage, increased difficulty of detecting an attack, and increased difficulty of catching the attackers. To better manage these changes, the CERT/CC is now part of the larger CERT Program, which develops and promotes the use of appropriate technology and systems management practices to resist attacks on networked systems, to limit damage, and to ensure continuity of critical services.

## The CERT Insider Threat Center

The objective of the CERT Insider Threat Center is to assist organizations in preventing, detecting, and responding to insider compromises. We have been researching this problem since 2001 in partnership with the DOD, the U.S. Department of Homeland Security (DHS), other federal agencies, federal law enforcement, the intelligence community, private industry, academia, and the vendor community. The foundation of our work is the CERT database of more than 700 insider threat cases. We use system dynamics modeling to characterize the nature of the insider threat problem, explore dynamic indicators of insider threat risk, and identify and experiment with administrative and technical controls for insider threat mitigation. The CERT insider threat lab provides a foundation to identify, tune, and package technical controls as an extension of our modeling efforts. We have developed an assessment framework based on the fraud, theft of intellectual property, and IT sabotage case data that we have used to assist organizations in identifying their technical and nontechnical vulnerabilities to insider threats, as well as executable countermeasures. The CERT Insider Threat Center is uniquely positioned as a trusted broker to assist the community in the short term, and through our ongoing research.

Dawn Cappelli and Andy Moore have been working on CERT insider threat research since 2001, and Randy Trzeciak joined the team in 2006. Dawn is the technical manager of the CERT Insider Threat Center, Andy is the lead researcher, and Randy is the technical lead for insider threat research. Although our insider threat team has now grown into an official Insider Threat Center, for many years the CERT Program's insider threat team consisted of Andy, Randy, and Dawn, which is why we decided to team up and capture our history in this book.

# Summary

The purpose of this book is to raise awareness of the insider threat issue from the ground up: staff members in IT, information security, and human resources; data owners; and physical security, software engineering, legal, and other security personnel. We strongly believe after studying this problem for more than a decade that in order to effectively mitigate insider threats it takes common understanding, support, and communication from all of those people across the organization. In addition, buy-in is needed from upper management, as they will need to support the cross-organizational communication required to formulate an effective mitigation strategy. And finally, it requires awareness and consideration by government leaders, as some of the issues are even larger than individual organizations. Employee privacy issues and mergers and acquisitions with organizations outside the United States are two such examples.

This book covers our extensive work in studying insider IT sabotage, theft of intellectual property, and fraud. Although it does not deal explicitly with insiders who committed national security espionage, many of the lessons in this book are directly applicable to that domain as well.

Most of the book can be read and easily understood by technical and non-technical readers alike. The only exception is Chapter 7. If you are not a "technical" person you are best off skipping this chapter. However, we strongly suggest you lend the book to your technical security staff so that they can consider implementing these controls.

Now that you understand the purpose of the book and its contents, we will begin to dig a little deeper into each type of insider crime, our modeling of insider threats, and the CERT Insider Threat Center in Chapter 1. We recommend that you read that chapter next so that you understand the basic concepts. After completing Chapter 1 you will have the foundation you need so that you can explore the rest of the book in any order you wish!

# Acknowledgments

We would like to start by thanking our amazing team at the CERT Insider Threat Center. This book represents the hard work of many brilliant people. First, thank you to our current team in the Insider Threat Center, listed here in the order in which they joined the team: Adam Cummings, Mike Hanley, Derrick Spooner, Chris King, Joji Montelibano, Cindy Nesta, Josh Burns, George Silowash, and Dr. Bill Claycomb. And a special thank you to Tara Sparacino and Cindy Walpole, who helped us to keep our heads above water at work while we wrote this book in our "spare time." The CERT Insider Threat Center is part of the Enterprise Threat and Vulnerability Management (ETVM) team in the CERT Program. The ETVM team is a very tight-knit group, and we would be remiss if we did not acknowledge these awesome, dedicated technical security experts, again listed in the order in which they started on the team: Georgia Killcrece (retired, but sorely missed!), Robin Ruefle, Mark Zajicek, David Mundie, Becky Cooper, Charlie Ryan, Russ Griffin, Sandi Behrens, Alex Nicoll, Sam Perl, and Kristi Keeler.

Thank you to the current and former CMU/SEI/CERT staff members who have participated in our insider threat work over the years: Chris Bateman, Sally Cunningham, Casey Dunlevy, Rob Floodeen, Carly Huth, Dr. Joseph ("Jay") Kadane, Greg Longo, David McIntire, David Mundie, Dr. Dan Phelps, Stephanie Rogers, Dr. Greg Shannon, Dr. Tim Shimeall, Rhiannon Weaver, Pam Williams, Bradford Willke, and Mark Zajicek. And a special thank you to Dr. Tom Longstaff, who was the CERT technical manager for the original Insider Threat Study, and worked on the CERT Program's original insider threat collaboration with the U.S. Department of Defense (DOD) Personnel Security Research Center.

Thank you to the many fabulous graduate students who have worked on our insider threat projects throughout the years, starting with our two current students: Todd Lewellen, Lynda Pillage, Jen Stanley, Chase Midler, Andrew Santell, Luke Hogan, Jaime Tupino, Tyler Dean, Will Schroeder,

Matt Houy, Bob Weiland, Devon Rollins, Tom Caron, John Wyrick, Christopher Nguyen, Hannah Joseph, and Akash Desai. Many of those students were from the Scholarship for Service Program—we commend the U.S. federal government for this program, which produces the most outstanding talent in the cybersecurity field.

A special thank you to Dr. Eric Shaw, who has been a Visiting Scientist in the CERT Program and a clinical psychologist at Consulting & Clinical Psychology, Ltd. Eric has been the guiding force in the psychological aspects of our research since the conclusion of our first Insider Threat Study with the Secret Service National Threat Assessment Center.

Thank you to Noopur Davis, Claude Williams, and Dr. Marvine Hamner, who worked for us as visiting scientists.

Thank you to the CERT Program's director, Rich Pethia, and deputy director, Bill Wilson, who have given us the autonomy and authority over the past decade to take our research in so many exciting directions. Thank you to our retired boss, Dr. Barbara Laswell, who helped us evolve from the Insider Threat Team of three people into the CERT Insider Threat Center. Thank you to SEI Director Dr. Paul Neilson and Deputy Director Clyde Chittister, for their support and recognition. We're extremely grateful to Terry Roberts for the visibility she has brought to our work. And thank you to Dr. Angel Jordan, former provost of Carnegie Mellon University, who has been an advocate for our work over the years.

We would like to thank the Secret Service, our original partner in this quest to understand and help organizations protect themselves from malicious insider attacks. Thank you to National Threat Assessment Center (NTAC) staff members who participated on the project, especially research coordinator Dr. Marisa Reddy Randazzo, who founded and directed the Insider Threat Study within NTAC; Dr. Michelle Keeney, who took over when Marisa left; Eileen Kowalski, who was the lynchpin throughout the project; and Matt Doherty, the Special Agent in Charge of NTAC. Also, thank you to Jim Savage, the sponsor of our original work with the Secret Service. Finally, a big thank you to our Secret Service liaisons for the Insider Threat Study, who moved to Pittsburgh and joined the CERT Program for a few years: Cornelius Tate, Dave Iacovetti, and Wayne Peterson. What great times we had in those good old days! And thank you to our current Secret Service liaisons, Tom Dover and Ryan Moore.

A special thank you to Dr. Douglas Maughan and the DHS Science and Technology (S&T) Directorate, who took over funding of the original CERT/Secret Service Insider Threat Study shortly after DHS was formed.

We're especially excited that Doug came back to us last year and told us he wanted to get the old team back together—and funded our current study of insider threats in the financial sector. In addition, we're receiving assistance on that project from the Secret Service, U.S. Department of the Treasury, and the financial sector. Thank you to Brian Peretti, who was in the very first financial sector review of our work for the original study, and is now back on the team in our current fraud project. And thank you to Ed Cabrera and Trae McAbee from the Secret Service—we could not possibly succeed in the current study without all of your hard work in gathering all of the case files and scheduling the interviews. Thank you to Pablo Martinez for being a strong supporter of our work, starting back in the original study, and continuing today.

Thank you to the Army Research Office and Carnegie Mellon CyLab, especially Dr. Pradeep Khosla, Dr. Virgil Gligor, Dr. Adrian Perrig, Richard Power, Gene Hambrick, and Dr. Don McGillen, who provided seed funding for many of our insider threat projects that have grown into full bodies of work. Your support sustained the insider threat database for years, enabled us to experiment with our modeling work, provided the infrastructure for the insider threat lab, and funded one of our most "fun" projects: our insider threat "video game."

We are especially grateful to our current sponsors at the U.S. DHS Federal Network Security (FNS) branch, Matt Coos and Don Benack, as well as the project leads, Rob Karas, Sean McAfee, and Will Harmon. Don and Matt had the vision to step up to the plate three years ago and fund our work "for the good of all." They realized the importance of our work and were willing to fund it before insider threats became a top-priority issue in the current cybersecurity environment. Thanks to their foresight, we can offer technical controls, assessments, and training to the community. We're excited about the opportunity to continue to make an impact together!

We are also thankful to our sponsors and collaborators in the DOD and intelligence community: Dr. Deborah Loftis, Laura Sellers, Dr. Stephen R. Band, Dr. Aaron J. Ferguson, Dr. Lynn Fischer, Dr. Howard Timm, Dr. Katherine Herbig, Dr. Ron Dodge, and Dr. Kirk Kennedy. Their expertise and experience have enabled a much richer treatment of the insider threat problem than would have otherwise been possible.

Our work in the system dynamics modeling of insider threats began and continues to be influenced by the Security Dynamics Network (SDN), a largely unfunded and loosely coordinated group of national laboratories and universities applying system dynamics to explore issues of cybersecurity. In the past, the group has focused on malicious insider threats and has been a source of expertise, information, and inspiration for the insider threat models developed in this book. We are very thankful to the members of the SDN, especially its founder, Dr. Jose Gonzalez of Agder University College; Dr. David Andersen and Dr. Eliot Rich of the University at Albany; Dr. Ignacio Martinez-Moyano of Argonne National Laboratory; Dr. Stephen Conrad of Sandia National Laboratories; and Dr. Jose Maria Sarriegui of the University of Navarra. A special thank you goes to Dr. Elise Weaver of the Human Resources Research Organization, who worked with us as a Visiting Scientist at the CERT Program and assisted us in our very first system dynamics modeling efforts.

We would also like to thank all of the SEI business development staff members who have helped us with our insider threat work over the years: Jan Philpot, Mike Greenwood, Joe McLeod, Frank Redner, David Ulicne, Bob Rosenstein, Greg Such, Dave Scherb, and Angela Llamas-Butler. Thank you to Summer Fowler and Lisa Marino, who have helped us with project management activities that have become increasingly complex over the years, and Michele Tomasic, who has helped us with so many things over the years. Thank you to Bill Shore and everyone in the SEI Security Office, and Dave Thompson and everyone in SEI IT, especially Jerry Czerwinski and Craig Lewis; and thank you to Linda Pesante and her staff, especially Ed Desautels and Paul Ruggerio, who have helped us with editing and technical writing over the years. Also, thank you to David Biber for the wonderful graphics he has created for us over the years, including nice crisp images for this book!

Finally, we would like to thank Dr. Don Marinelli, cofounder of Carnegie Mellon's Entertainment Technology Center (ETC), and the ETC faculty and students who worked with us to create the first video game for insider threat training. Semester 1: faculty advisors Dr. Scott Stevens and Jessica Trybus; student team Ankur Ahlawat, Chris Daniel, Aditya Dave, and Todd Waits; and visiting scholars Soo Jeoung Kim and Michelle Macau. Semester 2: faculty advisors Dr. Scott Stevens and Dr. Ralph Vituccio; and student team Stephen Calender, Julie Charles, Evan Miller, and Todd Waits. We still hope to interest a sponsor in turning that prototype into an operational system someday!

If we forgot someone who has helped us throughout the years, we apologize profusely! We tried hard to include everyone, but if we overlooked you, please let us know.

**From Dawn:** Thank you to my wonderful husband and soul mate, Fred—you've been inspiring me for 35 years and without you I can't imagine where I would be! To my daughter and best girlfriend, Alyssa—I treasure all of our fun times together. To my son, Anthony—you are truly the happiest person I know! Thanks to my sister, Cindy, who has always been there for me. And finally, thank you to the greatest parents in the world—whom I miss terribly. Your faith and encouragement made me what I am today.

Thank you to Andy and Randy—how exciting to accomplish this together after all of those years as team "Andy, Randy, and Dawn!"

**From Andy:** My heartfelt thanks go, most of all, to my beautiful wife, Susan, for sharing our life adventure. Coming home to you each day is the best thing in my life! And thanks to my incredible son, Eric, who put up with my having my nose in a laptop during many early morning hours. Your achievements continue to amaze me and your love and friendship enrich our lives immeasurably. Finally, thanks to Dawn and Randy's steadfast dedication and friendship. It is hard to believe how far we've come in the ten years since it all started.

**From Randy:** Thank you, Marianne, for being my wife and best friend! You are truly a blessing to me, to our family, and to all the other lives you touch. To my daughter, Abbie, you are an amazing, intelligent, and strong young lady. To Nate the Great, always keep those around you laughing. To Luke, thank you for making every day fun. Thank you to my parents for all of the hard work and sacrifices you made over the years!

Finally, thank you to Dawn and Andy for bringing me into the circle of trust. It is truly a pleasure working with both of you!

# Chapter 1

# Overview

Insiders pose a substantial threat due to their knowledge of and access to their employers' systems and/or information. They bypass physical and electronic security measures through legitimate means every day. There is no demographic profile of a malicious insider—they are men and women, married and single, young and old, and cover a range of ethnicities. However, we have identified some distinct characteristics of insiders and their crimes, which can be used in designing mitigation strategies.

Insider IT sabotage is typically committed by technical users with privileged access, such as system administrators, database administrators, and programmers. The motivation in these crimes is usually revenge for a negative workplace event, and the crimes are often set up while still employed, but executed following termination.

Insider theft of intellectual property (IP) is usually committed by scientists, engineers, programmers, and salespeople. These insiders usually steal the information they worked on, and take it with them as they leave the organization to start their own business, take with them to a new job, or give to a foreign government or organization.

Insider fraud is usually committed by lower-level employees such as help desk, customer service, and data entry clerks. The crimes are motivated by financial need or greed, and they typically continue for a long period of time. Many of these insiders are recruited by outsiders to steal information. Collusion with other insiders is very common in crimes involving modification of information for payment from the outside.

In this chapter, we begin with true stories of insider attacks, which will help you to understand the different types of insider crimes as well as the potential consequences. We believe that the more actual cases you read, the more you will come to understand the patterns in the cases.

Next, we point out the expanding complexity of insider threats. Although we have broken the problem into three distinct crime profiles, and most incidents resemble those profiles, there are some complex issues that we must point out so you understand the scope of the problem. In this chapter we simply want to raise the issues so that you keep them in mind as you read the rest of the book. In Chapter 9, Conclusion and Miscellaneous Issues, we provide more detail on each of these issues.

The next section contains a breakdown of the cases in our insider threat database. Our database of more than 700 insider threat cases provides an unmatched wealth of information that can be useful to all of you in understanding insider threats and in designing mitigation strategies. If you are interested in additional details from our database, refer to Appendix B, Deeper Dive into the Data. In addition, Appendix C, CyberSecurity Watch Survey, contains detailed findings from the Cyber-Security Watch Survey, which we conduct annually with the Secret Service and *CSO* Magazine.[1]

Next, we explain the importance of our crime profiles and associated crime models. Over the years, we have heard that the first impression of some practitioners is that they are not interested in "academic models." The good news is that, although in some cases we started with complex academic models, we have translated them into straightforward, practical teaching tools that have raised awareness and resulted in successful mitigation strategies for practitioners for years. Those high-level models are the ones we use in this book.

We end this chapter with a brief description of the objective and work of the CERT Insider Threat Center. If you don't care where material in this book came from, you certainly can skip the end of this chapter and go on to Chapter 2, Insider IT Sabotage. However, some of you might feel better with a brief glimpse of the history of our research so that you deem the advice we give in the book to be trustworthy. We provide a brief timeline of the development of the Insider Threat Center in this chapter.

---

1. Note that in some years Deloitte and Microsoft also participated in the survey.

# True Stories of Insider Attacks

We have found over the years that true stories of insider attacks can be extremely valuable in raising awareness and in pointing out new areas of concern that must be considered in designing a mitigation strategy. Many members of the CERT Insider Threat Center have contributed to creating these case summaries as part of documenting cases in the database based on a wide variety of public records and media reports. We are thankful to everyone who helped elaborate on insider threat cases as a basis from which to learn.

In this section we use these stories to reinforce for you the breakdown of insider threats into three types of crimes: fraud, theft of IP, and sabotage. Therefore, we will start this chapter with one real-life example of each type of insider crime.

Many people also find these case examples to be very valuable tools in grabbing the attention of upper management and gaining support for an insider threat mitigation strategy. If you would like to peruse more case examples, see Chapter 8, Case Examples.

## Insider IT Sabotage

Recall that insider IT sabotage crimes are those in which an insider uses IT to direct specific harm at an organization or an individual. For example, insiders in these attacks have deleted critical information, brought down systems, and defaced Web sites to embarrass the organization. As you will see in the following example, however, these attacks are frequently not that straightforward.

> A network administrator who designed and created the network for a major U.S. city was not just the only person who fully understood the network, but also the only person who had the administrative passwords for the network devices. After being reprimanded for poor performance and for threatening a coworker, he was reassigned to a different job. He refused to provide the passwords to his replacement, however, and was subsequently terminated, then arrested. The city was unable to access the network devices for 12 days, although during that time, fortunately the infrastructure continued to function normally and such access was not necessary. It was also discovered during that period of time that he had installed rogue access points in wiring closets, and had programmed the network devices to fail if anyone attempted to reset them without the administrative passwords. Although he was imprisoned, he refused to

provide the passwords to anyone except the city's mayor, claiming that his behavior followed standard network security practices. After a 12-day standoff in which the case received significant media attention, the mayor visited him in prison and obtained the passwords.

This case may be familiar to some of you as it received significant media attention, and was extremely intriguing to technical security experts. Experts from the vendors of the network devices worked with city officials to attempt to formulate a solution to this problem. In the end, however, the best solution they could come up with was a personal visit to the perpetrator in jail by the city's mayor.

We have other cases similar to this in our database that occurred in smaller organizations. Previously, those types of cases were dismissed by technical security experts as not possible in larger organizations because they tend to have mature security practices. This case made many experts reconsider their security practices to ensure that this type of scenario couldn't happen to them! Specifically, this case drives home the point that any infrastructure should not have a single point of failure, whether that is a device or a human being.

## Insider Fraud

Insider fraud cases are those in which an insider uses IT for the unauthorized modification, addition, or deletion of an organization's data (not programs or systems) for personal gain, or theft of information, which leads to an identity crime (e.g., identity theft, credit card fraud). Examples of insider fraud crimes include

- Theft and sale of confidential information such as Social Security numbers or credit card numbers
- Modification of critical data in return for payment; for example, driver's license records, criminal records, or welfare status
- Stealing of money; for example, in financial institutions or government organizations

As you will see in the following example, however, not all cases are quite that clear-cut.

A manufacturer of computer networking products found that it had to issue recall notices to its customers for various products. In order to better serve its government customers, it offered to ship replacement products to them immediately upon request, and the defective parts could be returned later. The company had outsourced its help desk operations to another company. One of the help desk operators needed money to care for his elderly parents, and therefore carried out a scheme to earn some extra money. He created fictitious email addresses, and used those email addresses to send requests for replacement parts, supposedly for government customers. He then had the replacement parts shipped to his home address, and to the home addresses of several relatives. Over a 20-month period, the manufacturer sent more than 90 shipments containing 500 products with a retail value of more than $8 million to the addresses supplied by the malicious insider. He then sold 90 of the products on an Internet auction site for more than $500,000. He was arrested, convicted, and ordered to pay more than $8 million in restitution, plus serve 51 months in prison.

This case demonstrates the insider threat risk posed by trusted business partners. It is important that you consider the insider threat risk not only from within your organization, but also from other organizations that you allow access to your systems, network, or information, or whose employees play key roles in your critical business processes. In fraud cases, business process gaps often provide the means for end users to commit crimes, as in the case just described. It is important that you carefully analyze your business processes for vulnerabilities that end users can use to commit fraud. These crimes are described in greater detail in Chapter 4, Insider Fraud, and insider threats from trusted business partners are explored in Chapter 9.

## Insider Theft of Intellectual Property

We define insider theft of IP as an insider's use of IT to steal intellectual property from the organization. This category includes industrial espionage involving insiders; information stolen often includes proprietary engineering designs, scientific formulas, source code, and confidential customer information. The following is a representative case involving customer information.

After working for his company for more than four years, a sales representative was approached by a competitor regarding employment with them. For the next two months, the sales rep emailed proprietary information from his current employer to his home, including customer lists, quotes, customer passwords, marketing and sales plans, material costs and profit margins, and a computer program used to configure quotes for customers. He then visited his potential employer and used a stolen password to access a secure area on his current employer's Web site. This access enabled the competitor to access confidential information regarding customer orders, quotes requested, and more. The next day, he received a formal employment offer. He sent an email accepting the offer, and included a copy of the program he had emailed to his home earlier. Next, he deleted the contents of his hard drive at work, thinking that would destroy the evidence of his crime, and turned in his resignation. After starting his new job a few days later, he continued to access the secure customer area of his previous employer's Web site using the passwords he had stolen.

This case fits our profile of insider theft of intellectual property perfectly, as you will see in Chapter 3, Insider Theft of Intellectual Property. In addition, it highlights a specific area of concern: passwords and account management. It is well known that an employee's account should be disabled, and passwords for shared accounts should be changed immediately upon termination. This case points out other types of shared accounts that could be easily overlooked, however: Web site accounts, customer accounts, and so on. Does your termination process include consideration of these types of accounts? Do you even have a comprehensive list of the types of accounts that exist and need to be considered at termination? Based on our experience, it might be a good idea for you to double-check!

# The Expanding Complexity of Insider Threats

As our work matured, we began to realize that the insider threat is much more complex than it appears on the surface. The expanding complexity of insider threats includes the issues outlined in Table 1-1.

**Table 1-1**  *The Expanding Complexity of Insider Threats*

| | |
|---|---|
| **Collusion with Outsiders** | Insiders can be recruited by or work for outsiders, including organized crime and foreign organizations or governments. |
| **Business Partners** | It is important to control and monitor access to your information and systems by "trusted" business partners. |
| **Mergers and Acquisitions** | Consider heightened risk of insider threats when organizations are merged or acquired. |
| **Cultural Differences** | Behavioral indicators exhibited by malicious insiders who were born in different countries may differ. |

| | |
|---|---|
| **Foreign Allegiances** | Organizations operating branches outside their own country must consider the insider threats posed by employees with allegiance to another country. |
| **Internet Underground** | Some insiders seek technical assistance from the Internet underground. The Internet underground is a collection of individuals with shared goals where there is some degree of hierarchical structure and the primary communication mechanism or agent of electronic crime involves the Internet. Further, it may demonstrate some degree of pseudoanonymity and/ or secrecy, which may be useful for organizing and carrying out electronic crimes. |

We will address these issues throughout the remainder of the book. For example, collusion with outsiders is a factor in fraud cases where stolen information is sold to outsiders and outsiders often recruit insiders to commit the crime, and in theft of IP cases in which information is stolen to benefit a foreign government or competitor. Those types of issues are explored in Chapter 3 and Chapter 4.

Trusted business partners have been the source of insider fraud, theft of intellectual property, and IT sabotage committed by technical contractors. Collusion with the Internet underground can significantly multiply the potential impact of an IT sabotage crime; therefore, countermeasures should be considered to prevent or detect suspicious communication in the workplace. These issues are covered in Chapter 9.

Mergers and acquisitions increase the risk of insider threats; therefore, we recommend you carefully consider all of the best practices in Chapter 6, Best Practices for the Prevention and Detection of Insider Threats, before embarking on that activity.

Cultural differences and foreign allegiance could influence the behavioral models presented in Chapter 2 and Chapter 3.

## Breakdown of Cases in the Insider Threat Database

At the time of this writing, we have more than 700 cases in our insider threat database. Most of the work detailed in this book is based on the intentional insider crimes that occurred within the United States. The chart in Figure 1-1 depicts the breakdown of those cases by type of crime, including national security espionage crimes. Cases of industrial espionage are included but as part of the theft of IP category.

Note the Miscellaneous (labeled "Misc.") bar in the graph. These miscellaneous cases either don't fit into the other categories or are fairly new and we have not been able to gather much information on them. We like to track cases in our database as soon as we become aware of them, but categorize them under Miscellaneous until we have sufficient information to include them in our analysis.

Some crimes fall into multiple categories, as illustrated in this case example.

> A manager in the engineering department of a manufacturing company did not get along with his coworkers; one of them even quit his job because of conflicts with him. He actually bragged about the things he had done to infuriate the company's management. After a dispute with another colleague, the insider abruptly quit his job, but then found out he would not receive a severance package. He therefore chose another route to gain a form of severance pay: While at work he made a copy of the system backups, deleted all remaining traces of his company's premier

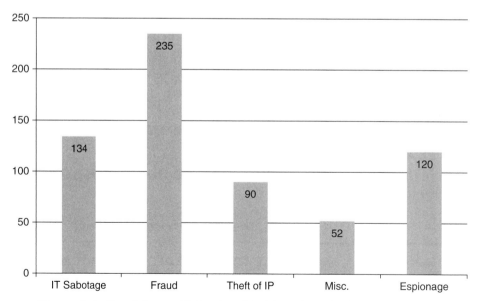

**Figure 1-1** *Breakdown of intentional insider crimes in the United States (including national security espionage)*

product, including the backups, and took the only remaining copy with him. He then offered to restore the data for $50,000, which he believed to be the amount of severance to which he was entitled. He threatened to retaliate with massive legal and personal attacks if the company contacted law enforcement or its lawyers; however, he was arrested and convicted. Unfortunately, the company went out of business because the information, valued at up to $10 million, was never recovered.

The insider in that example stole the information (theft of intellectual property) in order to harm the company (IT sabotage) and extorted money for its return (fraud). Therefore, it is important when considering the details of each type of crime as described in this book that some insiders carry out multiple types of crimes.

## CERT's MERIT Models of Insider Threats

MERIT stands for Management and Education of the Risk of Insider Threat. As part of the MERIT project we developed a series of models and associated tools that evolved into the assessments, workshops, and technical solutions you will read about in the remainder of this book.

> MERIT stands for Management and Education of the Risk of Insider Threat.

As you read this book, you will notice that we rely heavily on our insider threat models for designing the most effective mitigation strategies. Our insider threat database yields a wealth of information regarding the details of hundreds of insider crimes. It is quite useful to be able to determine the number of permanent employees versus contractors, the number of insiders who constructed **logic bombs,**[2] how many organizations experienced a reduction in force before an insider attack, and so on, directly from our database. However, because of the complexity of the insider threat issue, we feel that understanding the "big picture" of the problem is the key to success in overcoming it. The insider threat models help describe and communicate this big picture.

---

2. **Logic bomb:** malicious code implanted on a target system and configured to execute after a designated period of time or on the occurrence of a specified system action.

The purpose of our models is to identify patterns in the evolution of the cases over time. In short, we focused on the story behind the cases, and developed models that tell that story in a way that you can understand and act on.

> In short, we focused on the story behind the cases, and developed models that tell that story in a way that you can understand and act on.

## Why Our Profiles Are Useful

Here is an example of why we believe the profiles and associated MERIT models are critical to designing a successful insider threat mitigation strategy.

> A programmer at a telecommunications company was upset because he did not get the anticipated promotion to leader of his software development team. In order to exact revenge, he added two additional lines of code to his employer's premier telecommunications product. When triggered, the new code would randomly insert the letter *i* into the transmission stream. He checked-in the modified code, but did not set it to execute. Five months later, he found a new job and quit. Before he left, however, he set the **malicious code**[3] to begin execution six months in the future. At that time, the malicious code began corrupting the organization's communication stream and disrupting customer services.

The crime in that case had significant consequences for the victim organization. Its primary service for its customers was disrupted, with no obvious explanation for the problem. If you are a software engineer, you know how you approach a problem like this: What changes did we release yesterday? How about the day before, or last week, or last month? The investigation required examination of logs spanning almost a year, at which point the company finally found evidence of the crime.

Now let's examine how our profiles could have been useful in detecting this malicious code before it executed. The simple addition of two lines of source code would probably not have appeared to be malicious, as this programmer was responsible for maintaining that code. Code reviews of every change to this system could certainly have identified the malicious code, but we find that most organizations do not perform code reviews once a system is in stable, production mode. Could this happen to you? Could one of your software engineers put two lines of code into your most critical

---

3.  **Malicious code:** intended to execute a malicious function. Also commonly referred to as **malware**.

production system and cause it to fail or disrupt operations? Do you do code reviews of every change to that system?

The good news is that by understanding our insider threat profiles, you will have a chance of preventing this from happening to you. This is an example of an IT sabotage attack, so please read Chapter 2 for mitigation strategies for this type of incident. You will learn that disgruntled technical employees who exhibit concerning behaviors in the workplace over an extended period of time should not be taken lightly. In addition, many of them set up their attack while still employed but execute the attack following termination. Our mitigation strategies for insider IT sabotage are based on those patterns.

## Why Not Just One Profile?

As we worked on the Insider Threat Study we came to realize that all insider threats are not alike. However, we also realized that there appeared to be distinct similarities in how each type of insider crime evolved over time. Therefore, we chose one type of insider crime to profile first: insider IT sabotage. The cases of insider IT sabotage intrigued us because they were among the more technically sophisticated attacks examined in the study and resulted in substantial harm to people and organizations.

> **NOTE**
>
> It is important that you understand that the crime profiles and associated models are very different for each type of insider threat. Who does it, when, why, how—these are very different for each of the three types of crimes: insider IT sabotage, theft of intellectual property, and fraud.

In performing the "big picture" analysis of insider IT sabotage, we first reviewed all insider IT sabotage cases to identify those with sufficient information for this type of analysis. We needed case files that contained details regarding why the insider attacked, what events surrounded the attack, what technical actions the insider took to set up and carry out the attack, what concerning behaviors did the insider exhibit at work prior to the attack, and so on. We discovered a very strong pattern that applied to almost every IT sabotage case in our database.

> **NOTE**
>
> Insider IT sabotage crimes have happened in every sector and no organization should disregard this type of threat.

Next, we validated those patterns against the data in our database and identified general observations about the majority of the cases, and then we were ready to create our models. We chose system dynamics modeling; we found that the system dynamics approach helped to structure and focus the team's discussion. We used a group modeling approach with experts from both psychology and information security. Appendix F, System Dynamics Background, contains a more in-depth discussion of system dynamics for readers who are interested in more details.

Our MERIT model of insider IT sabotage was published in 2008: *The "Big Picture" of Insider IT Sabotage Across U.S. Critical Infrastructures* [Moore 2008]. The information from that report is covered in Chapter 2. Our next insider threat model was for national security espionage and is not included in this book. In 2011 we published our MERIT model of insider theft of intellectual property, *A Preliminary Model of Insider Theft of Intellectual Property* [Moore 2011a]. The information from that report is covered in Chapter 3.

We will soon be creating a fraud model as part of a current project with the Secret Service, the U.S. Department of Homeland Security (DHS) Science and Technology (S&T) Directorate, and U.S. Department of the Treasury. We have included a preliminary analysis of our fraud cases prior to that study in Chapter 4, which is being published in the *CERT Research Annual Report* [Moore 2011b].

## Why Didn't We Create a Single Insider Theft Model?

After the success of our insider IT sabotage model, we decided to create an insider theft model. We went through the same steps as before: We identified cases with rich information available, identified key elements in the cases, and then attempted to identify the prevalent patterns in a group modeling session. However, in examining all of our theft cases, we found that there was not a strong pattern like the one we identified for the IT sabotage cases. Instead, we discovered two different patterns that seemed to be based on the type of information stolen.

We realized that insiders who steal information that is used to commit identity theft or credit card fraud tend to be lower-level employees in the organization who find a way to make extra money on the side by stealing information. They usually sell the data to someone outside the organization who actually uses the data to commit identity theft or credit card fraud. These tend to be long, ongoing schemes that continue until the insider is caught.

The insiders who steal intellectual property are totally different! They tend to be engineers, scientists, programmers, and salespeople who steal information as they are leaving the organization. Furthermore, they steal the information to take to their new employer, usually a competitor, or to start their own competing business.

Thus, we ended up creating the model for insider theft of intellectual property, and the insider fraud model. Oh, but wait: There's just a bit more!

As we explored the data further, we discovered more interesting patterns. First, we found that the insider theft of intellectual property crimes actually did fall into two overlapping groups: insiders who acted alone, and those who actually led a "ring" of insiders to steal the information. See Chapter 3 for more details.

Second, we found that cases in which insiders modified information for financial gain fit the same model as the ones who stole information to commit fraud; they were lower-level employees. They simply found a way to make extra money by modifying information rather than stealing it. For instance, they created fake driver's licenses, modified criminal histories, or changed salaries. There are obviously differences in the technical methods used to steal versus modify information, but the other patterns in the crimes are the same. Therefore, our insider fraud model includes both types of crimes. See Chapter 4 for details.

## Overview of the CERT Insider Threat Center

The objective of the CERT Insider Threat Center is to assist organizations in preventing, detecting, and responding to insider compromises. Figure 1-2 depicts the malicious insider at the start of the incident timeline, and the damage at the end of the timeline. Our ultimate goal is to help you prevent the insider from attacking. However, if he should decide to attack, our objective is to provide you with the understanding and solutions you need to detect the illicit activity as early in the timeline as possible. Unfortunately, some malicious insiders will succeed in their attack; in those cases we want to arm you with policies, practices, and technical measures so that you can respond to the attack as quickly as possible. Response measures include recovering from the attack, identifying the perpetrator, and implementing new measures for improved incident management in the future.

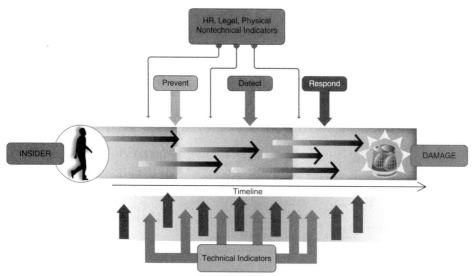

*Opportunities to prevent, detect, and respond to an insider attack*

**Figure 1-2** *Objective of the CERT Insider Threat Center*

Figure 1-2 also illustrates how we hope to achieve those objectives: through detection of both technical and nontechnical indicators. If you learn only one thing from this book, let it be this: *Insider threats cannot be prevented and detected with technology alone.* Insiders use authorized access to the systems and information they access every day to carry out their attacks; therefore, automated detection based solely on online actions is extremely difficult if not impossible.

> If you learn only one thing from this book, let it be this: *Insider threats cannot be prevented and detected with technology alone.*

We feel it is important that you understand the basis of the information presented in the remainder of this book. Many books and articles have been written about insider threat, many of them posing elaborate scenarios in which technically privileged users use sophisticated means to exfiltrate information or sabotage their employer's networks. It is important that you understand that all of our work in the CERT Program is based on empirical data. What have insiders *actually* done? How have they done it?

Our database provides the foundation of all of our work in the CERT Insider Threat Center as depicted in Figure 1-3. Our models, which are used to describe how the crimes evolve over time, provide the next layer in that foundation upon which all of our work is based.

The CERT Insider Threat Center consists of three teams, and all three teams base their work on the insider threat database and models. Specifically, the Insider Threat Research Team bases its research on empirical data from the cases in the database and our models. The insider threat lab develops new technical solutions and standards to fill gaps in the current tools market; they focus on gap areas as dictated by the means of execution of crimes in the database and the patterns captured in our models. The Insider Threat Outreach and Transition Team develops insider threat assessments, workshops, and exercises based on cases in the database and the models.

In addition, all three teams share information and collaborate with one another, as shown in Figure 1-4. For example, the Research Team performs

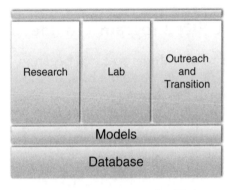

**Figure 1-3**  *CERT Insider Threat Center body of work*

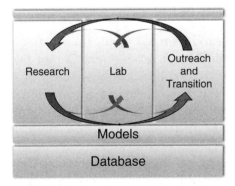

**Figure 1-4**  *Information sharing in the CERT Insider Threat Center*

policy and legal research and applies science-based approaches to analyze the efficacy of solutions developed in the lab. The lab tackles difficult problems uncovered by the Outreach and Transition Team doing assessments in the field. The Outreach and Transition Team gathers information about what is actually working and not working for practitioners and conveys those issues to the other teams, and so on.

Over the years we have built a structure in the Insider Threat Center that enables us to stay in touch with what's happening in the field, take advantage of our unique position in one of the leading research universities in the world, and partner with government and industry to develop solutions that are having an immediate impact on insider threat mitigation.

## Timeline of the CERT Program's Insider Threat Work

The CERT Program's insider threat research began in 2000 and has continued to grow. In this section we present a brief timeline of the history of the CERT Program's work in this area. Figure 1-5 summarizes the evolution of the body of work of the CERT Insider Threat Center.

### 2000 Initial Research

The CERT Program's original insider threat research was sponsored by the U.S. Department of Defense (DOD) in 2000, and focused on insider threats in the military services and defense agencies.

### 2001 Insider Threat Study

Our insider threat research ramped up the following year, in 2001, when the Secret Service National Threat Assessment Center (NTAC) and the CERT Program joined efforts to conduct a unique study of insider incidents, the Insider Threat Study (ITS). The Department of Homeland Security, Office of Science and Technology (DHS S&T) provided financial support for the completion of the study in 2003 and 2004. Four reports were produced as a result of that effort focusing on the banking and finance sector [Randazzo 2004], the information technology sector [Kowalski 2008a], the government sector [Kowalski 2008b], and the analysis of insider IT sabotage across all critical infrastructure sectors [Keeney 2005].

## 2001 Insider Threat Database

After the completion of the Insider Threat Study with the Secret Service, we realized the enormous value of our database. Following the study, Carnegie Mellon's CyLab[4] agreed to sponsor the ongoing maintenance and evolution of the database, and in 2009 the DHS Federal Network Security (FNS) branch became the sponsor of the CERT insider threat database.

## 2005 Best Practices

In 2005, CyLab provided funding to us for the "Common Sense Guide to Prevention and Detection of Insider Threats." Our best practice work is now being sponsored by DHS FNS. The best practices from the "Common Sense Guide" are detailed in Chapter 6.

## 2005 System Dynamics Models

After publishing the Insider Threat Study reports with the Secret Service, we felt that people were looking for a few nuggets they could take back to their IT staff for technical resolution, and were not seeing the "big picture" of how these crimes evolve over time. We convinced CyLab to fund us to develop models of insider threat. The project, titled MERIT (for Management and Education of the Risk of Insider Threat), resulted in groundbreaking models that have influenced researchers and practitioners around the world ever since. Those models have become another foundation upon which all of our work is based.

We discuss our system dynamics modeling work in more detail in Appendix F.

## 2006 Workshops

In 2006, CyLab continued its support of our insider threat work by funding us to develop an insider threat workshop. What started out as a half-day workshop has expanded over the years so that we now offer several versions: a two-day public offering, on-site workshops for individual organizations, half-day and one-day versions, and custom workshops, including an executive workshop for C-level executives and academically oriented workshops focused on a specific research objective.

---

4. www.cylab.cmu.edu/

Appendix A, Insider Threat Center Products and Services, contains more details about the CERT insider threat workshops.

## 2006 Interactive Virtual Simulation Tool

In 2006, we developed MERIT *InterActive* (MERIT$_{IA}$), a prototype of an interactive virtual simulation tool—essentially a video game to teach insider threat mitigation with Carnegie Mellon's Entertainment Technology Center (ETC). Appendix E, Insider Threat Training Simulation: MERIT *InterActive*, contains more details about the MERIT *InterActive* insider threat training simulation prototype.

## 2007 Insider Threat Assessment

We created the first version of our insider threat assessment instrument, sponsored by CyLab, based on more than 4,000 issues of concern (organized into more than 130 categories) that we identified from cases in our database. We created a series of six assessment workbooks for Information Security/Information Technology, Human Resources, Software Engineering, Legal, Data Owners, and Physical Security. In 2009, DHS FNS recognized the value of our assessment process, and sponsored an effort to enhance the insider threat assessment into a more scalable process with measurable results.

Appendix A contains more details about the CERT insider threat assessments.

## 2009 Insider Threat Lab

In 2009, CyLab funded creation of our insider threat lab, where our technologists could test existing technical solutions for the insider threat problem and identify new or refined solutions in gap areas. CyLab funded the lab hardware and software infrastructure in 2009, and in 2010, DHS FNS funded us to begin developing solutions using the lab.

See Chapter 7, Technical Insider Threat Controls, for more details about technical controls we created in the insider threat lab that you can implement in your own organization.

## 2010 Insider Threat Exercises

The CERT Program has developed XNET, a platform that allows organizations to create customized, realistic, interactive simulations on an isolated network.[5] In 2010, DHS FNS funded us to create insider threat exercises using XNET. These exercises are now offered to government and industry practitioners at workshops and conferences.

See Chapter 7 for more information about our insider threat exercises.

## 2010 Insider Threat Study—Banking and Finance Sector

In 2010, DHS S&T brought together the CERT Insider Threat Center, the Secret Service, and the Department of the Treasury to repeat the original Insider Threat Study. This time, however, the focus was solely on cases that occurred in the banking and finance sector. At the end of the study, a report will be published much like the original study. In addition, we will publish a system dynamics fraud model that will evolve the preliminary fraud model presented in this book.

Chapter 4 contains a preliminary fraud model that was developed previously as part of the CyLab MERIT project.

Figure 1-5 shows a summary of the history of the CERT Insider Threat Center body of work.

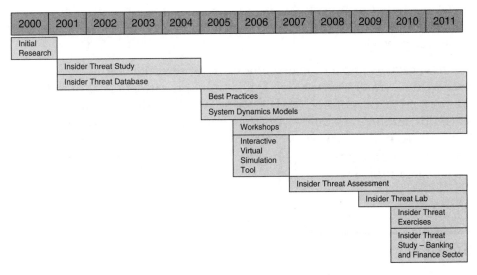

**Figure 1-5** *CERT Insider Threat Center timeline*

5. For more information on CERT's XNET capability, see http://xnet.cert.org/.

## Caveats about Our Work

Organizations are often reluctant to report incidents of illicit insider cyberactivity, even to law enforcement. Therefore, the actual number of insider cases is most likely significantly greater than those that we have been able to identify. Our work is largely based on reported cases, although our assessments have exposed us to additional cases not reported to law enforcement. This limits the ability to generalize our findings to *all* organizations and underscores the difficulty other researchers have faced in trying to better understand insider threat. Nevertheless, this limitation does not diminish the value of the knowledge that we gained from analyzing these incidents. We provide insight into actual criminal and other illicit acts committed by insiders. This insight has been found to be quite useful to individuals who are charged with protecting critical assets as they begin to examine ways to improve their defenses against insider threats.

The other limitation of our work is that we have only collected data for malicious insiders. We have not been able to collect similar data for "good guys." We know how the convicted insiders acted in our cases, and have identified definite patterns in their behavior, both online and socially. But we have no idea if "normal" people exhibit those same behaviors. This is an area of research that is widely recognized to be lacking in the insider threat domain, but unfortunately no one has come up with a good way to collect the comprehensive types of data we have without violating employee privacy.

Do these caveats impact the usefulness of our research? From an academic perspective, yes. However, feedback from practitioners since 2001 has encouraged us to continue forging ahead in our study of malicious actors, since our findings resonate with the community. In addition, our countermeasures have received overwhelmingly positive feedback from those tasked with keeping their organizations' systems, data, and networks safe from insider threats.

## Summary

By now you should understand that there are three distinct types of insider threats: insider IT sabotage (covered in detail in Chapter 2), theft of intellectual property (covered in detail in Chapter 3), and fraud (covered in detail in Chapter 4). You have been exposed to some actual case examples for each, so you should now understand which of those threats are of most concern to you. You should now know which chapter—2, 3, or 4—you want to read next in the book. We do recommend that you understand the nature of the insider threat problem before you jump to the solutions offered in Chapter 6 and Chapter 7.

Chapter 5, Insider Threat Issues in the Software Development Life Cycle, is devoted to that specific type of insider threat. These crimes can be quite destructive and difficult to detect, so we strongly recommend you read that chapter if you do any software development in your organization.

You should now recognize the expanding complexity of insider threats, including threats from trusted business partners, dangers posed by collusion with the Internet underground and organized crime, and impacts of foreign allegiances and cultural issues. If these issues are of concern, you will find them addressed in more detail throughout the book.

We discussed our system dynamics modeling, and explained that the descriptions of our models in this book are written for managers and practitioners. We described the high-level patterns we observed for each type of crime. We have presented these models for years to diverse audiences, including technical and nontechnical, management and nonmanagement, as well as CISOs, CSOs, and personnel in legal, HR, physical security, software engineering, and so on. The feedback is always overwhelmingly positive.

Finally, we provided a brief overview of the CERT Insider Threat Center. We wanted to give you enough background on the breadth of our capabilities so that you would be comfortable that we know what we're doing, and you can trust the material in this book!

# Chapter 2

# Insider IT Sabotage

*Insider IT sabotage: insider incidents in which the insider uses information technology (IT) to direct specific harm at an organization or an individual.*

Cases of insider IT sabotage include the most technically sophisticated attacks in the CERT insider threat database, and have caused substantial harm to people and organizations. Insider IT sabotage has occurred in almost every critical infrastructure sector, and poses a threat to virtually every organization in government and industry—to any organization reliant on information technology. In one insider IT sabotage case, a former system administrator wiped out 18 months of cancer research, which was never recovered. In another, a company lost $10 million, laid off 80 employees, and nearly went out of business. In yet another, billions of critical files were deleted from a financial institution's servers around the world when a logic bomb went off on every server at 9:00 a.m. just when the banks opened for business. In this chapter we describe the profile of insider IT sabotage and present strategies for mitigating insider IT sabotage crimes.[1]

These crimes are committed by technically sophisticated system administrators or programmers, using the same types of online actions typically used by those same employees or contractors in the course of their normal activity. Therefore, some say that stopping these types of

---

1. Material in this chapter includes portions from previously published works. The primary source was written by the authors of this book as a chapter in *Insider Attack and Cyber Security: Beyond the Hacker* edited by S.J. Stolfo et al., Springer Science + Business Media, LLC [Moore 2008]. Earlier versions of the insider IT sabotage model were published in [Moore 2007, Cappelli 2006, Band 2006].

attacks is next to impossible. Fortunately, we have identified distinct patterns in nearly every insider IT sabotage case. In this chapter we describe those patterns and present mitigation strategies that use those patterns to your advantage. These techniques include both technical and nontechnical measures. In addition, some are proactive across the enterprise, while others are targeted at specific employees triggered by indicators that could suggest an increased risk of attack.

> Fortunately, we have identified distinct patterns in nearly every insider IT sabotage case. In this chapter we describe those patterns and present mitigation strategies that use those patterns to your advantage.

For example, we suggest countermeasures such as periodic account audits, since a number of these insiders created **backdoor accounts**[2] prior to being fired so that they could get back in and exact their revenge following termination. With more and more **identity management systems**[3] available, we would expect to see a reduction in the use of this technique. However, during the week this chapter was written, a former system administrator at a large, multinational corporation used a **VPN token**[4] he had created for a nonexistent employee prior to being fired to break back into his employer's network and sabotage its systems.

On the other hand, we realize that account audits are time consuming and difficult to perform, especially at times of reduced staffing levels. Therefore, we also suggest that when a system administrator is sanctioned and "on the HR radar" you perform a detailed audit of all accounts that have been created since he first became disgruntled and began exhibiting concerning behaviors in the workplace.

The bottom line is that we believe there is a good chance to thwart these attacks, but it requires careful planning and implementation of mitigation strategies across your organization. We do have some "good-news" cases.

---

2. **Backdoor account:** an unauthorized account created for gaining access to a system or network known only to the person who created it.

3. **Identity Management System:** a system or technology that supports the management of identities. It is generally accepted that an IMS will establish identities, describe identities through one or more attributes, follow identity activity, and be capable of removing an identity from the system it manages (adapted from Future of Identity in the Information Society).

4. **Virtual private network (VPN):** a virtual network, built on top of existing physical networks, that provides a secure communications tunnel for data and other information transmitted between networks (NIST SP 800-46). A **VPN token** is a device, possibly physical, that an authorized user of the VPN is given to ease authentication.

- **A logic bomb would have wiped out every file on every server on the network.** Fortunately, the organization reacted swiftly to a suspicious comment made by a system administrator who was to be fired the following Monday, took all systems offline over the weekend, and discovered the logic bomb before it executed.

- **A logic bomb would have destroyed information on more than 70 servers, including a critical patient-specific, drug-interaction conflict database.** Fortunately, a computer system administrator, while investigating a system error, discovered the logic bomb, notified IT, and the malicious code was neutralized before impacting the organization.

The impacts of an insider IT sabotage attack can be devastating: Companies have gone out of business, lost millions of dollars, lost entire product lines, or had to undergo massive layoffs. Impacts of these attacks in government agencies and critical infrastructure organizations have ranged from embarrassing reputational impacts to serious threats to national security. Financial impacts in the 123 cases in the CERT database at the time this was written averaged $1.7 million, ranging from $1,000 to $87 million. (Note that half of the organizations suffered $50,000 or less in financial losses.) However, the impacts are not limited to financial losses; operational and business impacts were devastating in many of these cases.

We strongly suggest that you pay close attention to this chapter. We find that many people do not fully understand the risk of insider IT sabotage to their organization. For instance, financial institutions are understandably concerned with internal fraud. But what if a financial institution's customers could not use their debit or credit cards, use ATMs, or access any of their money for an entire weekend after a fired system administrator sabotaged critical servers on a Friday night? That's what happened to one unfortunate financial institution.

Likewise, manufacturing, pharmaceutical, and chemical organizations seem to be most concerned with protection of their trade secrets—formulas, manufacturing processes, and engineering information. But what if, as in one company, a rogue system administrator sabotaged the manufacturing process, resulting in the disruption of critical machinery and the ultimate collapse of the company?

Finally, national security espionage arguably receives the most attention in the U.S. government, but consider multiple cases in which government employees helped undocumented immigrants obtain citizenship and government credentials for profit.

## Impacts of Insider IT Sabotage Attacks

The impacts of insider IT sabotage attacks have included the following.

- Electricity between power grids was shut down in one area of the United States.
- A safety hotline was disabled.
- More than 50,000 customer records were corrupted.
- Thirty thousand copies of a newspaper had to be reprinted.
- A company's **domain name**[5] was added to **anti-spam blacklists.**[6]
- Critical data was lost and the company went out of business (multiple cases).
- The organization's network was inaccessible—ranging from hours to days to three months (multiple cases).
- A person was marked as being deceased in a large government database, causing major problems for the person.
- Cars inexplicably shut down or their horns beeped nonstop.
- A company's voice-mail system was redirected to a pornographic phone service.
- Customers' credit card numbers were posted to the Internet along with other proprietary information.
- All administrative passwords at a company were changed, system files were deleted, a billing system was destroyed, and two internal databases were deleted.
- A company's international e-commerce site was unavailable (multiple cases).
- Hundreds of staff hours were required to recover from backups or reenter data manually (multiple cases).
- A company's clients' Web pages were modified to contain embarrassing information.

These are documented cases.

Unfortunately, all of these things really did happen, and much to the surprise of the victim organizations. It does not take much imagination to envision the potential for a threat of even greater harm, such as malicious software that results in the release of toxic chemicals by a manufacturer, or mass casualties of our armed forces.

Now that we have caught your attention, let's look at the characteristics and "big picture" of insider IT sabotage attacks.

---

5. **Domain names:** host names tied to IP resources such as Web sites (adapted from ICANN/Wikipedia).

6. **Anti-spam blacklists:** a system designed to block spam messages through a system of IP address filtering. Often functions in tandem with a content-recognition system.

By their very nature, these attacks require technical sophistication and privileged access, so it is not surprising that they are usually carried out by system administrators, database administrators, and programmers. What is surprising, however, is that the majority of the attacks occur after the insider has been terminated or quit the organization.

One-fourth of the cases were contractors, and almost all worked full time. Ages ranged from 17 to 65, and only seven IT saboteurs in the CERT database are female. However, according to the U.S. Bureau of Labor Statistics, most people in such technical positions are men. In 2010,

- 16.5% of all network and computer system administrators were women.
- 36.4% of all database administrators were women.
- 22% of all computer programmers were women.
- 20.9% of all computer software engineers were women.[7]

Therefore, we are not suggesting that men are more likely than women to commit these types of crimes. On the contrary, we suggest that rather than focusing on demographic characteristics, you should focus on

- Understanding the positions at risk for these crimes
- Recognizing the behavioral patterns and organizational factors that influence an insider to commit IT sabotage attacks
- Implementing mitigation strategies based on those patterns

We will assist in that effort by describing the CERT Program's MERIT[8] model of insider IT sabotage. The MERIT model describes the profile of an insider IT sabotage attack by identifying common patterns in the evolution of the incidents over time. These patterns are strikingly similar across the cases in our database. After describing those patterns, we will present mitigation strategies that you should consider based on those patterns. The difficulty in preventing an IT sabotage attack is that these are technically sophisticated users who have the access, ability, and motivation not only to carry out the attack, but also to conceal their activities. The good news is that, based on the patterns we have identified, a combination of technical and nontechnical countermeasures can enhance your chances of thwarting

---

7. ftp://ftp.bls.gov/pub/special.requests/lf/aat11.txt

8. Recall as described in Chapter 1, Overview, that MERIT stands for *Management and Education of the Risk of Insider Threat.*

these attacks. Even better: It is very likely that you already own all of the technology you need in order to implement our suggestions!

# General Patterns in Insider IT Sabotage Crimes

The intent of the MERIT model of insider IT sabotage is to describe the general profile of insider IT sabotage crimes. The MERIT models describe the patterns in the crimes as they evolve over time—profiling the life cycle of the crime, rather than profiling only the perpetrator. Our study of insider IT sabotage cases brought to light how the problem of malicious insider retribution arises and escalates within an organization. The key elements of the model were observed in a majority of cases in the CERT database.

The MERIT model of insider IT sabotage was first published in 2008. It has been widely accepted by industry and government as being representative of these types of attacks. The model was created using system dynamics modeling, which is described in the original report. Over the years, however, we have found that a higher-level view of that model is more useful in describing the patterns to practitioners so that clear, actionable guidance can be provided for mitigating these attacks. That higher-level form of the model and accompanying countermeasure guidance is presented is the remainder of this chapter. We have broken the model into small pieces in this chapter in order to make it more understandable. The full model is shown in Figure 2-1. Figure 2-2 shows the system dynamics model with mitigating factors noted.

## Personal Predispositions

> **NOTE**
>
> Most insiders had personal predispositions that contributed to their risk of committing IT sabotage.
>
> **Personal predisposition:** a characteristic historically linked to a propensity to exhibit malicious insider behavior.

Personal predispositions help explain why some insiders carry out malicious acts, while coworkers who are exposed to the same events and conditions do not act maliciously. Personal predispositions can be recognized by certain types of observable characteristics [Band 2006].

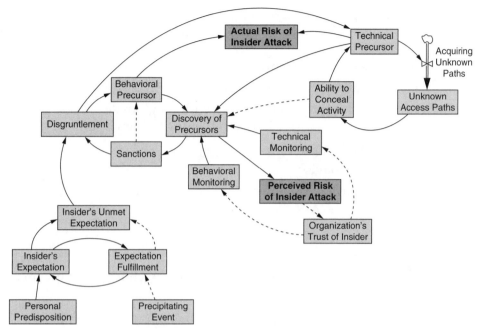

**Figure 2-1** *MERIT model of insider IT sabotage*

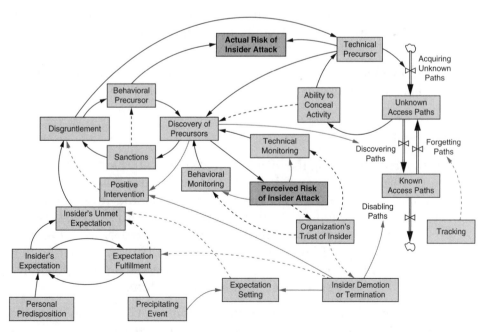

**Figure 2-2** *Insider IT sabotage mitigating measures*

Example personal predispositions found in the insider cases that may be observable within the workplace include the following:

- Conflicts with fellow workers
- Bullying and intimidation of fellow workers
- Refusal to confront supervisors with legitimate work-related complaints due to shyness while complaining to competitors
- Serious personality conflicts
- Unprofessional behavior
- Inability to conform to rules; for example, a history of
  - Arrests
  - Hacking
  - Security violations
  - Harassment or conflicts resulting in official sanctions or complaints
  - Misuse of travel, time, and/or expenses
- Difficulties controlling anger with bursts of inappropriate temper

Predispositions differ from one person to the next, and influence the rate that expectations rise and fall. Personal predispositions may explain why one employee ends up attacking an organization while coworkers do not. Understanding this distinction is the first important step in recognizing heightened insider threat risk in an organization.

All of the insiders in the CERT database who committed IT sabotage exhibited personal predispositions.

### What Can You Do?

Your approach to reducing the insider threat should start in the hiring process by performing background checks and evaluating individuals based on the information received. Background checks should investigate previous criminal convictions and include discussions with prior employers regarding the individual's competence and approach to dealing with workplace issues. This type of investigation can yield valuable information that could suggest that the prospective employee has personal predispositions, which could increase risk for insider threat in the future.

Thirty percent of the insiders who committed IT sabotage in the CERT Program's original study with the Secret Service had a previous arrest history, including arrests for violent offenses (18%), alcohol- or

> **TIP**
>
> To reduce the insider threat, begin in the hiring process by performing background checks and evaluating individuals based on the information received.

drug-related offenses (11%), and nonfinancial/fraud-related theft offenses (11%) [Keeney 2005]. (Note that some of the insiders had been arrested for multiple offenses.) The relatively high frequency of previous criminal arrests underscores the need for background checks. These proactive measures should not be punitive in nature; rather, you should indoctrinate the employee into the organization with appropriate care. In addition, this information should be used as part of a risk-based decision process in determining whether it is appropriate to give the new employee privileged access to critical, confidential, or proprietary information or systems.

You should require background checks for all potential employees, including contractors and subcontractors. In one case in the CERT database, an organization employed a contractor to perform system administration duties. The hiring organization was told by the contractor's company that a background check had been performed on him. The contractor later compromised the organization's systems; during the investigation it was discovered that the contractor had a criminal history of illegally accessing protected computers.

## Disgruntlement and Unmet Expectations

> **NOTE**
>
> Most insiders who committed IT sabotage were disgruntled due to unmet expectations.
>
> **Unmet expectation:** an unsatisfied assumption by an individual that an organization action or event will (or will not) happen, or a condition will (or will not) exist.

Disgruntlement is a recurring factor in the CERT insider IT sabotage cases, predominately due to some unmet expectation by the insider. For example:

- The insider expected certain technical freedoms in his[9] use of the organization's computer and network systems, such as storing

---

9. Most of the insiders who committed IT sabotage were male. Therefore, male gender is used to describe the generic insider in this chapter.

personal files, but was reprimanded by management for exercising those freedoms.

- The insider expected to work for the hiring supervisor or work on a certain project, but over time a new supervisor was hired or he was moved to a different project.
- The insider expected a certain financial reward for his work, but bonuses or raises were lower than expected due to the organization's financial status.

Figure 2-3 depicts the insider's personal predisposition leading to heightened expectations; then a precipitating event results in unmet expectations that lead to insider disgruntlement.

Over time, employees and contractors come to expect certain things in the workplace based on past history. In IT sabotage cases, a precipitating event leads to unmet expectations, triggering disgruntlement in insiders. A precipitating event is anything that removes or restricts the freedom or recognition to which the employee or contractor has become accustomed. For instance, a new supervisor who suddenly enforces the organization's acceptable-use policy may cause extreme disgruntlement in certain employees. Other precipitating events include the insider being passed up for a promotion, as well as sanctions by management, transfer, demotion, or termination of the insider.

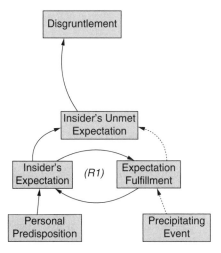

**Figure 2-3** *Expectation escalation*

Note that some precipitating events, such as raises that are lower than expected, lack of bonuses, and downsizing, simply cannot be avoided, especially in times of economic downturn. It is very important that organizations appreciate the influence such factors can play in insider IT sabotage attacks by planning carefully and increasing vigilance as such steps are executed. In one CERT case, a system administrator planted a logic bomb designed to wipe out data on 70 company servers after finding out about planned layoffs due to the company's reorganization. Even after surviving the downsizing, the insider refined the logic bomb and set it to go off more than a year later. Fortunately, other IT personnel discovered the logic bomb while investigating a system problem and neutralized the destructive code.

Unmet expectations from the CERT cases include

- Salary/bonus
- Promotion
- Freedom of online actions
- Work ethic
- Project requirements (deadlines, milestones)
- Overestimated abilities
- Access to information following termination
- Use of company resources
- Job dissatisfaction
- Supervisor demands
- Coworker relations
- Responsibilities

Precipitating events in the CERT cases include

- Being passed over for promotion
- Demotion due to project completion
- Transfer between departments
- Supervisor issues:
  - New supervisor hired
  - Disagreement with supervisor
- Access changed

- Financial:
  - Disagreement over salary and compensation
  - Bonuses lower than expected
- Termination of subcontractor contract
- Termination of partnership because of financial issues
- Coworkers overriding decisions
- Outsourcing of project

## What Can You Do?

Responsibilities and constraints of your employees and consequences for violations need to be clearly communicated and consistently enforced. Policies or controls that are misunderstood, not communicated, or inconsistently enforced can breed resentment among employees, lead to unmet expectations, and potentially result in harmful insider actions. A consistent, clear message on your organization's policies and controls will help reduce the chance that employees will lash out for a perceived injustice.

> **TIP**
>
> Clearly communicate and consistently enforce responsibilities and constraints of your employees and consequences for violations.

As individuals join your organization, they should receive a copy of organizational policies that clearly lays out what is expected of them, together with the consequences of violations. Evidence that each individual has read and agreed to the organization's policies should be maintained.

Consistent enforcement of policies is essential to maintain a harmonious work environment. When employees see inconsistent enforcement of policies, it quickly leads to animosity within the workplace. In many of the cases analyzed, inconsistent enforcement or perceived injustices within organizations led to insider disgruntlement. Coworkers often felt that "star performers" were above the rules and received special treatment. Many times that disgruntlement led the insiders to commit IT sabotage.

In one case, employees had become accustomed to lax policy enforcement over a long period of time. New management dictated immediate strict policy enforcement, which caused one employee to become embittered and strike out against the organization. In other words, policies should be enforced consistently across all employees, as well as consistently enforced over time.

Of course, organizations are not static entities; change in your policies and controls is inevitable. Employee constraints, privileges, and responsibilities change as well. You need to recognize times of change as particularly stressful times for employees, appreciate the increased risk that comes along with these stress points, and mitigate it with clear communication regarding what employees can expect in the future.

It is important that you anticipate and manage negative workplace issues, beginning with preemployment, continuing through employment, and especially at termination. When employees have issues they need an avenue within your organization to seek assistance. Employees need to be able to openly discuss work-related issues with a member of management or human resources without the fear of reprisal or negative consequences. Managers need to address these issues when discovered or reported, before they escalate out of control.

When employee issues arise because of outside issues, including financial and personal stressors, it can be helpful to use a service such as an employee assistance program. These programs offer confidential counseling to assist employees, allowing them to restore their work performance, health, or general well-being.

Finally, contentious employee terminations must be handled with utmost care, as most insider IT sabotage attacks occur following termination.

## Behavioral Precursors

> **NOTE**
>
> Behavioral precursors were observable in insider IT sabotage cases.
>
> **Behavioral precursor:** an individual action, event, or condition that involves personal or interpersonal behaviors and that precedes and is associated with malicious insider activity.

Often, the first sign of disgruntlement is the onset of concerning behaviors in the workplace. Some examples of concerning behaviors in the CERT cases were

- Conflicts with coworkers or supervisors
- A sudden pattern of missing work, arriving late, or leaving early
- A sudden decline in job performance
- Drug use

- Aggressive or violent behavior
- Mood swings
- Bizarre behavior
- Sexual harassment
- Poor hygiene

Unfortunately, in many of the incidents in the CERT database, the concerning behaviors were not recognized by management prior to the incidents, or the organization failed to take action to address the behaviors.

Note that the precipitating events in the CERT cases most likely affected many employees, not only the malicious insider. Therefore, it is likely that many employees were similarly disgruntled, and also exhibited concerning behaviors similar to the insider. Therefore, at this point in the model, it is most likely difficult to distinguish between insiders who might eventually attack, and those employees who are simply disgruntled. It is important that you do not rely on only one portion of the model to identify a person who may be at risk of committing IT sabotage, but instead recognize the escalating risk as an employee or contractor progresses along the path in the model.

### What Can You Do?

You should invest time and resources in training supervisors to recognize and respond to inappropriate or concerning behavior in employees. In some of the CERT cases, less serious but inappropriate behavior was noticed in the workplace but not acted on because it did not rise to the level of a policy violation. However, failure to define or enforce security policies in some cases emboldened the employees to commit repeated violations that escalated in severity, with increasing risk of significant harm to the organization. It is important that you consistently investigate and respond to all rule violations committed by employees.

---

**TIP**

Train supervisors to recognize and respond to inappropriate or concerning behaviors.

---

Policies and procedures should exist for employees to report concerning or disruptive behavior by coworkers. While frivolous reports need to be screened, all reports should be investigated. If an employee exhibits suspicious behavior, you should respond with due care. Disruptive employees should not be allowed to migrate from one position to another within the organization, evading documentation of disruptive or concerning activity. Threats, boasting about malicious acts or capabilities ("You wouldn't believe how easily I could trash this net!"), and other negative sentiments should also be treated as concerning behavior. Many employees will have concerns and grievances from time to time, and a formal and accountable process for addressing those grievances may satisfy those who might otherwise resort to malicious activity. Specifically, any employee or contractor with privileged access who is experiencing difficulties in the workplace should be aided in the resolution of those difficulties.

Once concerning behavior is identified, several steps might assist you in managing risks of malicious activity. First, the employee's privileged access to critical information, systems, and networks should be evaluated. Logs should be reviewed to carefully examine recent online activity by the employee. While this is done, the organization should provide options to the individual for coping with the behavior, perhaps including access to a confidential employee assistance program.

## Stressful Events

> **NOTE**
>
> In most cases stressful events, including organizational sanctions, contributed to the likelihood of insider IT sabotage.
>
> **Stressful events:** events that cause concerning behaviors in individuals predisposed to malicious acts.

The IT saboteurs in the CERT cases experienced one or more stressful events, including sanctions and other negative work-related events, prior to their attack. The majority of insiders who committed IT sabotage attacked after termination or during suspension from duties. Stressful events observed in cases include poor performance evaluations, reprimands for unacceptable behavior, suspensions for excessive absenteeism, demotions due to poor performance, restricted responsibilities, disagreements about salary or bonuses, lack of severance packages, being passed over for a promotion, and new supervisors.

As shown in Figure 2-4(a), the insider's disgruntlement is exhibited through behavioral precursors (concerning behaviors), which can be

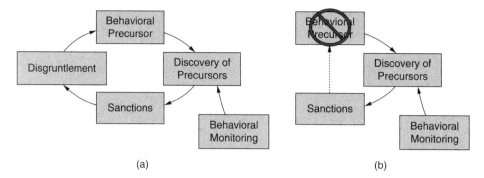

**Figure 2-4** *Typical escalation of disgruntlement (a) and intended effect of sanctions (b)*

discovered provided the organization has sufficient behavioral monitoring in place. In some cases in the CERT database, management did not even notice the insider's escalating disgruntlement, which gave them little chance of mitigating the escalating threat. In most cases, however, the organization's response to inappropriate behaviors was punitive in the form of sanctions. Sanctions were technical, such as restricting system privileges or the right to access the organization's systems from home, or nontechnical, such as demotion or formal reprimand.

Examples of sanctions in the CERT cases are

- Demotions
- Reprimands
- Suspensions
- Responsibilities removed from projects
- Suspension of Internet access

The intended effect of sanctions, as shown on the right in Figure 2-4, is to prevent additional behavioral precursors. In most "normal" people, sanctions most likely have the intended effect. In the malicious insiders in our database, however, sanctions often had unintended consequences, such as further increasing the insider's disgruntlement. Whether sanctions curb behavioral precursor activity or spur the insider to greater disgruntlement and disruption depends largely on the personal predispositions of the person. This is a key aspect of the model in which we begin to more easily distinguish between insiders who might retaliate and those who most likely will not. We believe that in most nonmalicious employees and contractors, imposition of sanctions will serve as a "wake-up call," and they either accept the circumstances or seek a new job, rather than planning an attack.

## What Can You Do?

It is important that managers and human resources staff members understand and consider the potential for insider IT sabotage when there are ongoing, observable behavioral precursors that continue or even escalate following employee sanctions. In the remainder of this chapter we will discuss technical monitoring that should be considered once this escalating pattern of disgruntlement by technically privileged users is recognized.

> **TIP**
>
> Managers and human resources staff members must understand and consider the potential for insider IT sabotage when there are ongoing, observable behavioral precursors.

It is also important to point out that sanctions can be quite important when they involve contractors rather than employees. The following example illustrates important physical security and legal/contracting issues regarding contractors.

> An energy management facility subcontracted with a company for system administrator support. One such system administrator, who worked physically on-site at the energy management facility, was suspended by his employer late on Friday afternoon due to an employee dispute. His employer decided to wait and inform the energy management facility of the suspension on Monday morning. Late Sunday night he used his authorized physical access to the energy production facility, used a hammer to break the glass case enclosing the emergency power off button, and hit the button. Some of the computer systems were shut down as a result, including computers that regulated the exchange of electricity between power grids. For a period of two hours, the shutdown denied the organization access to the energy trading market, but fortunately didn't affect the transmission grid directly.

In order to protect yourself from this type of risk, consider contractually requiring advance notification of pending employee sanctions by your subcontractors.

## Technical Precursors and Access Paths

> **NOTE**
>
> In many cases organizations failed to detect technical precursors.
>
> **Technical precursor:** an individual action, event, or condition that involves computer or electronic media and that precedes and is associated with malicious insider activity.

> **NOTE**
>
> Insiders created or used access paths unknown to the organization to set up their attack and conceal their identity or actions. The majority of insiders attacked after termination.
>
> **Access path:** a sequence of one or more access points that lead to a critical system.

Most of the insiders in the CERT insider IT sabotage cases were clearly headed toward termination through an escalating series of concerning behaviors and associated sanctions. In light of this somewhat predictable outcome, many of them created access paths unknown to the organization to enable them to set up and carry out their attack, even after termination. For example, insiders created backdoor accounts, installed and ran **password crackers,**[10] installed **remote network administration tools**[11] or modems to access the organization's systems, and took advantage of ineffective security controls in termination processes.

These technical precursors could serve as an indicator of a pending attack if you detect them. Recall that most IT sabotage attacks actually occur following the insider's voluntary or involuntary termination. Therefore, it is important that you recognize the patterns in the MERIT model, and be especially vigilant for technical precursors prior to termination of a disgruntled system administrator or other technical, privileged user.

Figure 2-5 depicts the progression from insider disgruntlement to technical precursors that may indicate a pending attack. Some of these actions

10. **Password cracker:** a program used to identify passwords to a computer or network resource; used to obtain passwords for other employee accounts.

11. **Remote network administration tools:** tools to allow the administration of a computer from a location other than the computer being administered.

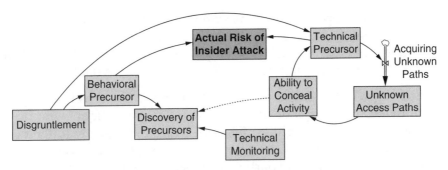

**Figure 2-5** *Technical precursors due to disgruntlement*

also contribute to the damage potential of the attack. Examples include sabotage of backups and decreases in the redundancy of critical services or software. Insiders often acquire access paths unknown to the organization—"unknown access paths." This increases their ability to conceal their activity, making it more difficult for you to discover the precursors. To make matters worse, this ability to hide their actions may actually embolden the risk-averse insiders to continue, or even increase, their efforts to attack.

Examples of methods used by insiders to create unknown access paths to set up their attack include

- Creating backdoors before termination or after being notified of termination
- Installing a modem for access following termination
- Disabling anti-virus programs on desktops and testing a virus
- **Network probing** (any number of practices in which a particular network is either passively surveilled or actively scanned)
- Installing a remote network administration tool
- Downloading and installing malicious code and tools (e.g., a **rootkit**,[12] password cracker, or virus)
- Planting a logic bomb while still employed—here the logic bomb is performing on behalf of the insider and thus is a virtual access path to disrupt systems

---

12. **Rootkit:** software that enables continued privileged access to a computer while actively hiding its presence from administrators by subverting standard operating system functionality or other applications.

We have had the opportunity to interview several convicted insiders. One described the situation as a "downward spiral" where he could "see the end coming." In other words, these employees are "on the HR radar" and realize that termination, voluntary or involuntary, is inevitable.

The extent to which insiders rely on unknown access paths to set up and execute their attack depends on their risk tolerance. Insiders who do not care whether they are caught, or insiders acting impulsively (often out of the passion of the moment), may use both known and unknown paths in their attack. Insiders who are particularly risk-averse may only attack using access paths that are unknown to the organization. Of course, an insider may not know whether the organization is aware of a particular access path. Nevertheless, in either case, insiders who commit IT sabotage generate technical precursors that, if observed, may indicate suspicious activity. Just as with behavioral precursors, the detection of technical precursors depends on having a sufficient level of technical monitoring in place.

In addition to creating unknown access paths, the following technical precursors in the cases in the CERT database enabled the insiders to carry out their attacks or conceal their activity or identity:

- Changing all passwords right before resignation
- Disabling system logs
- Removing history files
- Failing to create backups as required
- Failing to document systems or software as required
- Unauthorized accessing of customers' systems
- Unauthorized use of coworkers' machines left logged in
- Sharing passwords with others and demanding passwords from subordinates
- Refusing to swipe badges to record physical access
- Accessing Web sites prohibited by the organization's acceptable use policy
- Refusing to return a laptop upon termination

## What Can You Do?

Techniques that promote nonrepudiation of action ensure that online actions taken by users, including system administrators and privileged users, can be attributed to the person who performed them. Therefore, if malicious insider activity occurs, nonrepudiation techniques allow each and every activity to be attributed to a single employee. Policies, practices, and technologies exist for configuring systems and networks to facilitate nonrepudiation. However, keep in mind that system administrators and other privileged users will be the ones responsible for designing, creating, and implementing those policies, practices, and technologies. Therefore, **separation of duties**[13] is also very important: Network, system, and application security designs should be created, implemented, and enforced by multiple privileged users.

> **TIP**
>
> **Nonrepudiation**[14] techniques must be implemented to attribute all actions to the person that performed them.

In addition, policies, procedures, and technical controls should enforce separation of duties and require actions by multiple users for releasing all modifications to critical systems, networks, applications, and data. In other words, no single user should be permitted or be technically able to release changes to the production environment without online action by a second user. These controls would prevent an insider from releasing a logic bomb without detection by another employee.

Note that in order to enforce separation of duties for system administration functions, you must employ at least two system administrators. There are several case examples in the CERT database in which the organization was victimized by its sole system administrator. Although many small organizations cannot afford to hire more than one system administrator, it is important that they recognize the increased risk that accompanies that situation.

Finally, the majority of the insiders who committed IT sabotage were former employees. You must be particularly careful in disabling access, especially for former system administrators and technical or privileged users. Thoroughly documented procedures for disabling access can help ensure that stray access points are not overlooked. In addition, the **two-person rule** should be considered for the critical functions performed by these

---

13. **Separation of duties:** the separation of tasks among various individuals.

14. **Nonrepudiation:** ability to verify a particular user is accessing a system or performing a particular action; the goal being to make it more difficult for a user to hide illicit activity.

users to reduce the risk of extortion after they leave the organization. The two-person rule is a control mechanism that requires the involvement of two persons for a particular operation (adapted from Wikipedia).

Some unknown access paths used by malicious insiders included compromised accounts. They used password crackers, obtained passwords through **social engineering,**[15] and used unattended computers left logged in. Password policies and procedures should ensure that all passwords are strong, employees do not share their passwords with anyone, employees change their passwords regularly, and all computers automatically execute password-protected screen savers after a fixed period of inactivity. As a result, all activity from any account should be attributable to its owner. In addition, an anonymous reporting mechanism should be available and its use encouraged for employees to report all attempts at unauthorized account access.

Some insiders created backdoor accounts that provided them with system administrator or privileged access following termination. Other insiders found that shared accounts were overlooked in the termination process and were still available to them. System administrator accounts were commonly used. Other shared accounts included database administrator (DBA) accounts. Some insiders used other types of **shared accounts,**[16] such as those set up for access by external partners like contractors and vendors. One insider also used training accounts that were repeatedly reused over time without ever changing the password.

Periodic account audits combined with technical controls enable identification of the following:

- Backdoor accounts that could be used later for malicious actions by an insider, whether those accounts were specifically set up by the insider or were left over from a previous employee

- Shared accounts whose password was known by the insider and not changed after termination

- Accounts created for access by external partners such as contractors and vendors whose passwords were known by multiple employees, and were not changed when one of those employees was terminated

---

15. **Social engineering:** a nontechnical form of intrusion that relies heavily on human interaction and often involves tricking other people to break normal security procedures (Whatis.com).

16. **Shared account:** an account used by two or more people.

The need for every account should be reevaluated periodically. Limiting accounts to those that are absolutely necessary, with strict procedures and technical controls that enable auditors or investigators to trace all online activity on those accounts to an individual user, diminishes an insider's ability to conduct malicious activity without being identified. Account management policies that include strict documentation of all access privileges for all users enable a straightforward termination procedure that reduces the risk of attack by terminated employees.

It is important that your password and account management policies are also applied to all contractors, subcontractors, and vendors that have access to your information systems or networks. These policies should be written into contracting agreements, requiring the same level of accountability in tracking who has access to your systems. Contractors, subcontractors, and vendors should not be granted shared accounts for access to your information systems. They should not be permitted to share passwords, and when employees are terminated at the external organization, your organization should be notified in advance so that account passwords can be changed. Finally, be sure to include contractor, subcontractor, and vendor accounts in the regularly scheduled password-change process.

## The Trust Trap

> **NOTE**
>
> The "Trust Trap" contributed to organizations being victimized in IT sabotage attacks.

In addition to insider predispositions and behaviors, organizational predispositions and behaviors—such as excessive trust of employees, a reluctance to "blow the whistle" on coworkers, or inconsistent enforcement of organization policies—can also influence an organization's exposure to malicious insider acts. Figure 2-6 depicts a trap in which organizations sometimes find themselves. We call this the Trust Trap and have described its role in previous models [Andersen 2004, Cappelli 2006, Band 2006].

To understand the Trust Trap, we need to distinguish between the actual and perceived risk of an insider attack. As shown in the top portion of Figure 2-6, actual risk depends on the behavioral and technical precursors exhibited by the insider. However, your perceived risk of insider attack is influenced by the extent that you discover and understand behavioral and technical precursors.

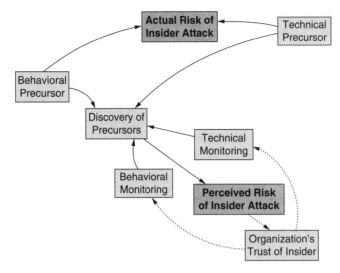

**Figure 2-6** *Trust Trap*

A key factor in the Trust Trap is your trust of your employees, as shown in Figure 2-6. Clearly, there are good reasons why you want to create a workplace in which individuals can trust one another and there is a good trust relationship between the organization and its employees (e.g., to increase morale and productivity). However, managers who strive to promote trusting workplace relationships sometimes shortcut essential behavioral and technical monitoring procedures, or allow them to erode over time due to competing pressures and priorities. Lower levels of monitoring lead to undiscovered precursors, resulting in an overall lower perceived risk of attack. This false sense of security reinforces managers' trust in the individuals working for them. The cycle continues, with your monitoring ability steadily deteriorating until a major compromise becomes obvious to all involved. It is essential that you trust your employees, but you must balance trust with verification, by applying consistent levels of behavioral and technical monitoring.

## Mitigation Strategies

The intent of the MERIT models is to communicate the patterns of each specific type of insider threat over time based on our in-depth analysis of empirical case data. We believe the models also suggest key mitigation strategies for you to defend yourself against someone from within.

We therefore propose countermeasures based on expert opinions in behavioral psychology and information security.

It is critical that all levels of management recognize and acknowledge the threat posed by insiders and take appropriate steps to mitigate malicious attacks. While it may not be realistic to expect that every attempt at insider IT sabotage will be stopped before damage is inflicted, it is realistic to expect that you can build resiliency into your infrastructure and business processes to allow you to detect the attacks earlier, thereby minimizing the financial and operational impact.

> **TIP**
>
> All levels of management must recognize and acknowledge the threat posed by insiders and take appropriate steps to mitigate malicious attacks.

The remainder of this chapter describes potential countermeasures that we believe could be effective in mitigating insider IT sabotage. Figure 2-7 depicts organizational issues of concern in the sabotage cases in our database.

The suggestions that follow apply to identifying and mitigating the most prevalent areas of concern from the graph, as well as some of the other issues that were relevant in a number of cases.

## Early Mitigation through Setting of Expectations

First, you should recognize the personal predispositions of employees and understand the impact they can have on insider threat risk. Second, you should actively manage the expectations of employees to minimize unmet expectations. This can be achieved through communication between managers and employees, especially in the form of regular employee reviews, taking action to address employee dissatisfaction when possible. Consistent enforcement of policies for all employees is also important so that individual employees do not come to feel that they are above the rules or that the rules are inconsistently enforced.

> **TIP**
>
> Managers should recognize the personal predispositions of employees and understand the impact they can have on insider threat risk.

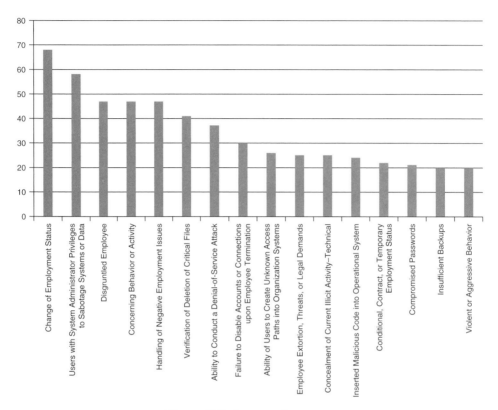

**Figure 2-7** *Issues of concern*

When the expectations of the insider are in line with your practices and policies, unmet expectations are not an issue. However, if a precipitating event impacts expectation fulfillment, proactive actions by management to reset expectations may decrease the level of unmet expectations. If you fail to reset expectations, the level of unmet expectations may continue to rise, increasing disgruntlement on the part of the insider.

For example, you can attempt to lower the level of unmet expectations regarding system use and job responsibilities by a number of proactive countermeasures.

- You institute an acceptable use policy, describing the employee's roles and responsibilities when using the organization's information systems. The policy should be given to each employee as part of his or her orientation to the organization. As changes to the policy occur, employees need to be made aware of the changes and the impact to them. Finally, the policy must be consistently enforced for all employees so that no employees feel that they are "above the rules."

- Management, in conjunction with human resources, should clearly define job responsibilities for each employee in the organization. Processes such as performance reviews should be used to check and set expectations periodically.

## Handling Disgruntlement through Positive Intervention

First of all, management should be trained to pay attention to employee behaviors in the workplace, and to recognize the fact that ongoing concerning behaviors in the workplace could signal potential problems. Remember that insiders who commit IT sabotage are typically very technical, privileged users. It is important that managers of information technology and software engineering teams receive management training so that they are trained to manage *people*, not just technology.

> **TIP**
>
> Managers should be trained to pay attention to employee behaviors in the workplace.

As managers observe ongoing concerning behaviors exhibited by an employee or contractor, they should consider utilizing positive intervention strategies to lower the disgruntlement of the insider. While the intent of employee sanctioning may be to reduce undesirable behaviors, it may backfire in some cases, causing disgruntlement to increase and leading to more disruptive behaviors. When positive intervention is used, the disgruntlement may be reduced, eliminating additional behavioral precursors, as well as the escalation to technical actions to set up an attack.

One positive intervention strategy is an employee assistance program. These programs are sometimes offered by organizations as an employee benefit, to assist employees in dealing with personal or work-related issues that may affect job performance, health, and general well-being. Employee assistance programs can include counseling services for employees and/or their family members.

To explore another positive intervention strategy, let's say an employee is passed over for a promotion. Management could proactively anticipate that the employee may become disgruntled, and attempt to come up with some type of compensating measure. For example, perhaps the employee could be given increased responsibility or professional development, in order to better position him for the next opportunity for promotion.

## Eliminating Unknown Access Paths

Careful tracking and monitoring of access paths available to each employee and contractor is critical so that they can be disabled upon termination. Recall that unknown access paths used by insiders to carry out IT sabotage attacks include backdoor accounts, shared accounts, malicious code planted by the insider, logic bombs, and remote access via remote access systems. Note that some of those access paths, such as shared accounts, are legitimate paths, while others, such as logic bombs, are solely for illegitimate purposes.

---

**TIP**

Careful tracking and monitoring of access paths is critical so that they can be disabled upon termination.

---

Figure 2-8 reflects the relationship between access paths unknown to the organization and access paths known to the organization. These important relationships are explained in the following section.

### Forgetting Paths

Management or the IT staff may forget about known paths, making them unknown. For example, a manager might authorize a software developer's request for the system administrator password during a time of heavy development. Therefore, the system administrator password is an access path known to you at that point in time. If a formal list of employees with access to that password is not maintained, the manager could forget that decision over time. The manager may also resign from the organization, leaving no organizational memory of the decision to share the system administrator password. In either case, the software developer's knowledge of the system administrator password has become an access path unknown to you, and a potential attack vector following termination.

### Discovering Paths

You should institute proactive auditing practices to discover access paths that might otherwise be forgotten. Access paths can be discovered by

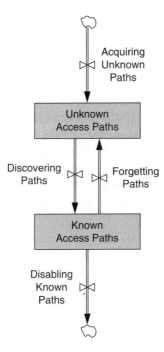

**Figure 2-8** *Access paths available to the insider*

monitoring network traffic or by computer system account auditing, for example. Monitoring network traffic facilitates discovery of suspicious network traffic for further investigation. Account auditing facilitates discovery of unauthorized accounts. Once these access paths are discovered, they can be investigated to determine if they are simply forgotten access paths that should be tracked or disabled, or if they have been created deliberately by an insider for potential malicious activity.

### Acquiring Unknown Paths

Insiders can acquire new access paths unknown to the organization by, for example, creating a backdoor account or stealing passwords. Note that privileged users frequently perform actions such as installing new software and systems, and creating accounts. Therefore, it is important that clear policies exist to govern these actions, and technical controls are used to detect these paths and enforce the policies so that you can discover new access paths and assess their legitimacy.

### Disabling Known Paths

Finally, you can disable access paths that you know about by, for example, removing backdoor accounts or changing shared passwords. It is important that you carefully track access paths, audit them periodically, and disable those that are no longer needed. A key vulnerability exists when you do not know about all of the access paths each of your employees has to your critical systems.

Access paths unknown to the organization provide a mechanism that can be used by the insider to facilitate a future attack, even following termination. For example, organizations often did not know about (or did not think about) insiders' access to shared accounts such as system administrator or database administrator accounts; overlooking such accounts during an insider's termination process often allowed an insider's attack following termination. In addition, unknown access paths can make it more difficult for you to attribute the attack to the insider. If you are unaware of the paths that can be used by an insider for attacks, the task of protecting yourself is significantly more complex.

Diligent tracking and management of access paths into your systems and networks is a critical mitigation strategy for insider IT sabotage. As tracking increases, the likelihood that you will forget about the existence of specific access paths and who has access to them decreases. If precursor technical activity is detected, unknown access paths can be discovered and disabled, further reducing the number of unknown access paths available to the insider. This makes it more and more difficult for the insider to conceal unauthorized or malicious online activity. Conversely, if technical precursors are not discovered, the insider can accumulate unknown access paths, making it easier for him to conceal his actions.

In the cases we examined, the access paths often used by the insider but unknown to management were accounts secretly created by the insider or shared by other coworkers. Compounding the problem, lack of tracking led to unknown access paths that were overlooked in the termination process and later used by the insider to attack. Therefore, we consider ongoing and thorough account management an important practice for tracking access paths and reducing the occurrence of unknown access paths. Account management is a complex task that encompasses verifying new accounts, changing account authorization levels, tracking access to shared accounts, and decommissioning old accounts. Unfortunately, it takes a significant amount of time and resources for organizations to recover from obsolete account-management practices.

## More Complex Monitoring Strategies

Some access paths require a more complex detection program. For instance, a good number of insiders planted logic bombs to conduct their attacks.

Logic bombs are often planted in a place where they are sure to execute, such as operating system scripts or stable, production systems. Note that these are files that should not be modified on a frequent basis, and therefore, triggering an alert when such files are modified is a practical monitoring strategy. Commercial configuration-management and change-management software provide the technical solutions for implementing these triggers. While configuring such a system takes some time up front to determine what files should be changed infrequently, if ever, the time spent will be well worth it should malicious code be discovered when planted by a malicious insider *or outsider.*

---

**TIP**

Some access paths require a more complex detection program, such as monitoring for logic bombs or other malicious code.

---

Likewise, one insider disabled the anti-virus software on his desktop, tested a virus, and planted it in his company's production source code. He then proceeded to release the new production executable directly to all of the customers' systems. When they double-clicked on his company's icon the next morning, it destroyed hardware and software, forcing manual travel to each customer site to recover the systems. Obviously, it would have been to the company's benefit to detect the planting of the virus in the code *before* it was released to the customers' systems. The detection strategy actually is very practical. Is there a good reason for users to disable the anti-virus tool on their desktops, even if they are privileged users? Not likely in most organizations. Therefore, an alert could be triggered when services are disabled on the host, and an investigation initiated by the information security team.

Similarly, configuration-management software could trigger an alert when unauthorized software is installed. This control would detect the insiders who installed a remote network administration tool, password crackers, and other software that they used after termination to attack.

## A Risk-based Approach to Prioritizing Alerts

Some insiders in the CERT cases were especially devious and their actions would be very difficult to detect. One insider sabotaged the source code for an exception handling screen that was only to be used in extenuating circumstances because it overrode *all* security controls that were built in to the system. The screen was so dangerous that anytime it was used an alert was immediately sent to Security for investigation, to make sure the use was legitimate. The insider simply commented out the one line of code that sent the alert to Security, and then used the screen to attack the organization. That action would be extremely difficult to detect. First, he was authorized to modify the source code, so that action alone would not look like anomalous activity. Second, how many organizations do code reviews of every change made to the source code for production systems? In our experience, not many do. Fortunately, there is a solution.

As we discussed previously, configuration-management systems can detect changes to files, including source code; in fact, this organization used such a system and the change was in the logs. However, it is not usually practical to investigate every change to every source code file. In this case, however, that particular source code was in a critical file, and any changes to it could have triggered an alert. We recommend that system owners take the time to prioritize the most critical source code files in their systems—the ones that should trigger a code review anytime a change is made. The change-control system can be set up to report alerts in order of priority, which would make it easy for information security teams to investigate suspicious changes quickly.

In another case, a securities trader for a bank, who was previously a computer specialist, inserted malicious code into a risk model program that he had created. This caused other employees to make increasingly riskier financial deals. The malicious code was discovered by a programmer who was making legitimate modifications to the source code. As in the previous case, the file modified was arguably one of the most critical source code files in their system. Prioritized alerts by a configuration-management system could have alleviated this problem by immediately triggering an investigation of the change.

Prioritizing assets is a time-consuming activity, and one that many organizations do not take the time to do. Rather than trying to prioritize everything, we suggest that each system and data owner tackle only their areas, and focus on identifying the highest-priority files. In this way, prioritized alerts can be generated for changes to those files—the ones posing the highest degree of risk to the organization.

---

**TIP**

System and data owners should focus on identifying their highest-priority assets and implement prioritized alerting when changes to those files occur.

## Targeted Monitoring

It is probably not practical for you to monitor every behavioral and technical action taken by each employee and contractor. However, a reasonable level of proactive logging of online activity across your network provides data that can be monitored or audited for suspicious activity proactively, or targeted to monitor people who have raised the suspicions of their managers.

> **TIP**
>
> Since it is not practical to monitor every behavioral and technical action, proactive monitoring of people who are on the HR radar should be implemented.

As the perceived risk of an insider attack increases, due to detection of behavioral or technical precursors, the amount of technical and behavioral monitoring should also increase. Increased monitoring could lead to discovery of precursor activity, enabling you to identify individuals at a higher risk for malicious behavior and implement more targeted individual monitoring.

If a manager notices an employee progressing through the pattern of behavior described in this chapter, he might consider an audit of that employee's online activity. If the employee's behaviors, either technical or nontechnical, are extreme enough, managers may need to escalate the level of logging and monitoring of that employee's online activity.

Note that very clearly defined policies should be in place in advance of such targeted logging and monitoring; an organization should not perform these actions without consulting with its legal department in advance. Thresholds for beginning targeted monitoring must be very clearly defined. In addition, such policies must be consistently enforced. If you institute targeted monitoring of one employee, and do not implement it for another employee exhibiting the same behaviors, there could be legal repercussions.

Targeted monitoring should be part of a comprehensive insider threat incident-management plan, which should be developed by management, working together with the human resources, information security, legal, and physical security departments.

## Measures upon Demotion or Termination

Termination or demotion was the final precipitating event in many cases we examined. It is important for you to recognize that such precipitating events may cause the insider to take technical actions to set up and carry out the attack, possibly using previously acquired unknown access paths. A clearly defined process for demotions and terminations in combination with proactive IT best practices for detecting unknown access paths and eliminating unauthorized access paths can reduce the insider's ability and/or desire to attack you.

> **TIP**
>
> Precipitating events, such as demotions or termination, may cause increased disgruntlement, so organizations should follow a consistent termination process.

Prior to the demotion or termination, you should be certain about what access paths are available to the insider. If the insider is to be terminated, you must disable all access paths prior to notifying the insider. It is important to understand that if you have been lax in tracking and managing access paths, it could be too late to confidently demote or terminate an employee without fear of retribution.

When a demotion occurs, you should analyze the roles and responsibilities of the new position and update authorization levels and access controls, including role-based access. Some organizations in the cases we analyzed overlooked the change in privileges, allowing the employee to retain privileges from his previous position, giving him access to information beyond that needed for his new position.

Setting expectations during a demotion or termination can be a deterrent against future attacks. Employees should be clearly told what the acceptable use policy is regarding their new positions, what their roles and responsibilities are in their new positions, what their performance improvement plans are (if applicable), and that future monitoring and auditing will be implemented to measure job performance against individual and organizational goals and objectives.

## Secure the Logs

In most insider threat cases, system logs are used to identify the insider, including remote access logs, file access logs, database logs, application logs, and email logs. Many insiders take steps to conceal their actions; some insiders, knowing that the logs would be used for identification, attempted to conceal their actions by modifying the logs. In some cases, they modified the logs to implicate someone else for their actions.

> **TIP**
>
> It is particularly important that you architect your systems to ensure the integrity of your logs by implementing continuous logging to a centralized, secure log server.

## Test Backup and Recovery Process

Prevention of insider attacks is the first line of defense. However, experience has taught us that there will always be avenues for determined insiders to successfully compromise a system. Effective backup and recovery processes need to be in place and operational so that if compromises do occur, business operations can be sustained with minimal interruption. Our research has shown that effective backup and recovery mechanisms affected the outcomes in actual cases, and can mean the difference between

- Several hours of downtime to restore systems from backups
- Weeks of manual data entry when current backups are not available
- Months or years to reconstruct information for which no backup copies existed

Backup and recovery strategies should consider the following:

- Controlled access to the facility where the backups are stored
- Controlled access to the physical media (e.g., no one individual should have access to both online data and the physical backup media)
- Separation of duties and the two-person rule when changes are made to the backup process

In addition, accountability and full disclosure should be legally and contractually required of any third-party vendors responsible for providing backup services, including off-site storage of backup media. It should be clearly stated in service level agreements the required recovery period, who has access to physical media while it is being transported off-site, as well as who has access to the media in storage.

When possible, multiple copies of backups should exist, with redundant copies stored off-site in a secure facility. Different people should be responsible for the safekeeping of each copy so that it would require the cooperation of multiple individuals to compromise the means to recovery. An additional level of protection for the backups can include encryption, particularly when the redundant copies are managed by a third-party vendor at the off-site secure facility. Encryption provides an additional level of protection, but it does come with additional risk. The two-person rule should always be followed when managing the encryption keys so that you are always in control of the decryption process in the event the employees responsible for backing up your information leave your organization.

System administrators should ensure that the physical media on which backups are stored are also protected from insider corruption or destruction. Insider cases in our research have involved attackers who have

- Deleted backups
- Stolen backup media (including off-site backups in one case)
- Performed actions that could not be undone due to faulty backup systems

Some system administrators neglected to perform backups in the first place, while others sabotaged established backup mechanisms. Such actions can amplify the negative impact of an attack by eliminating the only means of recovery. To guard against insider attack, you should do the following.

- Perform and periodically test backups.
- Protect media and content from modification, theft, or destruction.
- Apply separation of duties and configuration-management procedures to backup systems just as you do for other system modifications.
- Apply the two-person rule for protecting the backup process and physical media so that one person cannot take action without the knowledge and approval of another employee.

Unfortunately, some attacks against networks may interfere with common methods of communication, thereby increasing uncertainty and disruption in organizational activities, including recovery from the attack. This is especially true of insider attacks, since insiders are quite familiar with organizational communication methods and, during an attack, may interfere with communications essential to the organization's data-recovery process. You can mitigate this effect by maintaining trusted communication paths outside the network with sufficient capacity to ensure critical operations in the event of a network outage. This kind of protection would have two benefits: The cost of strikes against the network would be mitigated, and insiders would be less likely to strike against connectivity because of the reduced impact.

> **TIP**
>
> Effective backup and recovery processes need to be in place and operational so that if compromises do occur, business operations can be sustained with minimal interruption.

## One Final Note of Caution

You must be aware of the possibility that your employees could attack another organization, possibly a previous employer, using your systems. While not common, such crimes can and do happen—there are a few such cases in the CERT database. You need to consider the liability and disruption that such a case could cause.

One such attack by an insider against his former employer from his current employer's systems may have been a major factor in the current employer's downfall. The insider claimed that the attack was payback for misdeeds against him and his current company. Although the current employer disavows having anything to do with the attack, it too suffered as a result of the insider's action. The law enforcement surrounded its offices and told workers not to tamper with any company data or files, putting its work on temporary hold. In a panic, the insider started massive erasure of potential evidence. The insider received five years for computer hacking and 20 years for obstruction of justice.

## Summary

Insider IT sabotage crimes are the most technically sophisticated crimes in our database. They are committed by technically privileged users who have the access and ability to carry out such attacks. The impacts of these types of crimes can be devastating—organizations have gone out of business, lost millions of dollars, and suffered far-reaching negative media exposure as a result of these attacks.

Most of the insiders who commit these attacks have personal predispositions that are indicated through observable behaviors such as conflicts with coworkers, serious personality conflicts, and inability to follow the rules. These employees attack following some type of negative precipitating event in the workplace, such as no raises due to a poor economy, a new supervisor that no one cares for, or being put onto a new project. As a result, they become disgruntled. Chances are that others in the organization are similarly disgruntled, since they most likely are subjected to the same circumstances. For a certain period of time, the atmosphere at work is probably tense, but then most employees "get over it." The malicious insiders, however, do not get over it. Instead, they become more and more disgruntled. They continue to exhibit concerning behaviors in the workplace, basically caught in a downward spiral that continues to get increasingly worse until they make the decision to attack.

By the time they decide they want revenge, they realize they most likely will be fired, or they voluntarily quit the organization. They know they will need to get back into the organization's network following their termination, so they create what we call "unknown access paths." For instance, they create backdoor accounts, insert malicious code into source code, social-engineer passwords, download malicious code, or write logic bombs. It is at this point that you either detect the unknown access path and setup of the attack, or have little chance of preventing the attack from occurring.

Our recommendations for preventing these types of attacks involve multiple parts of your organization. Management needs to be trained to recognize the signs of a potential insider attack. They need to recognize the warning signs, and try to alleviate the problem if possible. If not, they need to work with human resources to carefully handle the problem. If the situation worsens, they need to be able to pull in the information security and IT departments to audit recent activity by the employee or contractor, and perform targeted monitoring of his activity on an ongoing basis.

It is important that you plan ahead, however, or you will be prohibited from performing those actions by employee privacy laws. You need to put policies in place that clearly define when you can conduct targeted auditing and monitoring of an individual employee or contractor's online activity. You also must have clearly defined practices that are consistently enforced to implement those policies.

Now that you understand insider IT sabotage, you have a choice of where to go next in this book. If you want to follow up immediately on the insider IT sabotage problem, you can go to Chapter 6, Best Practices for the Prevention and Detection of Insider Threats, or to Chapter 7, Technical Insider Threat Controls.

If you want to understand the whole landscape of insider threats, you can continue with Chapter 3, Insider Theft of Intellectual Property.

# Chapter 3

# Insider Theft of Intellectual Property

*Insider theft of intellectual property (IP): an insider's use of IT to steal proprietary information from the organization. This category includes industrial espionage involving insiders.*

*Intellectual property: intangible assets created and owned by an organization that are critical to achieving its mission.[1]*

## Types of IP Stolen

The types of IP stolen in the cases in our database include the following:

- Proprietary software/source code
- Business plans, proposals, and strategic plans
- Customer information
- Product information (designs, formulas, schematics)

---

1. While IP does not generally include individuals' Personally Identifiable Information (PII), which an organization does not own, it could include a database that the organization developed that contains PII.

What if one of your scientists or engineers walked away with your most valuable trade secrets? Or a contract programmer whose contract ended took your source code with him—source code for your premier product line? What if one of your business people or salespeople took your strategic plans with him to start his own competing business? And possibly worst of all, what if one of them gave your intellectual property to a foreign government or organization? Once your IP leaves the United States it's extremely difficult, often impossible, to get it back.

Those are the types of crimes we will examine in this chapter. Organizations in almost every critical infrastructure sector have been victims of insider theft of IP.

In one case of insider theft of IP, an engineer and an accomplice stole trade secrets from four different high-tech companies they worked for, with the intention of using them in a new company they had created with funding from a foreign country. In another, a company discovered that an employee had copied trade secrets worth $40 million to **removable media,**[2] and was using the information in a side business she had started with her husband. In yet another, a large IT organization didn't realize that it had been victimized until it happened to see a former employee at a trade show selling a product that was remarkably similar to the organization's!

When we began examining the theft of IP cases in our database we surmised that insiders probably stole IP for financial reasons. We were very wrong about that! We found that quite the opposite is true: Very few insiders steal intellectual property in order to sell it. Instead, they steal it for a business advantage: either to take with them to a new job, to start their own competing business, or to take to a foreign government or organization.

> Very few insiders steal intellectual property in order to sell it. Instead, they steal it for a business advantage: either to take with them to a new job, to start their own competing business, or to take to a foreign government or organization.

Another misconception about theft of IP is that system administrators are the biggest threat, since they hold "the keys to the kingdom." Not according

---

2. **Removable media:** computer storage media that is designed to be removed from the computer without powering the computer off. Examples include CDs, USB flash drives, and external hard disk drives.

to our data! We don't have a single case in our database in which a system administrator stole intellectual property, although we do have a few cases involving other IT staff members. However, keep in mind that we only have cases in which the perpetrator was discovered and caught; it is possible that system administrators *are* stealing IP and are simply getting away with it.

In fact, the insiders who steal IP are usually current employees who are scientists, engineers, programmers, or salespeople. Most of them are male. We checked the U.S. Bureau of Labor Statistics to determine if most of those types of positions are held by men, but the results, listed here for 2010, were inconsistent.

- 12.9% of all architectural and engineering positions were held by women.
- 45.8% of all biological scientists were women.
- 33.5% of all chemists and materials scientists were women.
- 26.2% of all environmental scientists and geoscientists were women.
- 39.5% of all other physical scientists were women.
- 49.9% of all sales and related occupations were held by women.[3]

> Insiders who steal IP are usually current employees who are scientists, engineers, programmers, or salespeople.

We are not suggesting that you assume men are more likely than women to commit these types of crimes. On the contrary, we suggest that rather than focusing on demographic characteristics, you should focus on the following:

- Understanding the positions at risk for these crimes
- Recognizing the patterns and organizational factors that typically surround insider theft of IP incidents
- Implementing mitigation strategies based on those patterns

These types of crimes are very difficult to detect because we found that these insiders steal information for which they already have authorized

---

3. ftp://ftp.bls.gov/pub/special.requests/lf/aat11.txt

> Insiders steal information for which they already have authorized access, and usually steal it at work during normal business hours. In fact, they steal the same information that they access in the course of their normal job. Therefore, it can be very difficult to distinguish illicit access from legitimate access.

access, and usually steal it at work during normal business hours. In fact, they steal the same information that they access in the course of their normal job. Therefore, it can be very difficult to distinguish illicit access from legitimate access.

Fortunately, we have come up with some good strategies based on our MERIT model of insider theft of intellectual property that we will detail in this chapter. The first half of this chapter describes the model at a high level. In the second half of the chapter we will dig deeper into the technical methods used in committing these crimes and mitigation strategies that you should consider based on all of this information.

The MERIT model describes the profile of insider theft of IP by identifying common patterns in the evolution of the incidents over time. These patterns are strikingly similar across the cases in our database. Unfortunately, we were not quite as lucky in creating our theft of IP model as we were in creating our insider IT sabotage model. While we found one very distinct pattern that was exhibited in almost every IT sabotage case, we could not identify a single pattern for theft of IP. Instead, we ended up identifying two overlapping models.

- **Entitled Independent:** an insider acting primarily alone to steal information to take to a new job or to his[4] own side business
- **Ambitious Leader:** a leader of an insider crime who recruits insiders to steal information for some larger purpose

The cases in our database break up just about 50/50 between the two models. In addition, the models have different but overlapping patterns; the Ambitious Leader model builds from the Entitled Independent model. This is good news, as our suggested mitigation strategies apply to both models.

---

4. Most of the insiders who stole IT property were male. Therefore, male gender is used to describe the generic insider in this chapter.

In this chapter we will describe the patterns identified in both models, and will present mitigation strategies that use those patterns to your advantage.[5] These techniques include a combination of automated and manual countermeasures. In addition, some are focused on protection of your most valuable information assets, while others are targeted at specific employees triggered by indicators that could suggest an increased risk of attack.

For example, if you can identify your most critical assets, technical solutions such as **digital watermarking,**[6] **digital rights management,**[7] and **data loss prevention systems**[8] can be implemented to prevent those assets from leaving your network. There are several drawbacks to these technical solutions, however. First of all, most organizations can't or haven't identified and located all of their most critical computer files. This can be an overwhelming task, particularly in a large organization. In addition, many of you have trusted business partners that legitimately move your critical files back and forth from their own networks to yours. Those types of environments can complicate use of those types of technologies.

Because of the complexity of implementing a purely technical solution focused on critical assets, we also suggest targeted monitoring of employees or contractors who are leaving your organization. We found that most insiders steal intellectual property as they are leaving the organization, suggesting that it could be beneficial to watch their actions more closely, specifically those involving removable media, email, and other methods used in exfiltrating information.

We will provide suggested countermeasures throughout this chapter, and detailed technical information for the theft of IP cases in the section Mitigation Strategies for All Theft of Intellectual Property Cases at the end of the chapter. The bottom line is that unlike IT sabotage, where the goal is to catch the

---

5. Material in this chapter includes portions of previously published works. Specifically, the insider theft of intellectual property modeling work was published by Andrew Moore, Dawn Cappelli, Dr. Eric Shaw, Thomas Caron, Derrick Spooner, and Randy Trzeciak in the *Journal of Wireless Mobile Networks, Ubiquitous Computing,* and *Dependable Applications* [Moore 2011a]. An earlier version of the model was published by the same authors in [Moore 2009].

6. **Digital watermarking:** the process of embedding information into a digital signal that may be used to verify its authenticity or the identity of its owners, in the same manner as paper bearing a watermark for visible identification (Wikipedia).

7. **Digital rights management (DRM):** a term for access control technologies that are used by hardware manufacturers, publishers, copyright holders, and individuals to limit the use of digital content and devices.

8. **Data loss prevention (DLP) systems:** refers to systems designed to detect and prevent unauthorized use and transmission of confidential information (Wikipedia). Also commonly called **data leakage tools.**

insider as he is setting up his attack—planting malicious code or creating a backdoor account—you cannot really detect theft of IP until the information is actually in the process of being stolen—as it is being copied to removable media or emailed off of the network. In other words, your window of opportunity can be quite small, and therefore you need to pay close attention when you see potential indicators of heightened risk of insider theft of IP.

We have some "good-news" cases that indicate that it is possible to detect theft of IP using technical measures in time to prevent disastrous consequences.

- An organization detected IP emailed from a contractor's email account at work to a personal email account, investigated, and discovered significant data exfiltration by the contractor. The organization found the contractor was working with a former employee to steal information to start a competing business. Obviously, the stolen IP was extremely valuable, as the contractor was arrested, convicted, ordered to pay a fine of $850,000, and sentenced to 26 years in prison!

- After a researcher resigned and started a new job, his former employer noticed that he had downloaded a significant number of proprietary documents prior to his departure. This led to his arrest before he could transfer the information to his new employer's network. The information was valued at $400 million.

- During an organization's routine auditing of **HTTPS traffic**[9] it discovered that an employee who had turned in his resignation had exfiltrated proprietary source code on four separate occasions to a server located outside the United States. Although the employee claimed the transfer was accidental, and that he had only uploaded open source information, he was arrested.

---

## Impacts

The impacts of insider theft of IP can be devastating: Trade secrets worth hundreds of millions of dollars have been lost to foreign countries, competing products have been brought to market by former employees and contractors, and invaluable proprietary and confidential information

---

9. **HTTPS traffic:** network traffic that is encrypted via the Secure Sockets Layer protocol.

has been given to competitors. More than half of our theft of IP cases involved trade secrets.

> More than half of our theft of IP cases involved trade secrets.

In addition, impacts in these cases can reach beyond the victim organization. Here are some examples.

- Source code for products on the U.S. Munitions List was shared with foreign military organizations.[10]
- A government contractor stole passwords that provided unauthorized access to sensitive, potentially classified information.
- Source code was added to software in a telecommunications company that enabled the perpetrators to listen in on phone calls made by 103 high-ranking government and nongovernment officials.

Estimated financial impacts in the theft of IP cases in the CERT database averaged around $13.5 million (actual) and $109 million (potential).[11] The median estimated financial impact was $337,000 (actual) and $950,000 (potential). This means that a few extremely high-impact cases skew the average significantly. The highest estimated potential financial losses were

- $1 billion in a high-tech case in the IT sector
- $600 million in a telecommunications company
- $500 million in a pharmaceutical company
- $400 million in a chemical company
- $100 million in a biotech company

The highest estimated actual financial losses were

- $100 million in a manufacturing business
- $40 million in a manufacturing business
- $6 million in the financial services sector
- $1.5 million in a high-tech software development organization

---

10. In U.S. law, the U.S. Munitions List is the list of weapons and similar items that are subject to licensing because of the danger they pose. The U.S. Munitions List is related to the International Traffic in Arms Regulations. Farlex Financial Dictionary. Copyright © 2009 Farlex, Inc.

11. Twenty-five of the 85 cases of theft of IP had known estimates on actual or potential financial impact.

These are only some of the cases with the highest financial consequences. We provided this list for several reasons. First, we are frequently asked how to calculate return on investment (ROI) for insider threat mitigation. That is a very difficult question, and one that has not yet been answered adequately for cybersecurity in general. To start, you should identify what your critical assets are, and estimate the potential loss if those assets were to leave your organization. The losses we listed from actual cases should help you to convince your management that insider threat is not to be taken lightly!

Second, although almost half of the insider theft of IP cases occurred in the IT sector, we want to emphasize that these types of crimes have resulted in significant losses in other sectors as well.

We strongly suggest that you pay close attention to this chapter if you are concerned about the security of your proprietary and confidential information. Now that we have caught your attention, let's look at the characteristics and "big picture" of insider theft of intellectual property.

## General Patterns in Insider Theft of Intellectual Property Crimes

The intent of our MERIT model of insider theft of intellectual property is to describe the general profile of insider theft of IP crimes. The MERIT models describe the patterns in the crimes as they evolve over time—profiling the life cycle of the crime, rather than profiling only the perpetrator.

The MERIT model of insider theft of IP was first published in 2009. The model was created using system dynamics modeling, which is described in the original report and in Appendix F, System Dynamics Background. Over the years, however, we have found that a higher-level view of that model is more useful in describing the patterns to practitioners so that clear, actionable guidance can be provided for mitigating these incidents. That higher-level form of the model and accompanying countermeasure guidance is presented in the remainder of this chapter.

As mentioned earlier, our overall model for theft of IP actually consists of two models: the Entitled Independent and the Ambitious Leader; we will present those one at a time. We have broken each model down into small pieces in this chapter in order to make it more understandable. The full model of the Entitled Independent is shown in Figure 3-1. Figure 3-2 shows the full model of the Ambitious Leader.

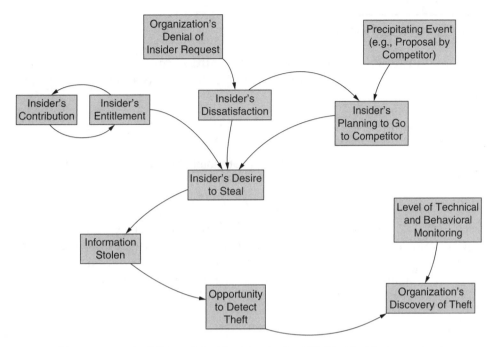

**Figure 3-1** *MERIT model of insider theft of IP: Entitled Independent*

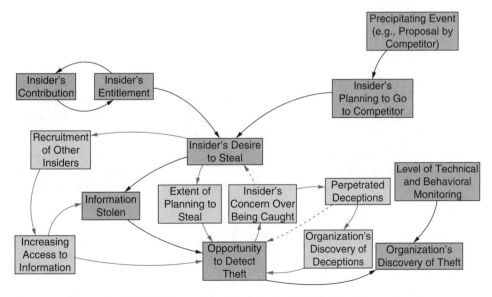

**Figure 3-2** *MERIT model of insider theft of IP: Ambitious Leader*

# The Entitled Independent

This section describes the model of the Entitled Independent, an insider acting primarily alone to steal information to take to a new job or to his own side business.

> **NOTE**
>
> Most insiders felt entitled to take the information they were accused of stealing.

Based on our review of incident descriptions and interviews with victim organizations, investigators, and prosecutors of insider cases, we determined that most insiders felt entitled to take the information they were accused of stealing. The majority of the insiders stole information that they had worked on while employed by the organization.

## Insider Contribution and Entitlement

Figure 3-3 shows how the insider's feeling of entitlement toward the information he develops escalates over time. The employee comes into your organization with a desire to contribute to its efforts. As time goes on and he develops information, writes source code, or creates products, his contribution becomes more tangible. These insiders, unlike most employees and contractors, have personal predispositions that result in a perceived sense of ownership and entitlement to the information created by the entire group. The longer he works on the product, the more his sense of entitlement grows.

This sense of entitlement can be particularly strong if the insider perceives his role in the development of products as especially important. If his work is dedicated to a particular product—for example, development of a software system, or the building of customer contact lists—he may have a great sense of ownership of that product or information. This leads to an even greater sense of entitlement. In addition, consistent with good management practice, individuals may receive positive feedback for their efforts,

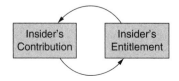

**Figure 3-3** *Insider entitlement*

which may further reinforce their sense of ownership, because of their predispositions.

Evidence of entitlement was extreme in a few cases. One Entitled Independent, who had stolen and marketed a copy of his employer's critical software, created a lengthy manuscript detailing his innocence and declaring that everyone at the trial had lied. After being denied a raise, another insider stole the company's client database and threatened to put them out of business on his way out the door.

## What Can You Do?

Knowing that insiders who steal IP tend to steal the assets they helped to develop is a key factor in designing a mitigation strategy. If you can identify your critical intellectual property, you can narrow down the list of employees and contractors who are at highest risk of stealing it to those who are working on it now or have worked on it in the past.

In addition, keep in mind that people move around within your organization. How good are you at adjusting access controls as those moves happen? Just because someone has moved to another project or area of the organization doesn't mean he doesn't still feel a sense of entitlement to his past work. Erosion of access controls is a problem that needs to be solved in order to reduce risk of insider theft of intellectual property. Almost three-quarters of the insiders in our theft of IP cases had authorized access to the information stolen at the time of the theft, but that doesn't mean that all of them *should* have had access. In many organizations, employees tend to transfer over time to different parts of the organization. They often accumulate privileges needed to perform new tasks as they move, without losing access they no longer need. Unfortunately, many insiders, at the time when they stole information, had accesses above and beyond what their job descriptions required.

We suggest that you periodically review and adjust your access controls for critical assets. We helped one organization set up an effective mechanism for controlling access once an employee transfers to another group. The organization realized that it couldn't disable the employee's access immediately upon transfer since there is typically a transition period in which the employee still needs access to his old team's information. So the organization set up an automated email to be sent from its HR system to the employee's previous supervisor three months after the date of transfer. This email lists all of the email aliases the employee is on, shared folders and collaboration sites to which the employee has access, and so on, and suggests that the supervisor contact IT to disable any access that is no longer necessary. This mechanism has been very successful in controlling the erosion of access controls in the organization.

Some insiders exhibited an unusual degree of possessiveness toward their work before stealing it. For instance, a few insiders kept all source code on their own laptops and refused to store it on the file servers, so they would have full control over it. This type of behavior should be recognized and remediated as early as possible.

### Insider Dissatisfaction

Dissatisfaction played a role in many of the Entitled Independent cases. Dissatisfaction typically resulted from the denial of an insider's request, as shown in Figure 3-4. Denial of an employee or contractor request can lead to dissatisfaction, which in turn decreases the person's desire to contribute. This also affects the person's sense of loyalty to you. Dissatisfaction often spurred the insider in our cases to look for another job; the majority had already accepted positions with another company or had started a competing company at the time of their theft. Once the insider receives a job offer and begins planning to go to a competing organization, his desire to steal information increases. This desire is amplified by his dissatisfaction with his current employer and his sense of entitlement to the products developed by his group.

> Dissatisfaction often spurred the insider in our cases to look for another job.

In one-third of the cases, the insider actually used the proprietary information to get a new job or to benefit his new employer in some way.

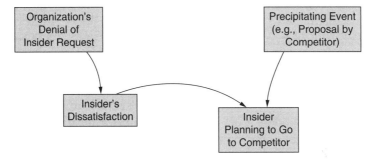

**Figure 3-4** *Insider dissatisfaction leading to compromise*

## Issues Leading to Dissatisfaction

Issues leading to dissatisfaction in the CERT database include the following:

- Disagreement over ownership of intellectual property
- Financial compensation issues
- Disagreement over benefits
- Relocation issues
- Hostile work environment
- Mergers and acquisitions
- Company attempting to obtain venture capital
- Problems with supervisor
- Passed over for promotion
- Layoffs

In more than one-third of the cases, the insider took the information just in case he ever needed it, with no specific plans in mind. One insider actually broke into his organization's systems after he was terminated to find out whether the organization had made any further progress on the product he had helped develop while he worked there.

### What Can You Do?

It is inevitable that many of your employees will find new jobs at some point in time. Now that you understand that these departing employees could pose increased risk of insider theft of intellectual property, you should consider a review of your termination policies and processes. As soon as an employee turns in his resignation, you need to be prepared to act, as you will see in the next section. If you can quickly and easily identify the critical information that employee has access to, you can kick into prevention and detection mode.

Also, food for thought: Some of the insiders who stole IP were contractors. How do you handle contractors when they leave your organization? In our insider threat assessments we have discovered a disturbing trend in ill-defined or loosely enforced procedures for contractor terminations. Although contractors only account for 12% of our insider theft of IP crimes, the risk they pose should not be disregarded. Contract award cycles can range from five years, to three, to even one year. Are you able to track access granted to contractors and ensure appropriate access even when contractors and contracting organizations change on a frequent basis?

## Insider Theft and Deception

> **NOTE**
>
> The insider's plan to leave the organization, dissatisfaction, and his sense of entitlement all contribute to the decision to steal the information.

As shown in Figure 3-5, eventually the desire to steal information becomes strong enough, leading to the theft and finally the opportunity for you to detect the theft. Perhaps someone observes an employee's actions, or consequences of those actions, that seem suspicious in some way. The most likely person to discover an insider theft according to our data is a nontechnical employee; in cases where we were able to isolate the person who discovered the incident, 72% were detected by nontechnical employees. Therefore, you should have processes in place for employees to report suspicious behavior, employees should be aware of those processes, and you should follow up on reports quickly, particularly if they concern an employee who fits the profile described in our models.

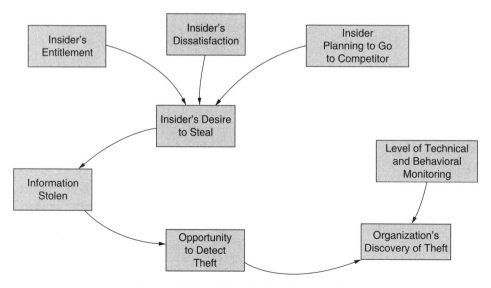

**Figure 3-5** *Insider theft and deception*

Our Entitled Independents did not exhibit great concern with being caught. Even though signed IP agreements were in place in around 40% of the cases, fewer than one-quarter of the Entitled Independents tried to deceive the organization while taking their information. While explicit deception is not a major factor in most of these crimes, the fact that it did occur in one-fourth of them suggests that you need to anticipate it when designing your countermeasures.

For example, upon announcing his resignation, one insider lied to his manager and said he had no follow-on employment, even though he had told a coworker about his new job at a competitor. If you become aware of deliberate deception like this, it may be an indicator of problems to come. Deceptions generally make it harder for you to sense the risk of theft, and that is why the insider does it. But if you are vigilant, deceptions may be discovered, alerting you to increased risk of insider threat. If the organization in this example had known that the insider had given contradictory information to his manager and coworker, it may have been forewarned of the heightened risk.

In general, your accurate understanding of your risk is directly related to your ability to detect the insider's illicit actions. With sufficient levels of technical and behavioral monitoring, these actions may be discoverable.

> **NOTE**
>
> Most information was stolen within one month of resignation using a variety of methods.

Most of these crimes tend to be quick thefts around resignation. More than one-half of the Entitled Independents stole information within one month of resignation, which gives you a well-defined window of opportunity for discovering the theft prior to employee termination. It is important that you fully understand the one-month window, however, as it is a bit more complex than it first appears. First, the one-month window includes the month *before* the insider turns in his resignation and the month *after* he resigns; actually two months total. This means that you need to have technical measures in place at all times so that you can go back in time and review past online activity. Second, some of these insiders stole IP long before resignation; just because they stole it within one month of resignation doesn't mean that is when they first started stealing it. Some of them stole slowly over time, committing their final theft right before resignation. However, fewer than one-third of the insiders continued their theft for more than one month.

One insider planned with a competing organization abroad and transferred documents to the company for almost two years prior to her resignation. However, for the most part, the insiders did steal the information quickly upon resignation.

> **NOTE**
>
> The one-month window includes the month before the insider resigns and the month after he resigns—actually two months in total.

In one case the insider accepted a position with a competing organization, resigned his position, and proceeded to download proprietary information to take with him to the new company before his last day of work. He stole the information despite warnings by his new employer not to bring any proprietary information with him to his new position. When questioned about the theft, the insider admitted to downloading the information, saying that he hoped to use it if he ever started his own business.

In a similar case, the insider accepted a position with a competitor and started downloading documents containing trade secrets the very next day. A few weeks later, after several sessions of high-volume downloading, the insider left the organization and started working for the competitor. Just two days after starting his new job, the insider loaded the stolen files onto his newly assigned laptop, and within a month had emailed the trade secrets to his new coworkers. This exemplifies the lack of any effort to conceal the theft.

A wide variety of technical means were used in the theft cases to transfer information, including email, phone, fax, downloading to or from home over the Internet, malicious code collection and transmission, and printing out material on the organizations' printers. One particularly vengeful insider acted in anger when his employer rewarded executives with exorbitant bonuses while lower-level employees were receiving meager raises or being laid off. He began downloading confidential corporate documents to his home computer, carrying physical copies out of the offices, and emailing them to two competitors. Neither of the two competitors wanted the confidential information and both sent the information they received back to the victim organization. This insider also made no attempt to conceal or deny his illicit activity.

We will explore the technical details of the theft of IP cases later in this chapter, following the Ambitious Leader model.

### What Can You Do?

Our case data suggests that monitoring of online actions, particularly downloads within one month before and after resignation, could be particularly beneficial for preventing or detecting the theft of proprietary information. You need to consider the wide variety of ways that information is stolen and design your detection strategy accordingly. **Data leakage tools**[12] may help with this task. Many tools are available that enable you to perform functions such as the following:

- Alerting administrators to emails with unusually large attachments
- Tagging documents that should not be permitted to leave the network
- Tracking or preventing printing, copying, or downloading of certain information, such as PII or documents containing certain words such as new-product codenames
- Tracking of all documents copied to removable media
- Preventing or detecting emails to competitors, to governments and organizations outside the United States, to Gmail or Hotmail accounts, and so on

You might also consider a simple mechanism to protect yourself from being the unknowing recipient of stolen IP from another organization. As part of your IP agreement that you make new employees sign, you might want to include a statement attesting to the fact that they have not brought any IP from any previous employer with them to your organization. We are heartened by the fact that many of the theft of IP cases in our database were detected by the new employer, and reported to the victim organization and/or law enforcement. You should be sure that you have a process defined for how you would respond to that twist of insider threat. In addition, you may consider asking departing employees to sign a new

---

12. **Data leakage tools:** systems designed to detect and prevent unauthorized use and transmission of confidential information (Wikipedia). Also commonly called **data loss prevention (DLP) systems.**

IP agreement, reminding them of the contents of the IP agreement while they are walking out the door.

---

## The Ambitious Leader

This section describes the Ambitious Leader model. These cases involve a leader who recruits insiders to steal information with him—essentially a "spy ring." Unlike the Entitled Independent, these insiders don't only want the assets they created or have access to, they want more: an entire product line or an entire software system. They don't have the access to steal all that they want themselves, so they recruit others into their scheme to help.

We omitted the What Can You Do? section from most of the Ambitious Leader scenarios because it is so similar to the Entitled Independent model. But we provide extensive advice at the end of the chapter when we explore the technical details in all of the cases.

More than half of the Ambitious Leaders planned to develop a competing product or use the information to attract clients away from the victim organization. Others (38%) worked with a new employer that was a competitor. Only 10% actually sold the information to a competing organization.

About one-third of our theft of IP cases were for the benefit of a foreign government or organization. The average financial impact for these cases was more than four times that of domestic IP theft. In these cases, loyalty to the insider's native country trumped loyalty to the employer. Insiders with an affinity toward a foreign country were motivated by the goal of bringing value to, and sometimes eventually relocating in, that country.

In general, the cases involving a foreign government or organization fit the Ambitious Leader model. However, because the consequences of these crimes are much more severe, and both government and private organizations are so concerned about this threat, we have included a separate section at the end of the Ambitious Leader model that analyzes those crimes in a bit more depth.

> About one-third of our theft of IP cases were for the benefit of a foreign government or organization. The average financial impact for these cases was more than four times that of domestic IP theft.

The rest of this section describes additional aspects of the Ambitious Leader model not exhibited by Entitled Independents. These cases are more complex than the Entitled Independent cases, involving more intricate planning, deceptive attempts to gain increased access, and recruitment of other employees into the leader's scheme.

The motivation for the Ambitious Leader is slightly different from that of the Entitled Independent. There was little evidence of employee dissatisfaction in the Ambitious Leaders. Insiders in this scenario were motivated not by dissatisfaction, but rather by an Ambitious Leader promising them greater rewards.

In one case, the head of the public finance department of a securities firm organized his employees to collect documents to take to a competitor. Over one weekend he then sent a resignation letter for himself and each recruit to the head of the sales department. The entire group of employees started work with the competitor the following week.

In another case, an outsider who was operating a fictitious company recruited an employee looking for a new job to send him reams of his current employer's proprietary information by email, postal service, and a commercial carrier.

Except for the dissatisfaction of the Entitled Independent, the initial patterns for Ambitious Leaders are very similar. In fact, the beginning of the Ambitious Leader model is merely the Entitled Independent model without the "organization denial of insider request" and "insider dissatisfaction." Most Ambitious Leaders stole the information that they worked on, just like the Entitled Independents. The difference is that they were not content only to steal the information they had access to; they wanted the entire system, program, or product line, and needed a more complex scheme to get it.

Theft took place even though IP agreements were in place for almost half (48%) of the Ambitious Leader cases. In at least one case, the insider lied when specifically asked if he had returned all proprietary information and software to the company as stipulated in the IP agreement he had signed. He later used the stolen software to develop and market a competing product in a foreign country.

## Insider Planning of Theft

The Ambitious Leader cases involved a significantly greater amount of planning than the Entitled Independent cases, particularly the recruitment of other insiders. Other forms of planning involved creating a new business in almost half of the cases, coordinating with a competing organization in almost half of the cases, and collecting information in advance of the theft.

This aspect of the insider behavior is reflected in Figure 3-6, which describes the Ambitious Leader formulating plans to steal the information prior to the actual theft. This extensive planning is an additional potential point of exposure of the impending theft, and therefore results in measures by the insider to hide his actions. In most of the Ambitious Leader cases, the insider was planning the theft a month or more before his departure from the organization.

The one-month window surrounding resignation holds for most Ambitious Leaders just as it does for Entitled Independents.

## Increasing Access

In more than half of the Ambitious Leader cases, the lead insider had authorization for only part of the information targeted and had to take steps to gain additional access. In one case involving the transfer of proprietary documents to a foreign company, the lead insider asked her supervisor to assign her to a special project that would increase her access to highly sensitive information. She did this just weeks prior to leaving the country with a company laptop and numerous company documents, both physical and electronic.

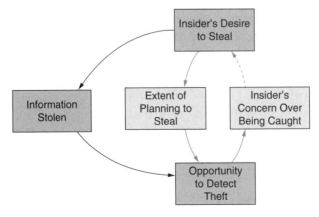

**Figure 3-6** *Theft planning by Ambitious Leader*

As shown in Figure 3-7, the recruitment of additional insiders is the primary means Ambitious Leaders use to gain access to more information. The need for recruitment increases the amount of planning activity necessary to coordinate insider activities.

## Organization's Discovery of Theft

There are many more avenues for you to detect heightened risk of insider theft of IP in Ambitious Leader cases than in Entitled Independent cases. Entitled Independents are often fully authorized to access the information they steal, and do so very close to resignation with very little planning. In addition, Entitled Independents rarely act as if what they are doing is wrong, probably because they feel a proprietary attachment to the information or product. Ambitious Leaders, on the other hand, often have to gain access to information for which they are not authorized. This involves, in part, coordinating the activities of other insiders and committing deception to cover up the extensive planning required.

### What Can You Do?

Figure 3-8 illustrates the avenues available for you to continually assess the risk you face regarding theft of IP. Because deception is such a prominent factor in Ambitious Leader cases, its discovery may be a better means to detect heightened insider risk here than in Entitled Independent cases.

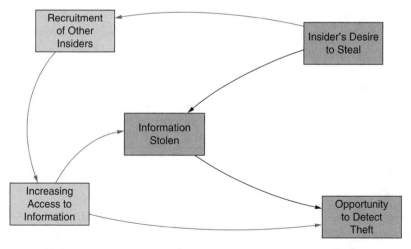

**Figure 3-7** *Increasing access by the Ambitious Leader*

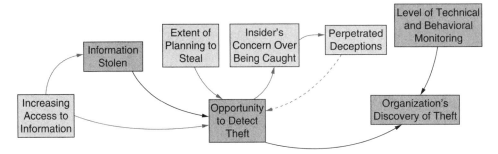

**Figure 3-8** *Organization's discovery of theft of IP in Ambitious Leader cases*

In some of the cases we reviewed, the organization only found out about the theft when the insider took his competing product to market or solicited business from his previous employer's customers. While this detection is later than one would prefer, it is still not too late to take action and prevent further losses. However, we strongly suggest that you consider the countermeasures at the end of this chapter to facilitate earlier detection. Many of the incidents in our database were detected by nontechnical means, such as the following:

- Notification by a customer or other informant
- Detection by law enforcement investigating the reports of the theft
- By victims
- Reporting of suspicious activity by coworkers
- Sudden emergence of new competing organizations

You can use technical monitoring systems to detect insider theft of IP. More than one-half of the Entitled Independents and almost two-thirds of the Ambitious Leaders stole information within one month of resignation. Many of these involved large downloads of information outside the patterns of normal behavior by those employees. In more than one-quarter of the Ambitious Leader cases, an insider emailed or otherwise electronically transmitted information or plans from an organizational computer.

Keeping track of backups of critical information is also important—in one case an insider took the backup media from his computer on his last day of work. Understanding the potential relevance of these types of precursors provides a window of opportunity for you to detect theft prior to employee termination.

Of course, the earlier you can become aware of illicit plans the better. Early awareness depends on behavioral as well as technical monitoring and is more likely to catch incidents involving Ambitious Leaders than Entitled Independents. In Ambitious Leader scenarios, you need to look for evolving plans and collusion by insiders to steal information, including attempts to gain access to information over and above that for which an employee is authorized. There were behavioral or technical precursors to the crime in all of the Ambitious Leader cases.

One insider, over a period of several years, exhibited suspicious patterns of foreign travel and remote access to organizational systems while claiming medical sick leave. It is not always this blatant, but signs are often observable if you are vigilant.

## Theft of IP inside the United States Involving Foreign Governments or Organizations

This section focuses on cases of malicious insiders who misused a company's systems, data, or network to steal intellectual property from an organization inside the United States for the benefit of a foreign entity— either an existing foreign organization or a new company that the insiders established in a foreign country.[13] These cases fit the problem described in the *Annual Report to Congress on Foreign Economic Collection and Industrial Espionage, FY07* prepared by the Office of the National Counterintelligence Executive.

> The United States remains the prime target for foreign economic collection and industrial espionage as a result of its worldwide technological and business leadership. Indeed, strong US international competitiveness underlies the continuing drive by foreign collectors to target US information and technology.[14]

---

13. Material in this section includes portions from a previously published work. Specifically, a joint CyLab and CERT Program article was published as "Spotlight On: Insider Theft of Intellectual Property inside the U.S. Involving Foreign Governments or Organizations" by Derrick Spooner, Dawn Cappelli, Andrew Moore, and Randy Trzeciak [Spooner 2008].

14. See www.ncix.gov/publications/reports/fecie_all/fecie_2007/FECIE_2007.pdf.

These cases also include activities defined by the Office of the National Counterintelligence Executive as economic espionage or industrial espionage.

> *Economic Espionage*—*the conscious and willful misappropriation of trade secrets with the knowledge or intent that the offense will benefit a foreign government, foreign instrumentality, or foreign agent.*[15]

> *Industrial Espionage*—*the conscious and willful misappropriation of trade secrets related to, or included in, a product that is produced for, or placed in, interstate or foreign commerce to the economic benefit of anyone other than the owner, with the knowledge or intent that the offense will injure the owner of that trade secret.*[16]

---

**NOTE**

We have not included any cases of national security espionage in this book.

---

Cases that involve foreign beneficiaries can differ from other theft of IP cases because the insiders may have a sense of duty or loyalty to their countries of origin that overrides any loyalty to their employer. Moreover, some of these cases suggest that some foreign entities appear to be interested in recruiting insiders to steal IP to advance businesses in that particular country. Competing loyalties, coupled with recruitment of employees in U.S. businesses by foreign nations or organizations, make this type of crime a potent threat for organizations that rely on IP for competitive advantage.

There are several reasons for heightened concern about this kind of crime. The impact of a crime that extends outside the jurisdiction of U.S. law enforcement on an organization can be substantially greater than a case that remains within U.S. jurisdiction. Insiders who leave the United States may be difficult or impossible to locate and arrest. And even if the insider were located and arrested, extradition to the United States would be required. Therefore, there can be more risk from an employee who intends to leave the United States following the theft than from employees contemplating criminal acts against their employer who remain in the United States.

---

15. Ibid.

16. Ibid.

In addition, it can be very difficult to recover stolen IP once it leaves the United States. In cases within U.S. borders, companies that receive the stolen IP can suffer similar consequences under the same laws as the insiders if they use the stolen IP for their own advantage. Thus, domestic organizations are under greater obligation to cooperate with authorities and return all stolen IP than foreign organizations might be.

## Who They Are

The majority of the insiders worked as either a scientist or an engineer. Males committed most of the incidents. Of the cases that identify citizenship, about half were foreign nationals, about 40% were naturalized U.S. citizens, two were U.S. citizens, and the rest were resident aliens or had dual citizenship.

The insiders' countries of origin, for cases in which the information was available, are shown in Table 3-1.

About one-fourth of the cases involved at least one accomplice who was also an insider. Some of those involved multiple insiders; one case involved 14 insiders in all! Almost 40% had at least one external accomplice.

**Table 3-1**  *Countries of Origin (When Known)*

| Country | Number of Cases |
| --- | --- |
| China | 13 |
| United States | 2 |
| Taiwan | 2 |
| Canada (naturalized citizen from China) | 2 |
| South Korea | 1 |
| Germany | 1 |
| Russia | 1 |
| Iran | 1 |
| Ecuador | 1 |
| India | 1 |
| Dual citizenship, China and United States | 1 |

Note that when multiple insiders are involved in a case we only code it as a single case, and code details for the primary insider. Additional information about conspirators is also coded for the case. If you are interested in a detailed description of the information coded for each case, please see Appendix D, Insider Threat Database Structure.

## What They Stole

All of these insiders stole intellectual property in digital form, physical form, or both. The methods used were consistent with those described elsewhere in this chapter.

Table 3-2 contains the details known for these cases. Damage amounts are supplied when they were available. We only used the term *trade secrets* when that term was used in the case file; otherwise, we used the description supplied in the case file.

**Table 3-2** *Breakdown of Cases*

| Sector | Number of Cases | Damages[17] | What Was Stolen |
|---|---|---|---|
| Information and telecommunications | 11 | 1 case, $1 billion | Trade secrets (4 cases) |
| | | 1 case, $600 million | Source code (3 cases) |
| | | 1 case, $1 million | Confidential product information (3 cases) |
| | | 1 case, $100,000 | |
| | | 1 case, $5,000 | Confidential manufacturing information(1case) |
| | | 6 cases, Unknown | Proprietary documents and source code (1 case) |

---

17. In the majority of the cases, damages reported were in the form of potential loss to the organization as reported in court documents.

| | | | |
|---|---|---|---|
| Chemical industry and hazardous materials | 7 | 1 case, $400 million | Trade secrets (5 cases) |
| | | 1 case, $100 million | Sensitive product information |
| | | 1 case, $50 million to $60 million | (1 case) |
| | | | Confidential documents |
| | | 4 cases, Unknown | (1 case) |
| Manufacturing | 3 | 1 case, $40 million | Trade secrets (2 cases) |
| | | 1 case, $32 million | Confidential documents (1 case) |
| Banking and finance | 1 | $5,000 | Source code |
| Commercial facilities | 1 | Unknown | Trade secrets |
| Defense industrial base | 1 | Unknown | Source code |
| Education | 1 | $3 million | Patentable proprietary information |
| Energy | 1 | Unknown | Sensitive software |
| Government–Federal | 1 | Unknown | Government restricted information |
| Public health | 1 | $500 million | Trade secrets |
| Water | 1 | $1 million | Trade secrets and source code |

## Why They Stole

The specific motives fall into several categories.

- **To form a new competing business:** One-third of the insiders stole the IP to establish a new business venture in a foreign country that would compete with their current employer. In all of these cases, the insiders had at least one accomplice who assisted them with their theft, with forming and/or running the new business, or with both. All but one of these insiders had already started their business before they left the victim organization; in fact, some of them had already established the business and had made money for quite some time.

- **To take to a new employer in a competing business:** More than 40% of these insiders stole IP to take to their new employers, businesses located outside the United States that competed with their current employer. In all but two of these cases, the insiders had already accepted jobs with the competitors before leaving the victim organization.

- **To take to their home country:** In three of the cases, this was the somewhat vague reason they gave for their theft. In another case, the insider stated he wanted to "benefit the homeland."

- **To sell to a competitor:** In two cases, the insider stole the information to sell to a competitor in another country outside the United States.

Mitigation strategies for these cases are the same as for any other cases of insider theft of intellectual property, which is covered in the next section.

# Mitigation Strategies for All Theft of Intellectual Property Cases

The intent of the MERIT models is to identify the common patterns of each type of insider threat over time based on our analysis of the cases in our database. We have found that the models suggest key mitigation strategies for you to defend yourself against these types of threats. We therefore propose countermeasures based on expert opinions in behavioral psychology, organizational management, and information security.

Your insider threat mitigation strategies should involve more than technical controls. An overall solution should include policies, business processes, and technical solutions that are endorsed by senior leadership in HR, legal, data owners, physical security, information security/information technology, and other relevant areas of the organization. It is critical that all levels of management recognize and acknowledge the threat posed by their current and former employees, contractors, and business partners, and take appropriate steps to mitigate the associated risk. It may not be realistic to expect that all intellectual property exfiltrated by insiders will be stopped before the information leaves your network, but it is realistic to expect that you can implement countermeasures into your infrastructure and business processes to allow you to detect as many incidents as possible, thereby minimizing the financial impact on your organization.

> An overall solution should include policies, business processes, and technical solutions that are endorsed by senior leadership in HR, legal, data owners, physical security, information security/information technology, and other relevant areas of the organization.

The remainder of this chapter describes potential countermeasures that we believe could be effective in mitigating insider theft of intellectual property.

## Exfiltration Methods

We begin this section by providing more in-depth details of the technical methods used by insiders to steal IP in our database. Methods varied widely, but the top three methods used were email from work, removable media, and remote network access. Table 3-3 describes the primary methods of exfiltration.

**Table 3-3** *Exfiltration Methods*

| Exfiltration Method | Description |
| --- | --- |
| Email | Insiders exfiltrated information through their work email account. The email may have been sent to a personal email account or directly to a competitor or foreign government or organization. Insiders used email attachments or the body of the email to transmit the sensitive information out of the network. |

*Continues*

**Table 3-3** *Exfiltration Methods (Continued)*

| Exfiltration Method | Description |
| --- | --- |
| Removable media | Common removable media types were USB devices, CDs, and removable hard drives. |
| Printed documents | Insiders printed documents or screenshots of sensitive information, and then physically removed the hard copies from the organization. |
| Remote network access | Insiders remotely accessed the network through a virtual private network (VPN) or other remote channel to download sensitive information from an off-site location. |
| File transfer | The insider was at work, on the company network, and transferred a file outside of the network using the Web, **File Transfer Protocol (FTP),**[18] or other methods. Although email could potentially fit this category, we thought that email should be considered separately due to the large number of crimes that used email. |
| Laptops | Insiders exfiltrated data by downloading IP onto a laptop at work and bringing it outside the workplace. For example, one insider was developing an application for his company on a laptop and later purposely leaked the source code. In other cases the insiders simply downloaded sensitive files onto their laptops for personal or business use later. |

We dug a little deeper into those methods to determine where our mitigation strategies need to be focused—on the host, the network, or the physical removal of information—and found that more than half involved the network, 42% involved the host, and only 6% involved physical removal.

## Network Data Exfiltration

Data exfiltration over the network was the most common method of removing information from an organization, used by more than half of

18. **File Transfer Protocol (FTP):** a communication standard used to transfer files from one host to another over a network, such as the Internet (Wikipedia).

the insiders in the database who stole IP. Removal methods included in this category were email, a remote network access channel (originating externally), and network file transfer (originating outside the network).

About one-fourth of the insiders used their work email account to send the IP outside the network, either sending IP to their personal email account, or directly emailing the IP to a competitor or foreign government or organization.

> About one-fourth of the insiders used their work email account to send the IP outside the network.

For example, an insider in one case sent customer lists and source code he had written from his work email account to his personal email account. During this time, he was being recruited by a competing organization. He accepted the competitor's offer and took the customer lists and source code to his new job to help him get a head start there.

In another case, an insider asked his superiors for confidential data about their product costs and materials. Two months later, he accepted a new job with a competitor. The original employer warned him against taking or distributing any of its proprietary information. However, the insider emailed internal business information from his work email account to two of his new supervisors before he started at the new company.

Interestingly, almost half of the cases involving email exfiltration also involved another type of exfiltration. This suggests that if you suspect an insider is stealing information you should check other communication channels for similar activity. Most frequently, the additional exfiltration path involved stealing information on a laptop, but use of remote access channels and theft of printed documents each happened a few times in combination with theft via email.

The second most frequent network exfiltration method was remote network access. As in the MERIT model, many of these cases occurred immediately before resignation or shortly after acceptance of a new job at a competitor. In more than one-third of these cases, the remote connections were established after normal work hours; in almost one-third of the cases, the time of exfiltration was unknown.

During the remote sessions, insiders downloaded sensitive documents to their remote computers. In one case, an insider and a coworker were employed as contract software developers for the victim organization. Their contracts were periodically renewed when modifications to the software were needed. Each time their contracts ended, the victim organization neglected to disable their remote access to the network since the organization knew they would be contracted again in the near future. However, at one point both insiders suddenly claimed that the programs they developed belonged to them, and requested that the organization cease using them. The company continued to use the applications, and the insider and accomplice were able to remotely access and download the proprietary source code they claimed to own.

The least common method of network data exfiltration was transferring data outside the network through outbound channels such as FTP, the Web, or instant messaging. These crimes were all perpetrated by more technically skilled insiders. Examples include the following.

- A computer programmer at an investment banking organization submitted his letter of resignation to his manager. He then used a script that copied, compressed, and merged files containing source code, and then encrypted, renamed, and uploaded the files using FTP to an external file hosting server.

- An insider transferred trade secrets and source code to a password-protected Web site using standard HTTP. The insider intended to start a side business with the company's stolen IP.

- An insider who failed to receive a raise and whose request for transfer was rejected submitted his resignation and downloaded proprietary information from his organization for potential use in a new job. He used FTP to transfer the data to his home computer.

### What Can You Do?

Most cases that involved use of the network to perpetrate the theft involved email and remote access over VPN. Given that several cases involved email to a direct competitor, you should consider at least tracking, if not blocking, email to and from competing organizations. Our cases did not explicitly show sophisticated concealment methods, such as use of **proxies**[19] or extensive use of personal, Web-based email services. However, we did find that insiders periodically leverage their personal, Web-based email as an

---

19. **Proxies:** A proxy server, more commonly known as a proxy, is a server that routes network traffic through itself, thereby masking the origins of the network traffic.

exfiltration method. You should carefully consider the balance between security and personal use of email and Web services from your network.

As mentioned, most insiders steal IP within 30 days of leaving an organization. You should consider a more targeted monitoring strategy for employees and contractors when they give notice of their exit. For instance, check your email logs for emails they sent to competitors or foreign governments or organizations. Also check for large email attachments they sent to Gmail, Hotmail, and similar email accounts.

Further, you should consider inspecting available log traffic for any indicators of suspicious access, large file transfers, suspicious email traffic, after-hours access, or use of removable media by resigning employees. Central logging appliances and **event correlation**[20] engines may help craft automated queries that reduce an analyst's workload for routinely inspecting this data.

## Host Data Exfiltration

Host-based exfiltration was the second most common method of removing IP from organizations; close to half of the cases involved an insider removing data from a host computer and leaving the organization with it. In these cases, insiders often used their laptops to remove data from the organization. We had difficulty determining the exact ownership and authorization of the laptops used. However, we do know that about one-sixth of the insiders who stole IP used laptops taken from the organization's site during normal work hours. Half of them transferred proprietary software and source code; the other half removed sensitive documents from the organization.

In one case, the insider worked for a consulting company and stole proprietary software programs from a customer by downloading them to a laptop. He attempted to disguise the theft by deleting references to the victim organization contained in the program, and then attempted to sell portions of the program to a third party for a large sum of money.

Another case involved an insider who accessed and downloaded trade secrets to his laptop after he accepted an offer from a foreign competitor. He gave his employer two weeks' notice, and continued to steal information until he left.

---

20. **Event correlation:** a technique for making sense of a large number of events and pinpointing the few events that are really important in that mass of information (Wikipedia).

By far, the most common method of host-based exfiltration in the database was removable media; 80% of these cases involved trade secrets, and the majority of those insiders took the stolen trade secrets to a competitor. The type of removable media used varied. Where information was available, we determined that insiders most often used writable CDs. Thumb drives and external hard disks were used in just 30% of the cases. However, the type of removable media used has changed over time. Insiders primarily used CDs prior to 2005. Since 2005, however, most insiders using removable media to steal IP use thumb drives and external hard drives. This trend indicates that changes in technology are providing new and easier methods of stealing data from host computers.

In one case, an insider resigned from his organization after accepting a position at another organization. He downloaded personal files as well as the organization's proprietary information onto CDs. Despite signing a nondisclosure agreement, the insider took the trade secrets to a competitor.

In a similar example, an insider received an offer from a competitor three months prior to resignation. He lied about his new position and employment status to coworkers. Only days before leaving the organization, he convinced a coworker to download his files to an external hard drive, supposedly to free up disk space. He came into work at unusual hours to download additional proprietary information onto a CD. Finally, he took this information with him to his new position at a competing organization.

### What Can You Do?

It is unlikely that the victim organizations in our database prohibited removable media in their daily computing environments. You should consider carefully who in your organization really needs to use removable media. Perhaps access to removable media is a privilege granted only to users in certain roles. Along with that privilege could come enhanced monitoring of all files copied onto such devices. In addition, understanding who requires removable media and for what purposes can help you to determine what may constitute normal and healthy business use, and to monitor for usage patterns that deviate from that. Inventory control, as it pertains to removable media, may also be helpful. For example, you could allow use of removable media only on company-owned devices prohibited from leaving your facility. Organizations requiring the highest-assurance environment should consider disallowing removable media completely, or allowing it only in special situations that are carefully audited.

Finally, recall the 30-day window in our theft of IP cases. Can you log all file transfers to removable media? You might not have the resources to review all of those logs (depending on how restricted your use of such media is). However, if the logs exist, you can audit them immediately on the hosts accessed by any employee who has announced his resignation. This would provide one quick mechanism for detecting IP that might be exfiltrated by an employee on his way out the door.

## Physical Exfiltration

Only 6% of the theft of IP cases involved some sort of physical exfiltration. We found that physical exfiltration usually occurs in conjunction with some other form of exfiltration that would have produced a more obvious network or host-based observable event.

## Exfiltration of Specific Types of IP

Once we determined what kinds of IP were stolen and how, we determined what methods of exfiltration were associated with the different types of IP. Several interesting findings surfaced. In particular, business plans were stolen almost exclusively through network methods, particularly using remote access. Conversely, proprietary software and source code involve a much higher use of non-network methods. This may be due in part to the volume of data associated with different asset types. Software and source code files are often large, but business plans are usually smaller documents that are easier to move over a VPN or as an email attachment. Enumerating the most frequent methods by which particular assets are exfiltrated may help steer monitoring strategies with respect to computers that house particular types of assets or are allowed to access given assets over the network.

## Concealment

Some insiders attempted to conceal their theft of IP through various actions. These cases signify a clear intent to operate covertly, implying the insiders may have known their actions were wrong. In one case, an insider was arrested by federal authorities after stealing product design documents and transferring them to a foreign company where he was to be employed. After being arrested, he asked a friend to log in to his personal email account, which was used in the exfiltration, and delete hundreds of emails related to the incident.

Another case involved an insider who used an encryption suite to mask the data he had stolen when moving it off the network.

## Trusted Business Partners

Trusted business partners accounted for only 16% of our theft of IP cases, but this is still a complicated insider threat that you need to consider in your contracting vehicles and technical security strategies.

For example, a telecommunications company was involved in a lawsuit, and had to hand over all of its applicable proprietary information to its attorneys, which it did in hard-copy form. The law firm subcontracted with a document imaging company to make copies of all of the information. One of the employees of the document imaging company asked his nephew, a student, if he would like to make a little extra spending money by helping him make the copies at the law firm. The nephew realized that he had access to proprietary access control technology that the telecommunications company used to restrict its services based on fees paid by each individual customer. He felt, like many others, that the company unfairly overcharged for these services, so he posted the information online to the Internet underground. This basically released the telecommunications company's "secret sauce," and now it was easy for members of that community to obtain free services. When the post was discovered, law enforcement investigated the source of the post and traced the activity back to the student.

It is important that you consider these types of threats when drawing up contracts with your business partners. Could that scenario happen to you? Do you write legal language into your contracts that dictates how your confidential and proprietary information can and cannot be handled?

It is important that you understand the policies and procedures of your trusted business partners. You establish policies and procedures in order to protect your information. When you enlist the support of a trusted business partner, you should ensure that their policies and procedures are at least as effective as your safeguards. This includes physical security, staff education, personnel background checks, security procedures, termination, and other safeguards.

In addition, you should monitor intellectual property to which access is provided. When you establish an agreement with a trusted business partner, you need assurance that IP you provide access to is protected. You need to get assurances that access to and distribution of this data will be monitored. You should verify that there are mechanisms for logging the dissemination of data, and review their procedures for investigating possible disclosure of your information.

These are just a few recommendations. We detail eight recommendations in Chapter 9, Conclusion and Miscellaneous Issues, regarding trusted business partners.

## Mitigation Strategies: Final Thoughts

We devoted a good deal of this chapter to technical countermeasures. Figure 3-9 depicts organizational issues of concern in the theft of intellectual property cases in our database. We addressed the technical issues in the previous section, but there are nontechnical issues worth noting as well. For instance, notice that the most prevalent issue of concern is an employee who went to work for a competitor. Therefore, you might want

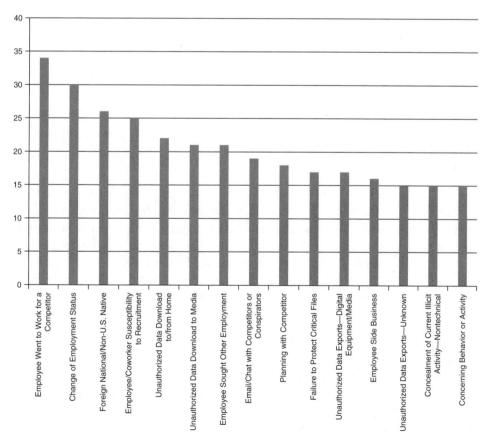

**Figure 3-9** *Issues of concern*

to monitor emails going to a competitor. We provide a control for doing that in Chapter 7, Technical Insider Threat Controls. Also, note the second most prevalent issue of concern: change in employment status, which would account for the insiders who stole information within 30 days of resignation. The third most prevalent issue is foreign national/non-U.S. native, which we covered in depth in the section Theft of IP inside the United States Involving Foreign Governments or Organizations earlier in this chapter. The fourth issue, employee/coworker susceptibility to recruitment, applies in all of the Ambitious Leader cases.

One final thought regarding the 30-day window: You should review your access-termination procedures associated with employee and contractor exit procedures. Several cases provided evidence that insiders remotely accessed systems by using previously authorized accounts that were not disabled upon the employee's exit. Precautions against this kind of incident seem to be common sense, but this trend continues to manifest in newly cataloged cases.

> **NOTE**
>
> For more details of technical controls you can implement to prevent or detect insider theft of IP, see Chapter 7, where we describe new technical controls from our insider threat lab.

## Summary

Insiders who steal intellectual property are usually scientists, engineers, salespeople, or programmers. The IP stolen includes trade secrets, proprietary information such as scientific formulas, engineering drawings, source code, and customer information. These insiders typically steal information that they have access to, and helped to create. They rarely steal it for financial gain, but rather they take it with them as they leave the organization to take to a new job, give to a foreign government or organization, or start their own business.

These insider threats fall into two groups. The first is the Entitled Independent, an insider who acts alone to take the information with him as he leaves the organization. The second is the Ambitious Leader, an insider who creates a "ring" of insiders who work together to steal the information. Ambitious Leaders want to steal more than just the information they created—they want the entire product line, or whole suite of source code, for example.

A portion of this chapter was devoted to insiders who stole IP to take to a foreign government or organization. These crimes can be particularly disastrous, since it is much more difficult to recover the information once it leaves the United States. We described the countries involved, the positions of the employees, and the methods of theft.

The most useful pattern we found in modeling these crimes was that most of the insiders stole at least some of the information within 30 days of resignation. That time frame actually encompasses a 60-day window: 30 days before turning in their resignation, and 30 days after. Our mitigation strategies use that time frame; we recommend logging of all potential exfiltration methods, especially emails off of the network and use of removable media, so that you can audit the information when an employee who has access to your critical information resigns. You need to be able to go backward in time when such an employee resigns to make sure he has not emailed your IP outside the network—for example, to competitors, to governments or organizations outside the United States, or to Gmail or Hotmail accounts. You also need to be able to identify information that was copied to removable media during that time frame. Finally, you need to do real-time alerting when such online activity takes place in that period between when the insider resigns and when his employment actually terminates.

The next chapter turns to insider fraud. Insider fraud involves theft as well, but theft of a different type of information: Personally Identifiable Information (PII), credit card information, and other data that could be used to commit fraud. It also includes crimes in which an insider modified information for financial gain, often for pay by outsiders.

# Chapter 4

# Insider Fraud

> *Insider fraud:* an insider's use of IT for the unauthorized modification, addition, or deletion of an organization's data (not programs or systems) for personal gain, or the theft of information that leads to an identity crime (identity theft, credit card fraud) [Weiland 2010].

> *Identity crime:* the misuse of personal or financial identifiers in order to gain something of value and/or facilitate some other criminal activity.[1]

We have two questions for you to consider. First, do you handle information that could be used to commit identity theft or credit card fraud? What would the repercussions be if that information was stolen? With current data breach notification laws, keeping the theft a secret is probably not an option, which means public exposure of the crime. How will your customers feel about your organization if that happens? Will loss of their trust affect your bottom line?

Second question: Do you handle any information that someone might wish to modify, delete, or add fraudulent information to? This information can range from the obvious financial data to less obvious information such as driver's licenses, criminal histories, credit histories, utility bills, food stamps, and so on. You need to take a minute to really think about this question. It is likely that the owner of a water company would not have

---

1. This definition comes from the Secret Service Web site: www.secretservice.gov/criminal.shtml.

anticipated that three of his meter readers would carry out a fraud scheme with 17 customers for 18 months for a total of $325,000. But that's exactly what happened. Take a minute to think about your information systems and which ones might provide an attractive means of earning some extra cash to your employees, contractors, or business partners.

Those are the types of crimes we will explore in this chapter. Recall from Chapter 1, Overview, that fraud crimes are by far the most prevalent in the CERT insider threat database. The data breach laws could account for the significant number of cases, because victim organizations can no longer handle those types of crimes quietly, internal to the organization. However, the fact remains that these types of crimes are definitely occurring, and not only in the financial sector as one might initially guess.

---

**NOTE**

By insider fraud we mean insiders who modify, add, or delete information for their own advantage, and those who relay information to others, either insiders or outsiders, who use it to commit fraud.

---

In our insider fraud cases, the insider is not necessarily the one who commits the actual identity crime, but the insider is often associated with others (possibly outsiders) who do commit an identity crime. In fact, all of the crimes in the CERT database that involved organized crime were insider fraud cases. In this chapter we describe the profile of insider fraud and present strategies for mitigating the insider fraud crimes.[2] We devote a section of this chapter specifically to the cases involving organized crime because the impacts of those were substantial: The average damages in these cases exceed $4 million, with one case resulting in almost $50 million in losses.

---

We devote a section of this chapter specifically to the cases involving organized crime because the impacts of those were substantial: The average damages in these cases exceed $4 million.

---

2. Material in this chapter includes portions from a 2010 *CERT Research Annual Report* article on insider fraud modeling work by Andrew Moore, Adam Cummings, and Derrick Spooner. See www.cert.org/cert/information/researchers.html.

We decided to exclude two types of insider fraud from our studies:

- Cases of corporate fraud, such as the Enron case, in which the fraud is pervasive throughout the organization and largely perpetrated for the (near-term) benefit of the organization
- Insider trading[3] cases that do not involve IT in carrying out the crime

Our insider fraud cases involve individuals or groups of individuals that act in the interests of that individual or group, and counter to the interests of the victim organization.

Fraud cases can have huge financial impacts, as exemplified by the following case in which an organization lost nearly $20 million.

> A customer service representative at a company that processed health insurance claims realized that he could take advantage of the lack of oversight or two-person control for checking claims entered into the system. He retrieved the names of medical care providers who rarely filed claims, changed their addresses, and then submitted false claims for them. The payments for those claims were sent to the new addresses he had entered—those of his associates in organized crime. Over a six-month period, the scheme diverted nearly $20 million in payouts to fraudulent Medicare claims from the company to the insider and his accomplices.

Insider fraud can also lead to the compromise of substantial personal information, as in the following case, in which almost 60,000 employee records were put up for sale on the Internet.

> A database administrator at an insurance company was responsible for a database containing personal employee information for all of the company's employees across the United States. After becoming frustrated over time by what he perceived to be unfairly low pay, he came up with a plan that enabled him to get revenge against his employer and make some extra money at the same time. He downloaded personal employee information from the database to removable media, resulting in the compromise of 60,000 employee records. Then, following a dispute with his employer, he quit his job.
>
> He solicited bids for the information over the Internet. He posted employee credit card numbers in newsgroups dedicated to credit card

---

3. From Wikipedia: "Insider trading is the trading of a corporation's stock or other securities (e.g., bonds or stock options) by individuals with potential access to non-public information about the company."

fraud, and encouraged the malicious use of those credit cards as well as others opened in the names of the victim employees. He continued to carry out his fraudulent activity for a two-year period before an under-cover agent posing as a potential buyer of the insider's stolen information arrested him.

It is important to note that this case was one of only three cases in the CERT database in which the insider stole an entire database as part of the fraud. This case was in the financial services sector; the other two cases were in the government sector and the water utilities sector.

Insider fraud can also compromise national security—for instance, by allowing unauthorized individuals access to the United States. The fol-lowing case shows how an insider compromised the process of granting foreign nationals access to the United States.

> The insider supervised employees processing asylum applications for the U.S. government. He fraudulently altered U.S. immigration asylum deci-sions in return for payments of up to several thousand dollars per case. He would approve an asylum decision himself and request that one of his subordinates approve the decision, or overturn someone else's denial of an asylum application. An outsider recruited the foreign nationals who wished to acquire political asylum. To conceal his activity, the insider often used his subordinates' computers and credentials. Several foreign nation-als either admitted in an interview or pleaded guilty in a court of law to lying on their asylum applications and bribing public officials to approve their applications. The insider received $50,000 for granting political asy-lum for 20 to 30 foreign nationals. The fraud was detected by the director of his office and was reported to law enforcement. The insider was con-victed and sentenced to 21 months of imprisonment.

Clearly the impacts of insider fraud can be wide-ranging—from purely financial to personal privacy, or even national security. The previous case examples are not unique in their impact: Many other organizations lost huge sums in money, assets, and employee security and privacy.

Like insider theft of IP, insider fraud is usually committed by current employees engaging in the same types of online activities that they per-form as part of their normal jobs. Unfortunately, instead of working toward the mission of the organization, they are working to benefit themselves. Most engage in fraud-related activities during normal work hours, while on-site, using their own authorized access.

Unlike crimes of insider theft of IP and IT sabotage, however, insider fraud crimes were often conducted by insiders in lower-level positions in the organization. These insiders were generally not professionals and were not

## Impacts of Insider IT Fraud

The impacts of insider IT fraud attacks include the following:

- Losses of almost $700 million hidden from a financial organization for five years
- More than $8 million worth of military equipment lost
- Driver's licenses provided to 195 people unable to obtain legal licenses
- Credit histories of 178 consumers modified or deleted, resulting in more than $4 million in high-risk loans that otherwise would not have been granted
- Loss to fraud of $335,000 among ten financial institutions and 25 retailers in multiple states
- More than $600,000 in fraudulent disability payments
- Loss of more than $250,000 by a city government through payments to fake vendors
- Almost $63,000 in fraudulent lottery winnings paid

technical insiders. About half of them were on the lower end of the pay scales, such as entry-level data entry clerks or administrative assistants. This makes some intuitive sense since many of the insider fraud cases were financially motivated, perpetrated by individuals in some level of financial difficulty.

Insider fraud crimes also had the greatest mix of perpetrators of both genders, with just slightly more female perpetrators than male. This could be due to the greater mix of people in nontechnical roles in organizations as well as people experiencing financial difficulties. We checked the U.S. Bureau of Labor Statistics for 2010 to determine the breakdown of those types of positions between men and women.

- 90.8% of all payroll and timekeeping clerks were women.
- 88% of all tellers were women.
- 75.9% of all court, municipal, and license clerks were women.
- 66.6% of all customer service representatives were women.
- 80.5% of all data entry keyers were women.[4]

As with the other types of crimes, the ages range quite broadly from people in their teens to those in their 70s. Again, we do not believe that demographic

4. ftp://ftp.bls.gov/pub/special.requests/lf/aat11.txt

characteristics are all that useful to identify likely perpetrators. Instead, we recommend focusing on general patterns of behavior that can provide insights into the nature of the crime and how to prevent it, or at least detect and respond to the crime to limit damage.

At the time this chapter was written, the U.S. Department of Homeland Security (DHS) Science and Technology (S&T) Directorate brought the original Secret Service/CERT Insider Threat Study team back together to study insider fraud in the financial sector. The U.S. Department of the Treasury also participated in the study to help us to connect with the financial sector. We are still in the case-gathering mode, and do not yet have analysis to report. However, this chapter reports preliminary findings based on our earlier fraud modeling work sponsored by CyLab, updated based on all of the fraud cases currently in the CERT database. Please keep checking our Web site at www.cert.org/insider_threat for our report and fraud model.

## General Patterns in Insider Fraud Crimes

The starting point for describing patterns of insider fraud, including the MERIT fraud model, is the Fraud Triangle, developed by the criminologist Donald Cressey in the early 1950s [Cressey 1974].[5] The Fraud Triangle evolved through Cressey's interviews with imprisoned bank embezzlers. His observation that many of these formerly law-abiding citizens had what he termed a "non-sharable financial problem" led to his development of the Fraud Triangle. As depicted in Figure 4-1, the Fraud Triangle involves three dimensions: pressure, opportunity, and rationalization. As the theory goes, all three elements must be present in order for fraud to occur.

- Pressure is what causes a person to commit fraud, often stemming from a significant financial need or problem. This problem or need can arise due to external pressures such as medical bills, addiction problems, or even just expensive tastes. While some fraud is committed simply out of greed, Cressey's observation was that there was often a need to resolve the problem in secret, that is, it was "non-sharable."

---

5. At the time we were writing this book, our insider fraud case files did not have sufficient data to support strong conclusions about the dynamic over-time nature of the crime, as is required for our modeling efforts. We therefore thought it was even more important to start the modeling efforts off in the existing, fairly well-established theory of the Fraud Triangle. Our current work expands insider fraud case data and we hope to validate these foundations as we move forward in refining the MERIT insider fraud model.

- Opportunity is the perpetrator's ability to commit fraud. Within an organization, weak security controls and inadequate oversight by management provide opportunities for some fraudsters. Organizations have more control over the opportunity dimension than the other two dimensions. Organizations can build processes, procedures, and controls that inhibit or deter an employee's ability to commit fraud and that effectively detect it when it does occur.
- Rationalization involves the process of overcoming any personal ethical hesitations to commit the fraud. It involves reconciling the bad behavior with commonly accepted notions of decency or trust. Rationalizing individuals may believe that, due to perceived mistreatment, the organization owes them something, or that committing the fraud is the only way to save their family from sure devastation. Rationalization may include beliefs that the fraudster is merely "borrowing" money until it can be paid back. At the other end of the spectrum, rationalization includes misunderstanding about the severity of the fraudulent acts or apathy about their consequences.

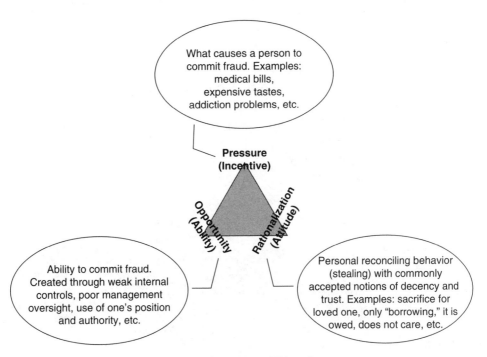

**Figure 4-1** *Fraud Triangle*

The Fraud Triangle has gained widespread support, most prominently from the American Institute for Certified Public Accountants [AICPA 2002]. We adopted the Fraud Triangle as the basis of our initial effort to model the primary patterns of insider fraud because the patterns in the cases in the CERT database support it. Figure 4-2 shows our interpretation of the Fraud Triangle for insider threat. Starting in the lower left, you can see that incentives for insider fraud stem from the insider's financial problems or the need to help family and friends, as well as other social networking pressures. Financial problems can lead to greater dissatisfaction with compensation. That dissatisfaction results in rationalization of the crime, feeling that the organization owes the insider for past mistreatment. Some insiders in our cases rationalized that their actions were only temporary and they would repay the organization later. Another common feeling was that the insider was at a turning point in his or her life and had no other option but to commit the crime.

Opportunity to commit the fraud is limited by the fraud prevention controls implemented by the organization.

The following sections further explain the three aspects of the Fraud Triangle based on observations from fraud cases in the CERT database.

### Origins of Fraud

The primary motivation for insider fraud is financial gain. Insiders stole information to sell it; modified data to achieve financial benefits for themselves, friends, or family; or were paid by outsiders to modify

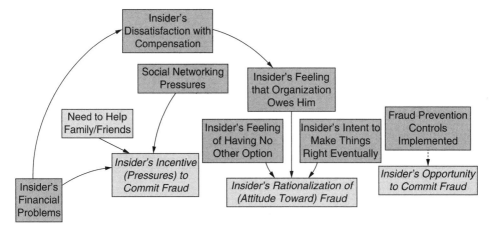

**Figure 4-2** *Insider Fraud Triangle*

> **NOTE**
>
> Fraud crimes involved theft and modification of information, often to solve the insider's financial problems.

information. Some insiders were motivated to provide additional income for their relatives, and a few insiders had large credit card debts or drug-related financial difficulties.

The most common and straightforward means used by insiders was stealing information to which they had access. Most thefts were not very sophisticated. Remember, these are largely not technical, and are not committed by highly educated individuals.

Some of them did use electronic means to exfiltrate information, however.

- They downloaded the information to home.
- They looked it up online and used it immediately.
- They copied it to removable media.
- They telephoned or faxed the information.
- They emailed the information.

A few fraud cases did involve more sophisticated methods. One insider was paid by an outsider to intentionally double-click on an email attachment that contained malicious code and a **software keystroke logger.**[6] The malicious code periodically transmitted customer information to a competitor. Another insider used an **anonymous remailer** to mask his involvement in a fraud scheme. An anonymous remailer is a server that receives email messages containing embedded instructions on where to forward them. The server then forwards the messages while also masking their originating location.

Some insider fraud crimes involved theft of information, but other insiders modified information, often paid for by outsiders who stood to benefit. For example, a series of insider crimes in the CERT database victimized credit history organizations; data entry clerks figured out that they could make money by "improving" the credit history of individuals trying to obtain loans for which they did not qualify.

---

6. **Software keystroke logger:** a software-based method of recording keystrokes entered from a keyboard.

Most modification cases involved changing information in a system, as in the previous example. However, some insiders added information—as in cases in which fake driver's licenses were created by adding false information to an application and generating the corresponding license. Very few cases involved the deletion of information, but some involved a combination of methods.

Figure 4-3 shows how financial problems, on the left-hand side of the figure, provide incentives for the insider to conduct fraudulent activities. The crime results in financial benefit, which helps to reduce the financial problems that originally motivated the crime. (The dotted line in Figure 4-3 indicates that the insider's financial problems are *reduced*.)

## Continuing the Fraud

A major difference between insider fraud and the other types of insider crimes is the time frame over which the crimes typically occur. Insider fraud is typically a long and ongoing crime. Insider IT sabotage and, to a lesser extent, theft of IP are largely big-bang events where the insider commits the crime and leaves the organization as fast as he can. Such smash-and-grab events do not work as well to perpetrate fraud, since insiders typically want to siphon off or modify information slowly and repeatedly for as long as possible so as not to be noticed. Since financial difficulty is often the motivating factor, losing or leaving one's job is not an attractive option.

Insider fraud is typically a long and ongoing crime.

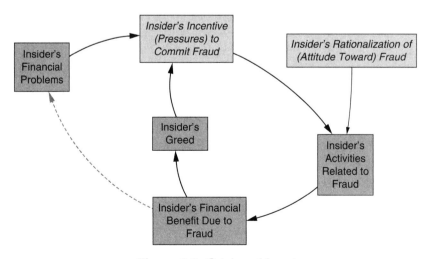

**Figure 4-3** *Origins of fraud*

The average insider fraud crime spanned about fifteen months, with half of the crimes lasting five months or more. More than half of the incidents were ongoing with frequent periods of significant compromise. Of the short, quick compromises, about half ended because the insider was caught quickly, and most of the others ended because the crime was committed as the employee was leaving the organization, or following termination.

Interestingly, many crimes involved the theft or modification of relatively small pieces of information—a credit card number, Social Security number, or credit history record—in contrast to the much larger thefts typical in the theft of IP cases. Each small piece of information brought the insider a small financial benefit, so the insider was motivated to keep the fraud going as long as possible and to "fly under the radar" of any organizational scrutiny.

Often, the insider's financial problems are eventually resolved, but the additional income is too good to resist and the fraud takes on a life of its own. This is where the insider's greed comes into play in Figure 4-3. The financial benefits, along with the ability to get away with the crime, result in an emboldening of the insider and the desire to keep things going.

## Outsider Facilitation

> **NOTE**
>
> Outsiders facilitated many of the fraud crimes and recruited the insider to commit the crime in about one-third of the cases.

Many of the insiders who committed fraud colluded either with people external to the organization or with other insiders. Some cases involved collusion with both insiders and outsiders. They colluded with at least one outsider in about 40% of the cases. Outsiders actually recruited insiders to help them commit fraud in about one-quarter of the cases. A recurring pattern involved outsiders recruiting an insider in a low-paying, nontechnical position who had access to Personally Identifiable Information (PII) or customer information. The insider stole the information and provided it to the outsider for pay; the outsider then used the information to commit the fraud.

The right-hand side of Figure 4-4 depicts the outsider facilitation of the fraud, which gives the insider the opportunity to commit the crime. Most of the insiders did not have the contacts or expertise needed to commit

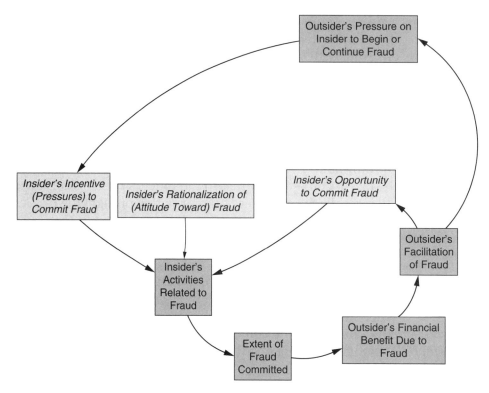

**Figure 4-4** *Outsider facilitation of insider fraud*

identity theft or credit card fraud, or to carry out other fraud schemes on their own. However, the outsiders who approached them had the knowledge and ability, and therefore were critical in actually carrying out the fraud using the information provided or modified by the insider. The bottom of Figure 4-4 depicts how the insider's actions result in financial benefit for the outsider, which encourages the outsider to pressure the insider to continue stealing or modifying information.

The loop around the outside of the figure illustrates how the growth of the fraud business will likely result in the outsiders pressuring the insider to increase their participation by stealing or modifying more and more information. While there are limits to growth of the fraud business, we often saw a period of escalation of fraud activities in the cases in the CERT database. Another incentive for the insider to continue could also come from the threat that the outsider could turn the insider in if he or she does not participate fully.

Identity crimes are the most prevalent type of fraud in the CERT database; in our cases there was no shortage of outsiders experienced in committing that type of crime. Outsiders recruited insiders to steal information more often than to modify it, probably because committing identity theft is much easier than coming up with a scheme for modifying an organization's information to their advantage. As you will see in the next section, not only was modification to commit fraud more likely the insider's idea, but insiders often recruited other coworkers to help.

> Outsiders recruited insiders to steal information more often than to modify it.

## Recruiting Other Insiders into the Scheme

> **NOTE**
>
> Coworkers facilitated many of the insider fraud crimes, especially for fraud involving modification of information.

Insiders recruited other insiders, often coworkers, in about one-fifth of our cases of insider fraud. The percentage is higher in insider fraud crimes in which information was modified as part of the crime than the theft cases. This makes sense for the following reason. Modification of information is a more detectable act than theft, at least from a technical point of view. Remember that insiders who committed fraud through theft stole small pieces of information such as credit card numbers or Social Security numbers. This type of theft may involve something as simple as opening a screen and manually copying the numbers down. We even had cases where the insider just remembered the information, and told it to an outsider so that he could commit the identity crime. Modifying information, at least online, requires technical action to change computer data. This action is easily auditable and more easily observable, especially by coworkers working with the insider using the same data or in close physical proximity.

Figure 4-5 depicts the insider's recruitment of other employees into the fraud crime. As the fraud crime grows, the insider's perceived risk of getting caught also grows, depending to some extent on the insider's knowledge of the organization's fraud controls. The recruitment is seen as a way to help conceal the expanded operations of the fraud crime. Another reason we've seen in cases for recruiting other employees is simply to handle the expanded workload of the crime. The insider recruitment in

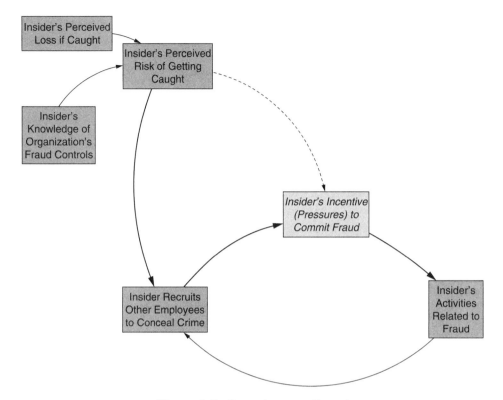

**Figure 4-5** *Coworker recruitment*

these cases results in real escalation of the fraud activities. Finally, some insiders recruit inside help to overcome separation of duties controls that exist within organizations. Often, actions of multiple employees are required to make a necessary change to the data.

As the fraud involves more and more people, the operation has more mouths to feed and the pressures on the insider to continue the fraud scheme grow accordingly. Here again, the crime can take on a life of its own, independent of the insider's desire to continue. As shown in the top-left portion of Figure 4-5, the insider's perceived risk of being caught, based on his perceived loss and knowledge of control, may cause him to want to stop the fraudulent activity—the incentive to continue is reduced (depicted by the dotted line). Several insiders told us that the crime felt like a downward spiral—it was actually a relief to be caught. But between the pressures provided by other complicit insiders and the pressure from the outsider to continue (as shown in Figure 4-4), the insiders found it extremely difficult to extract themselves.

We include both the perceived risk of being caught and the perceived loss if caught in the model since insiders may engage in fraud activities either because they do not believe they will be caught or because, even if they are caught, they do not expect significant repercussions. If the organization has a history of sweeping such incidents under the rug, then no matter their vigilance regarding detection, insiders may believe they have little to lose and a lot to gain by committing fraud.

### Insider Stressors

The lives of insiders who committed fraud in our cases were often in turmoil. As we discussed previously, insiders often had severe financial problems. In addition, insiders had other personal issues such as a family member with health problems, substance abuse, and physical threats

---

**NOTE**

Stressors both inside and outside the workplace were observable in insider fraud cases.

---

by outsiders. While the motivations for the crimes appeared to largely come from outside the workplace, some workplace issues were evident. Some insiders had disagreements over financial compensation or with supervisors. Such issues at times led to intense situations and what might be deemed as a hostile work environment. The threat of layoffs was also an issue in some cases. Here the insiders may have wanted to make as much money at the organization's expense as possible prior to being terminated.

## Insider Fraud Involving Organized Crime

The Federal Bureau of Investigation (FBI) defines organized crime as follows.

> Any group having some manner of a formalized structure and whose primary objective is to obtain money through illegal activities. Such groups

maintain their position through the use of actual or threatened violence, corrupt public officials, graft, or extortion, and generally have a significant impact on the people in their locales, region, or the country as a whole.[7]

The 24 insider threat cases facilitated by organized crime in the CERT database constitute about 10% of all of our fraud cases. These cases typically involve multiple insiders and/or outsiders committing long-term fraud. The average damages in these cases exceeded $4 million, and one case amounted to almost $50 million in losses. Criminal enterprises mask their fraud by involving multiple insiders who often work in different parts of the organization. These insiders know how to bypass critical processes and remain undetected.

In several cases, management was involved in the fraud. The insiders affiliated with organized crime either sell information to them for further exploitation or are directly employed by them to enable the fraud.

## Snapshot of Malicious Insiders Involved with Organized Crime

All of the insiders involved with organized crime in the 24 cases attacked the organization for financial gain. The insiders were usually employed in lower-level positions in the organization, were motivated by financial gain, and were often recruited by outsiders to commit their crimes. Sound familiar? Although these crimes fit the patterns we have already described for fraud, the impacts seem to be amplified by the involvement of organized crime.[8]

This section will discuss the two different types of insider organized crime activity.

- Insiders with ties to existing external organized crime groups.
- Insiders who form or participate in their own criminal enterprises. A criminal enterprise is a group of individuals with an identified hierarchy, or comparable structure, engaged in significant criminal activity.[9]

Here is a sample case involving a criminal enterprise.

> Five insiders worked for a credit reporting company. Each of them was a low-level employee with job responsibilities of data entry and

---

7. www.fbi.gov/about-us/investigate/organizedcrime/glossary

8. This section includes material authored by Christopher King in "Spotlight On: Malicious Insiders and Organized Crime Activity" published in *SEI Technical Note CMU/SEI-2011-TN-025* [King 2011].

9. www.fbi.gov/about-us/investigate/organizedcrime/glossary

modification of credit reports. A car salesman befriended one of the insiders while shopping for a car, and found out what the insider's job entailed. He offered to pay the insider $150 per customer to change credit reports of individuals who wished to purchase a car but had insufficient credit. The insider then recruited his colleagues to participate in the scheme. Each week the outsider dropped off the names of the individuals and associated payments. The organization had a business process in place to verify changes to credit reports, but two of the employees involved in the scheme had the authority to override the verification process. The fraud continued for more than a year until a routine audit discovered the discrepancy.

Here is an example case of a person affiliated with organized crime.

A teller at a large U.S. bank handled customer information on a daily basis and processed checks for customers. Heavily in debt, the insider was approached by individuals in the Mafia who offered to pay him to steal customers' PII. Over the course of several years, the insider sold PII to the organized crime group, who used it to create fraudulent checks, open unauthorized credit cards, and commit identity theft. The theft was caught when the bank became suspicious of the exceptionally high rate of fraud occurring in one of its local branches.

## Who They Are

This section is based on 20 cases that involved a criminal enterprise and four cases with ties to organized crime. The majority of the insiders were employed in nontechnical positions, although four held a management position. The crimes involving management went on for a longer period of time and the scale of the crime was much larger. The majority of the insiders were female, which is greater than the breakdown of all fraud cases in the CERT database (roughly 50% male/female). Finally, almost all cases involved collusion with outsiders. In cases involving existing organized crime groups there tended to be fewer insiders involved.

In the crimes involving management, the average loss was very high. One case involving a manager at a Department of Motor Vehicles (DMV) caused losses of $250,000; another DMV case resulted in a $1 million loss for the organization. The most damaging case involved an insider working for a city tax office, who was able to steal $48 million over the course of almost two decades. These insiders were lower- or mid-level managers with few technical skills. They used their deep knowledge of the organization's processes and systems to bypass the checks and balances in place and recruited their subordinates into the crime.

## Why They Strike

These insiders held low-level positions in the organization, and committed the crimes for financial gain.

## What They Strike

These insiders primarily copied or modified data for financial gain. Crimes included stealing customer information to sell for identity theft, modifying credit reports to give buyers a higher credit score, or creating fake credentials, such as driver's licenses. Insiders primarily modified data in organization databases and bypassed integrity checks.

## How They Strike

Nearly three-fourths of the attacks occurred on-site during normal work hours. For the most part, insiders used their authorized access to copy, modify, or delete critical data from the organization's systems.

Technical methods used included the following.

- Social engineering to obtain credentials or information

    The insider, after resigning from a law enforcement agency, convinced colleagues to run searches and gather information on companies to help him and his conspirators perform insider trading.

- Authorized use of the organization's systems

    An insider used his access to customer credit reports to sell the data to conspirators who would conduct identity theft.

- Bypassed secure processes

    An organization required two employees to issue tax-refund checks, but both insiders in the process were part of the same criminal enterprise and would issue fraudulent checks to their conspirators.

- Compromised account

    An insider working for a credit reporting agency performed modifications of customer credit in exchange for money. The insider used stolen passwords of coworkers to conceal evidence of the crime.

Table 4-1 contains summary information for all of the insider fraud cases in the CERT database that involved organized crime.

**Table 4-1** *Summary of Organized Crime Cases*

| Case # | Total # of Conspirators | # of Insiders | # of Outsiders | Impact | Insider-Led? |
|--------|-------------------------|---------------|----------------|--------|--------------|
| 1 | 10 | 4 | 6 | $48,115,451 | Yes |
| 2 | 94 | 1 | 93 | $10,000,000 | No |
| 3 | 4 | 3 | 1 | $6,775,434 | Yes |
| 4 | 3 | 1 | 2 | $2,700,000 | Yes |
| 5 | 14 | 13 | 1 | $2,288,946 | Unknown |
| 6 | 10 | 1 | 9 | $1,500,000 | Unknown |
| 7 | 7 | 2 | 5 | $1,000,000 | No |
| 8 | 4 | 1 | 3 | $841,164 | Yes |
| 9 | 10 | 5 | 5 | $800,000 | Yes |
| 10 | 6 | 1 | 5 | $638,000 | No |
| 11 | 6 | 2 | 4 | $335,000 | No |
| 12 | 16 | 6 | 10 | $287,500 | Unknown |
| 13 | 4 | 4 | 0 | $250,000 | Yes |
| 14 | 6 | 1 | 5 | $231,500 | Yes |
| 15 | 6 | 1 | 5 | $157,000 | Unknown |
| 16 | 16 | 1 | 15 | $77,300 | No |
| 17 | 6 | 2 | 4 | $75,000 | Yes |
| 18 | 2 | 1 | 1 | $10,000 | No |
| 19 | 8 | 2 | 6 | Unknown | No |
| 20 | 4 | 2 | 2 | Unknown | No |
| 21 | 9 | 5 | 4 | Unknown | Yes |
| 22 | 11 | 1 | 10 | Unknown | No |
| 23 | Unknown | 1 | Unknown | Unknown | No |
| 24 | 21 | 1 | 20 | Unknown | Unknown |

# Organizational Issues of Concern and Potential Countermeasures

Figure 4-6 depicts organizational issues of concern in the fraud cases in the CERT database.

The suggestions that follow apply to identifying and mitigating the five most prevalent areas of concern from the graph, as well as some of the other issues that were relevant in a number of cases.

## Inadequate Auditing of Critical and Irregular Processes

In close to half of the insider fraud cases, insiders remained undetected for long periods due to inadequate auditing of critical or infrequent business processes. In one incident, malicious insiders were able to modify records at the DMV because there was no auditing in place. In a second incident, an insider was able to submit false credit reports to the credit bureaus because

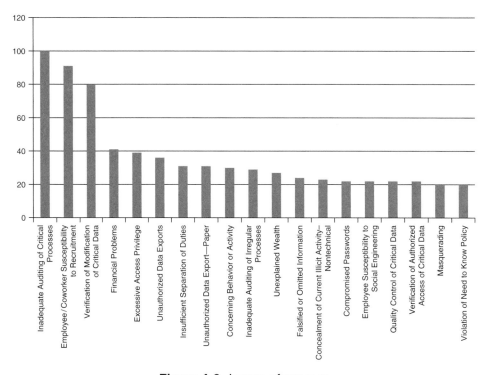

**Figure 4-6** *Issues of concern*

she social-engineered her management into leaving her department's activities out of the auditing process. Details of those cases follow.

> In the first case, a licensing-registration examiner at a DMV conspired with nine other accomplices to sell fraudulent IDs and driver's licenses by modifying a real customer's record with a picture of their client. This criminal enterprise included five DMV employees and five outsiders (three brokers and two recruiters). Most of their clients were undocumented immigrants desperate for driver's licenses or identity cards. The insiders were employees that had authorized access and occupied lower-level positions in the organization. The DMV's computer system was designed to cross-check Social Security numbers (SSNs) with the Social Security Administration, but the employees found a way to bypass that check. The insiders either used bogus SSNs or stole actual SSNs from the DMV system without being flagged by security. The ring made $800,000 in illicit profits from selling the fraudulent credentials.

> In the second case, an insider worked for a tax office preparing property tax refund checks. She generated tax refund checks to bogus companies and then gave the checks to her niece. Her niece deposited the checks into the bank accounts of the fake companies and then distributed the funds to various participants in the fraud scheme. Since the insider played a role in designing her organization's new computer system, she convinced management that her department should not be included in the auditing process. She was able to steal $48 million over the course of almost twenty years.

Both of these cases involved nontechnical overrides of critical processes. Vulnerabilities in critical processes should be included in your risk assessment. Periodic audits of the work products from these types of critical processes should be conducted to detect abuses of the system.

## Employee/Coworker Susceptibility to Recruitment

Many insider fraud cases involve outsiders, sometimes from organized crime, who approach employees of the victim organizations and offer to pay them in exchange for some service, often the unauthorized modification of data. The following incidents are examples of how an outsider was successfully able to recruit an insider to commit a crime.

> In the first case, the insider worked at an insurance company and began stealing PII that included banking information for the company's customers. The insider then sold this information to an outside coconspirator who created fraudulent checks for various banks using the customers' PII.

The insider and outsider then had "check-runners" cash the checks at various banks posing as legitimate customers, thus making fraudulent withdrawals from their accounts. The insider also passed on the customers' information to individuals who created fake IDs and counterfeit checks in the names of the bank customers. Multiple employees from several different banks were recruited for this scheme.

In another case, an insider was employed as a service representative for the victim organization. She sold personal information to the Nigerian Mafia to support identity theft. After several years, she was approached by a Nigerian male, and gave him her home phone number. The insider, facing financial difficulties, agreed to provide the man with personal information from her company's SSN records. The outsider paid her $15–$20 per SSN record. A few months later, several major financial institutions reported fraudulently issued and authenticated credit cards. The subsequent investigation led back to the insider, who confessed to law enforcement, resigned from her job, and was subsequently arraigned and pleaded guilty. She was sentenced to ten months in jail and two years of probation, and was ordered to pay $10,000 in restitution. The impact of this scheme is unknown, but several financial institutions had to reissue credit cards and implement fraud monitoring on customer accounts.

Both of these cases involved recruitment by outsiders, which can be hard for you to detect, particularly if it occurs outside the workplace. You should consider raising awareness in applicable managers and employees to this potential recruitment. You could let them know that they are susceptible to being recruited to steal the sensitive information to which they have access. They need to understand the types of crimes that could be committed with the information and that, although they would not actually commit the fraud, the evidence in your system logs will point directly to them. Furthermore, they will be turned over to law enforcement. Providing examples such as those we provide in this book, including the sentences the insiders received, might be helpful in reinforcing the potential consequences of these illicit actions.

In addition, you should encourage your employees to recognize and report suspicious contact in which an insider or outsider approaches them to join in a fraud scheme. Employees who have an understanding of the potential for recruitment by both insiders and outsiders and the consequences of committing such an act may decrease your risk and increase reporting.

Your training should be based on your policies, which should include a confidential means of reporting security issues. Confidential reporting allows reporting of suspicious events without fear of repercussions, thereby overcoming the cultural barrier of whistle-blowing. Employees need to understand that you have policies and procedures, and that managers will respond to security issues in a fair and prompt manner.

## Verification of Modification of Critical Data

In about one-third of the fraud cases, insiders were able to carry out their crime because the organization did not review critical data when it was modified. Insiders used authorized access and were able to change data without oversight. Two sample cases follow.

> In the first case, the insider worked at a consumer credit report agency. Her duty was to maintain the information stored in the consumer credit database. In exchange for money from outsiders, she inflated the credit scores of consumers to enable them to secure loans from third-party credit institutions and lenders. She also recruited other insider conspirators who helped her to modify or delete credit-history data for 178 consumers in return for a share of the payments. The purpose was to strengthen the consumers' creditworthiness; the impact was that lenders issued $4.2 million in new loans to these consumers.

> In the second case, six contractors pocketed $32,000 in food stamp kickbacks by issuing food stamps to 53 people who did not qualify for them, and increasing monthly allotments for existing cases. For payment, each recipient turned over an envelope to the insiders filled with a portion of the monthly food stamp allotment. They were able to carry out their crime by exploiting a weakness in exception handling in the system: If the food stamp request was coded as an "Expedited" case, the caseworker could open it without a supervisor's authorization.

Auditing database transactions may help to detect unauthorized access and modification of data. Frequent, random audits of critical database fields should verify the information entered since the last audit. But auditing data changes for all tables in a database is not practical and may in fact degrade performance. A monitoring strategy for fraud should include monitoring access and data modifications on critical tables, such as tables containing PII and/or customer information. Ideally a monitoring strategy should include logging successful and unsuccessful data access and modification attempts.

Additionally, automated flagging of mismatched data may detect improper modifications of the databases. Data integrity checks built in to your databases could be used as preventive measures. External audits of these databases can also uncover fraud that may be concealed by an internal audit. Finally, learn from the past. In assessments and workshops, we have worked with organizations that have been victimized multiple times by the same type of insider fraud. We recommend that part of your insider incident-management process include a lessons learned step in which you examine the illicit activities used by the insider to conduct the crime, and put into place automated scripts, triggers, and application-level controls to prevent the same thing from happening again.

The second case example also involved exploiting another issue of concern illustrated in Figure 4-6: inadequate auditing of irregular processes. The employees in that case were able to carry out their fraudulent activities using an "Expedite" function in the system that enabled them to get around all of the normal controls built in to the food stamp application. You should carefully examine your applications that could be used for fraud: Are there any "exception handling" functions that allow employees to override separation of duties and other controls? If so, you should consider having the system generate an automatic alert anytime that function is used, and someone should carefully audit that particular transaction.

## Financial Problems

Financial problems were the fourth most prevalent issue of concern in the fraud cases in our database. The first step to prevent this area of concern is to perform background checks on individuals before hiring them. Background checks should investigate previous criminal convictions, include a credit check, verify credentials and past employment, and if possible, include discussions with prior employers regarding the individual's competence and approach to dealing with workplace issues. This information should be used as part of a risk-based decision process in determining whether it is appropriate to give the new employee access to critical, confidential, or proprietary information or systems.

Background checks should be required for all potential employees, including contractors and subcontractors. In one case in the CERT database, an organization employed a contractor; the contractor's company told the organization that a background check had been performed on him. The contractor later compromised the organization's systems and obtained confidential data on millions of its customers. During the investigation it was discovered that the contractor had a criminal history for illegally accessing protected computers.

Other insiders developed financial problems after being hired. The CERT database includes single parents who couldn't make ends meet, insiders with "significant others" with drug problems or other financial problems, and so on. You might consider offering some type of employee assistance program that includes financial counseling, particularly in times of economic downturn, rather than risking that your employees and contractors will turn to criminal methods for solving their financial problems.

## Excessive Access Privilege

Some insiders accumulated excessive privileges that enabled them to carry out their crime. For example, a few of the insiders transferred to a different department in the same organization. When they transferred, they retained their old roles within an application, but also obtained new roles. This gave them multiple roles within the same application, enabling them to both enter and approve of data modifications—an oversight they used to conduct a lone fraud scheme. It is important that you carefully control and audit roles for systems that use **role-based access** control.[10]

## Other Issues of Concern

Other issues of concern from Figure 4-6 and suggested mitigation strategies follow.

- Insufficient separation of duties

  In some fraud cases, separation of duties was part of the formal business process, but with no technical enforcement. If possible, build your business processes into your online systems and enforce separation of duties via technical controls in your applications. For example, require that a supervisor approve of critical transactions electronically using his or her own account, rather than by signing a paper form.

- Compromised passwords

  In some of the fraud cases we found that employees shared their passwords in order to be more efficient. Even supervisors shared their passwords in a few cases so that their employees could log in to the supervisor's account and approve of transactions, resulting in "increased productivity." They asserted that they were overworked, and this was the only way that they could possibly handle their workload. It is important not only that you train employees not to share their passwords with *anyone,* but also that you explain what might happen if they do. Stress to them that if someone else uses their computer account to commit a crime, all of the evidence is going to point to them.

---

10. **Role-based access:** access required by a person's duties. Typically, a person's access to data/systems should be no greater than what is required the person's role.

They will have a very difficult time proving that they did not commit the illegal activity when all of the evidence points directly to them!

- Employee susceptibility to social engineering

  In some of the fraud cases, employees unwittingly assisted other employees in committing crimes by falling for social engineering. In one case, an insider who worked for a credit card point-of-sale terminal vendor used social engineering to obtain authentication information from the credit card company help staff. He posed as a distraught individual (with a fabricated identity) working for a particular, authorized merchant needing help with a malfunctioning terminal. He was then able to credit his own credit card by reprogramming a terminal using the information he had obtained. It is important that your employees are educated to understand potential social engineering techniques, not only from outsiders, but from other insiders as well.

## Mitigation Strategies: Final Thoughts

Mitigation strategies for insider fraud need to include prevention, detection, and response approaches just as they do for the other insider crimes.

Preventive controls for insider fraud take away the insider's opportunity to commit the crime; refer back to Figure 4-2. For example, screening and identification of at-risk employees at hiring is an option for reducing the number of high-risk employees with an opportunity for committing fraud. Certainly if individuals have a criminal history of fraud, they may be more likely to commit fraud against their employer. Individuals with chronic financial problems may also be more at risk. Since fraud crimes often involved database transactions, either viewing or modifying data, some level of role-based access control or multiperson transaction verification may help prevent some insider fraud crimes. Certainly these measures will make it more difficult to perpetrate the crime, may deter individuals from getting involved, or at least may make them think twice about it.

However, as evidenced in our cases, motivated insider fraudsters may find their way around these measures. We had cases in which the insider recruited other insiders precisely to get around role-based access controls. So detection of ongoing fraud activities is going to be essential for most organizations. The fact that insider fraud crimes are often long and ongoing is bad news for the victim organizations. However, it does afford the organization with ample opportunity to discover the crime, and possibly curtail the activity to limit damage.

There are two means for detecting insider fraud. The first is external discovery of the crime, potentially as a result of investigation into financial losses incurred by the fraud victims. As we have explained previously, the actual fraud crime is often conducted by an outsider to the victim organization. Detection of these activities is likely to be a point where law enforcement is brought in to investigate the potential problem. The second is the discovery of the internal crime—the insider's or accomplice's malicious actions. Here the organization has the opportunity to detect the illicit insider activity at any point from planning to insider recruitment to online execution.

## Summary

Insiders who commit fraud are usually low-level employees who use authorized access during normal work hours to either steal information or modify information for financial gain. Stolen information is usually PII or customer information that is then sold to outsiders who commit the actual fraud against the victims. Information is sometimes modified for the direct financial benefit of the insider, and sometimes is done for payment by outsiders.

All of the insider crimes in the CERT database involving organized crime fit into the fraud category. Most of these involve insiders who form their own criminal enterprise, but some involve insiders being recruited by external organized crime groups. These crimes have a significant impact, with average losses of more than $4 million.

Insiders who commit fraud are primarily motivated by financial difficulty. They start the crime due to mounting financial pressures, but then tend to carry out their scheme for as long as possible. Outsiders play a role in many of these crimes, either paying for stolen information, or finding "customers" who are willing to pay the insider to modify information.

In this chapter we explored technical methods used, as well as mitigation strategies.

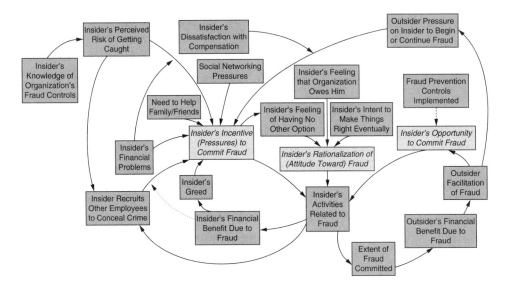

**Figure 4-7**  *Preliminary MERIT model of insider fraud*

A preliminary MERIT model of insider fraud is presented in Figure 4-7.

We have now explored each of the three types of crimes, insider IT sabotage, theft of intellectual property, and fraud, in detail. Next, we will dig a little deeper into one specific method of committing insider crimes: in the Software Development Life Cycle.

Chapter 5

# Insider Threat Issues in the Software Development Life Cycle

*Software Development Life Cycle (SDLC): Synonymous with "software process" as well as "software engineering," it is a structured methodology used in the development of software products and packages. This methodology is used from the conception phase through to the delivery and end of life of a final software product.[1]*

*Insider threat issues in the Software Development Life Cycle: those aspects of an organization's software development or maintenance policies and processes that insiders exploited to carry out their attack.*

You might think that this chapter is going to address software engineers who inject malicious code into the source code as they develop a new system. On the contrary, this chapter starts with the requirements and design phases of the SDLC, and points out how oversights in these phases can lead

---

1. Webopedia.

to exploitation later by end users of the system. Then it addresses malicious software engineers.

One critical requirement of most software systems should be that the system ensures the confidentiality, integrity, and availability of the underlying information. Unfortunately, in today's tumultuous economic conditions, time to market is often the driving factor in product development, often sacrificing important stages of the SDLC designed to address security issues. Software engineers, including both employees and contractors, have intentionally and unintentionally bypassed critical processes in the SDLC, leaving vulnerabilities in software that allowed exploitation by end users once it was in production.

In addition, software engineers and data owners often do spend a good bit of time anticipating and addressing information security issues. However, in many cases in the CERT insider threat database we have observed that the system designers neglected to anticipate how *authorized users* could commit illicit activity using the software. Finally, once the software is in production, developers tend to have free reign in many organizations, releasing changes to source code without any two-person control.

Neglecting to consider insider threat security requirements in software systems has allowed insiders to sabotage critical systems, defraud organizations of large sums of money, and modify data in systems to create false identity documents. While the impact in some incidents can be measured in dollars, other incidents impact organizational operations or threaten the national security of the United States.

The following case demonstrates the potential of an employee with software development skills and access to cause financial impact.

> A foreign currency trader in a financial institution started losing money on trades. Fearing job-related consequences, he executed a complex fraud scheme by modifying the source code of the trading system to hide fake trades he entered to counterbalance his losses. Since his undergraduate degree was in computer science, he had convinced the development team that it would be easier on all of them if he could just modify the source code himself when needed. Therefore, he had been given authorized access to the source code, and was able to modify it to hide his illicit activity.
>
> His scheme ended up continuing for more than five years; making it appear that the bank was profiting instead of losing close to $700 million. The insider was convicted, ordered to pay almost $700 million in restitution, and sentenced to more than seven years of imprisonment followed by five years of probation.

It is important for you to carefully consider this case. Many controls are built in to your software systems so that your end users cannot perform illicit activity. Therefore, it is very important that you do not allow your end users to have access to your source code. This is a new slant on the concept of separation of duties!

Given that most organizations are reliant on IT systems for achieving their mission, it is easy to see why the integrity of the software underlying those systems is critical. If the organization does not incorporate adequate security controls in its SDLC processes or an insider is able to bypass existing security controls, the potential for sabotage, fraud, or theft of information is increased.

Twenty-eight of the cases in the CERT database had issues related to exploiting a vulnerability in the SDLC. The majority of those cases involved an insider who sabotaged a previous employer's critical system. In a few of the cases the insider's malicious actions resulted in fraud or theft of intellectual property.

By looking at the 28 incidents, it became apparent that the vulnerabilities exploited could be broken down into two general categories:

- Requirements definition and system design
- System implementation and maintenance

## Requirements and System Design Oversights

Many systems automate business and workflow processes. When defining the requirements for such systems, the processes to be automated must be carefully defined. In the cases examined, many of the insiders, who were part of the development team, were able to carry out their illicit activities because they recognized instances in which protection from insider threats was not considered. For example, in some cases, there was no requirement for separation of duties in automated processes. In others, authentication and role-based access controls were not required for system access. System requirements should also include specification of data integrity and consistency checks for all changes made to production data by end users. Automated checks should also be run periodically to detect suspicious modifications, additions, or deletions. In other words, requirements should consider proactive data integrity mechanisms, as well as periodic auditing functions that can be implemented and run automatically on a more frequent basis than manual system audits.

Exception handling, or authorized system overrides, which were designed to accommodate unusual, special circumstances that could not follow the standard business processes, provided an easy mechanism for some insiders in the CERT database to commit malicious activity.

Note that all of the recommendations detailed here for defining system requirements apply to both systems built by the organization and those the organization acquired. When evaluating new systems for acquisition, the types of requirements detailed here should also be considered. Once requirements have been defined and potential systems are evaluated for purchase, the ability of each system to meet those requirements is an important part of the evaluation process.

## Authentication and Role-Based Access Control

> **NOTE**
>
> Neglecting to require authentication and role-based access control simplified insider attacks.

In some cases, even though authentication was required to access a critical system, users' access rights within the system were not restricted consistent with job responsibilities. Therefore, insiders were able to access data outside their need to know, allowing them to view, modify, or delete data for friends, relatives, high-profile celebrities, and others.

It is important that software systems use authentication to determine who a user is. Once the user's identity is determined, role-based access should ensure that each user has the minimum privileges needed to perform his or her job duties. The following case details how an employee at a law enforcement organization was able to exploit inadequate access controls in the suspect tracking system.

> One responsibility of a police communications operator was to look up and communicate information regarding driver's licenses to police officers in the field. This case began when a communications operator was approached by an acquaintance and asked if she would be willing to look up information in that system for three people, and she agreed. Over time, she proceeded to look up information on people in return for payment by her acquaintance. At some point she discovered that she not only

could read information from the database, but also could use other system functions. At that point, at the request of her accomplice, she began to create, in return for payment, illegal driver's licenses in the system for people who were unable to gain legitimate licenses. Fortunately, a confidential informant led to her arrest for fraudulently creating approximately 195 illegal driver's licenses.

This case is a "low-tech" incident that was enabled by oversights in defining and implementing access controls within a critical application. All system users had the same level of access, even to perform a critical function such as adding a driver's license to the database.

## Separation of Duties

> **NOTE**
>
> Neglecting to define security requirements/separation of duties requirements for automated business processes provided an easy method for insider attack.

Most organizations implement separation of duties in business processes to reduce the risk of fraud. Separation of duties should require that more than one person be involved in a critical business process. For example, one employee is given authorized access to generate a payment, but a second employee is required to approve and finalize the payment. Failure to identify requirements for separation of duties enabled some insiders to commit crimes against their organization.

> The office manager for a large trucking firm fraudulently added her husband to the payroll each week for weekly payouts, and then deleted him from the system and erased all records of the payments. This scheme went on for more than a year and resulted in more than $100,000 in losses to the firm.

In this case, the office manager had the ability to add employees to the payroll, generate paychecks, and delete records of payments from the database. One might expect this type of situation in a small organization, but this case example described a *large* trucking organization. Nonetheless, we realize that some organizations, especially smaller ones, can't afford to have multiple people involved in functions such as payroll. However, it is still important to use security controls to protect the records, payroll records in this case, from being modified by that single user, and to periodically audit those records for fraudulent activity.

## Automated Data Integrity Checks

> **NOTE**
>
> Neglecting to define requirements for automated data integrity checks made it difficult to detect malicious insider actions.

Automated data integrity checks are essential to ensuring the integrity of the data collected in organizations' systems. Defining the appropriate data integrity rules is the foundation for the software development team prior to any code being written. If the software systems supporting the organization do not enforce the business rules of the organization, they will allow malicious insiders to proceed undetected. The following case illustrates the need to enforce data integrity checks.

> A software administrator for a financial organization had full access to the organization's source code. He modified the source code to make changes to certain accounts and forward funds to his own private loan accounts, which he then used to move money into his checking account. The incident was detected when a fellow staff member was conducting a routine system audit and noticed a ten-year car loan in the insider's name. This was alarming because the organization did not issue car loans for that long of a time frame. Management confronted the insider after conducting a further investigation, and he admitted to stealing $90,000. He then turned himself in to law enforcement.

In this case, the organization failed to implement automated data integrity checks that could have either prevented or detected this fraudulent activity. For example, car loans were not issued for ten-year terms—an automated data integrity check could have caught that discrepancy. In addition, database triggers could have detected the suspicious transfer of funds into an employee account.

In short, any fraudulent activity that happens once should be analyzed to see how it can be prevented from ever happening again. Anything detected in a manual audit should be implemented as an automated script whenever possible.

Also, in some cases, although separation of duties was implemented, there was no design to "check the checker." Due to the high degree of collusion observed in fraud cases, it is recommended that system designers consider how they might implement yet another layer of defense on top of separation of duties, to discover incidents in which two employees are working together to commit a crime. Most of these types of crimes continue over a prolonged period, so although detection might not be immediate, patterns of suspicious activity can be discovered to catch the activity sooner rather than later.

## Exception Handling

> **NOTE**
>
> Neglecting to consider security vulnerabilities posed by "authorized system overrides" resulted in an easy method for insiders "to get around the rules."

Several insiders used special system functions created for exception handling to carry out their crimes. They realized that these functions were created for exceptional situations in which changes had to be made quickly, thus bypassing the usual mandated security checks. This type of functionality provided an easy way for insiders to get around the rules. The following case describes how insiders were able to bypass automated data integrity checks by using the system's "Expedite" function. This same case example was used in the previous chapter, as we believe that this issue is important enough to be included in both chapters, and this is the best case to illustrate the concept.

> Six contractors were case workers for an organization that distributed child care vouchers. The insiders issued food stamps to people who did not qualify for the assistance and increased monthly allotments on existing cases for payment. Over a six-month period, they pocketed $32,000 in kickbacks for issuing food stamps to 53 unauthorized beneficiaries. They were able to evade the business processes enforced in the system without a supervisor's authorization by opening the cases as "Expedited." They were only caught when someone that the insiders attempted to solicit reported their activity to local law enforcement. The victim organization's incident-related loss was $75,000.

It is important to design special data integrity checks for any data modified, added, or deleted using these exception-handling functions.

# System Implementation, Deployment, and Maintenance Issues

Very few insiders actually introduced intentional vulnerabilities or malicious code into source code during the initial development process; that type of activity was more often carried out during the maintenance phase of the SDLC. It is not uncommon for organizations to follow stringent development practices during initial development but allow the practices to erode once the system moves into operation.

## Code Reviews[2]

> **NOTE**
>
> Lack of code reviews allowed insiders to insert backdoors into source code, especially for stable, production systems.

There is only one case in the CERT database in which the insider committed malicious activity during the initial development phase of a project, but it is still a risk that we cannot overlook. An 18-year-old Web developer used a backdoor he had inserted into his source code during software development to access his former company's network, spam its customers, alter its applications, and ultimately put it out of business. Code reviews and strict change control, a part of any solid software development process, could have detected the backdoor and perhaps saved the company.

More insider incidents occurred during the maintenance phase of the SDLC than during initial system implementation. It appears that organizations impose more stringent controls during the initial development process, but once a system has been in production and stabilized following initial release, those controls tend to become more lax. Insiders in the cases in the CERT database took advantage of those relaxed controls in a variety of ways.

> A hardware engineer was unhappy with his new boss because he had modified the organization's bonus system. To exact revenge, he downloaded a virus from the Internet and embedded it inside the company's production executable. That night, he released the new executable to customers' systems. The next day, one by one, the organization's customers executed

---

2. **Code review:** a process to examine source code, typically by someone other than the original coder, with the purpose of identifying and addressing mistakes.

the infected software, requiring that someone be flown on-site to each customer location around the country to repair the damage.

While many organizations institute mandatory code reviews for development of new systems or for significant new modules in existing systems, several insiders were able to inject malicious code into stable production systems without detection. Ineffective configuration or change control processes contributed to their ability to do so. A few organizations in the cases examined implemented configuration-management systems that recorded a detailed log of the malicious insider activity. However, there was no proactive process for actually controlling system releases using those systems or reviewing the logs to detect malicious activity after the fact.

## Attribution

> **NOTE**
>
> Inability to attribute actions to a single user enabled insiders to sabotage projects.

During the software development process, organizations are vulnerable to the same types of insider attacks that can occur on production systems. One software development project manager, recognizing there was no way to attribute actions to a single user in the development environment, repeatedly sabotaged his team's project. The motivation in this case is unique: His team was falling behind in the project schedule, and he used the repeated sabotage as a convenient excuse for missed deadlines. It is important that organizations consider security during the development process just as on production systems.

## System Deployment

> **NOTE**
>
> Oversights in moving a system from development to production provided avenues for attack by insiders.

A variety of oversights in the process of moving a system from development to production provided avenues for attack by insiders. Examples from several different cases follow.

The lead developer for a new safety-related system being developed at a government agency refused to adhere to the procedures for documentation and backups. Management was aware of his negligence, repeatedly requesting that he rectify the situation, but he ignored them with no consequences. The system was put into production, and after a few months was in stable, production mode. At that time the team was to be disbanded, as they had been brought together as a temporary team for the sole purpose of developing the system. The lead developer, who was disgruntled with the situation, wiped all of the files from his laptop—the only copy of the source code that existed. Fortunately, law enforcement discovered an encrypted disk at his home containing the source code, but for several months he refused to decrypt the files and the agency was only able to run the executable version of the software. In the meantime, without access to the source code, they had no ability to make modifications or enhancements to the running version of the mission-critical safety system.

In the preceding case, the organization moved a system into production even though it was fully aware that the lead developer had not followed its process for documenting and backing up the source code. This SDLC oversight left the organization in a vulnerable position when the developer used that situation to "hold it hostage" for the only copy of the source code.

A government agency hired a team of contractors to develop a new system for them. The system was to process sensitive information, and therefore the developers were only supposed to have access to the development system and test data. The system was moved into production, however, and the same password file was used for the production system as in the development environment, enabling one of the developers to access and steal sensitive data after it had been entered into the production system.

In this case, the organization put sensitive information at risk when it moved the system into production. Security requirements need to be revisited during deployment to ensure that oversights such as this will not provide a vulnerability that could be exploited by insiders in the production environment.

A government agency used a Web content management system to manage and control all changes to its public-facing Web site. No one could change the agency's Web content without going through that system. Although the agency used a change control system to track content changes, it had no process for approval of changes before they were released to the Web site. As a result, a college intern, before leaving at the end of the summer, published material intended to be a joke on the agency's Web site, causing quite a scandal and damage to the agency's reputation.

This case is SDLC-related in the deployment of the Web content-management software. We chose this case because we want you to consider these types of issues for any infrastructure technologies you have acquired. It is important that you carefully consider these types of issues as you move systems from development to production because employees using those systems on a daily basis will likely notice the vulnerabilities.

## Backups

> **NOTE**
>
> Ineffective or lack of backup processes amplified the impact of insiders' mass deletion of data.

Insiders were able to sabotage backup systems that were left unprotected to amplify their attack. Risk management of critical systems needs to extend beyond the system itself to surrounding support systems, such as backups.

# Programming Techniques Used As an Insider Attack Tool

In this section we do a deep dive into insiders who used programming techniques as an attack tool.[3] We find these cases to be very interesting, and think that they might open your eyes to new attack vectors. Most of these attacks were conducted by system administrators or programmers, although a few were conducted by managers and other technical staff members. Most were current employees when they committed their crimes, although in some cases the impact was not realized until after the insider left the organization. The majority of the employees struck at the workplace, but many launched their attack remotely.

The majority of the insiders were motivated by revenge against their employers, but more than one-third were motivated by financial gain. Other motives include recognition and ideology.

The following case summaries describe how some of the insiders modified production source code or scripts to perpetrate their attacks. The methods used to achieve these objectives suggest countermeasures that should be considered to help mitigate risks associated with these types of insider attacks.

---

3. Material from this section includes portions from the joint CyLab and CERT Program article "Spotlight On: Programming Techniques Used as an Insider Attack Tool," authored by Dawn Cappelli, Thomas Caron, Randy Trzeciak, and Andrew Moore [Cappelli 2008a].

## Modification of Production Source Code or Scripts

Here are several cases of modification of production source code or scripts.

Case 1: A consultant modified source code used by his former employer, an Internet service provider (ISP), and disabled its communications capability for three weeks. He gained remote access to the ISP's radio-tower computer, and then used administrator passwords to reprogram the wireless access points of 110 of its customers, cutting off their Internet service. He reprogrammed the access points to complicate repair efforts, requiring that the service provider dispatch technicians to the premises of the subscribers who lost Internet access, an effort that extended over a three-week period. His actions also disrupted the communications of other ISPs outside the victim's network.

Case 2: A system administrator, fearing company layoffs, embedded malicious code within scripts on the organization's servers. The code was set to execute on his next birthday, approximately six months in the future. Had he been successful, the code would have wiped out critical data on more than 70 servers and caused widespread financial damage. It also would have caused potential health risks to the organization's customers. Even after surviving the layoffs a few days later, the insider did not remove the malicious code; in fact, he modified it one month later. The malicious code contained a programming error and failed to execute on his birthday as scheduled. However, the insider allegedly corrected the programming error six months later, setting the code to execute on his next birthday. Fortunately, a few months before the intended execution date, another system administrator investigating a system error discovered the malicious code and disabled it.

Case 3: A contractor hired as a system administrator wrote a logic bomb to delete all of the organization's files. He placed the logic bomb in two different scripts. The first was in an operating system script that rotated log files when a volume reached a certain point; rather than rotating log files it would execute his logic bomb. He placed the second logic bomb in his supervisor's log-in script. The logic bomb was set up to display a threatening and insulting message to his supervisor during login, execute the logic bomb, and remove all traces of the logic bomb from the system, including log files.

Case 4: Following termination, a former application developer at a consumer data marketing firm remotely logged in to the organization's systems and modified its Web site by inserting pornographic images. While this attack did not definitively use programming techniques, we chose to include it in this chapter due to the serious consequences.

## Obtaining Unauthorized Authentication Credentials

Here are two cases of obtaining unauthorized authentication credentials.

Case 1: An IT manager modified the password synch program that propagated password changes between the production and development systems. The insider was the only person on staff who knew this program existed. By removing a single line of code, he altered the program to store all password changes (account, old password, and new password) in a file as clear text, thereby gaining access to all account passwords that had been changed using the program.

Case 2: A student employed multiple methods for gaining access to unauthorized credentials; the most devious involved programming methods. First, he decrypted the password file on a departmental computer system and obtained the password for his professor's account. Using one of the passwords he obtained, he was able to gain access to the professor's personal account on Yahoo.com. The student wrote and installed a program in the professor's computer account that would run when the professor logged in, requesting the professor to enter his user ID and password for the university's administrative computer system, a separate network and computer system. That program enabled him to surreptitiously capture the professor's user ID and password for that network and computer system.

## Disruption of Service and/or Theft of Information

Here are several cases of disruptions of service and/or theft of information.

Case 1: A computer science major wrote a malicious program that, on several occasions, shut down the university server that was used as a portal for enrollment services. His real intention was theft: Over a two-year period, he accessed a database on the server and stole 8,000 names and Social Security numbers along with 37,000 personal records.

Case 2: A contractor working as a system administrator planted several logic bombs on the organization's network after the organization rejected his proposal to replace one of his fellow system administrators. When the organization decided to award the work to another firm, he planted logic bombs on five servers scheduled to detonate after he left. Three of the servers went offline when they executed, but the system administrator located the malicious code and prevented it from executing on the other two targeted computers.

Case 3: A consultant hired as a software developer accessed his client's servers remotely and removed some code needed to run the system, rendering the organization's systems inaccessible. This action followed a year of unmet demands and threats by the consultant. The insider intended to return the code once his demands were met.

Case 4: A system administrator, disgruntled because his yearly bonus was not as large as he expected, built and deployed a logic bomb that deleted 10 billion files and took down more than 2,000 servers around the country. He was able to distribute the malicious code by using the standard software distribution methods.

# Mitigation Strategies

Mitigation strategies for insiders who exploit vulnerabilities in the SDLC to sabotage critical systems include the following.

- Resilient system architecture that allows for efficient recovery or sustains the organization during disasters. The requirements for the architecture should be defined at the beginning of each project so as to set expectations for recovery in the event an incident occurs that disrupts operations.
- Configuration and access control of source code. All attempts to access source code in development and production should be tracked and regular audits of access to source code should be performed.
- Formal code review/inspection to prevent malicious code from being inserted into production systems.

The mitigation strategy for insiders who exploit vulnerabilities in the SDLC to commit fraud involves automated workflow processes. These processes should enforce proper authorizations, approvals, and separation of duties for critical business functions.

Mitigation strategies for insiders who exploit vulnerabilities in the SDLC to steal source code focus on configuration and access control of source code. Source code in development and production should be monitored closely to ensure it is not being moved off the organization's network without knowledge and approval of the organization.

# Summary

In this chapter we presented one specific type of insider threat: those that exploited the Software Development Life Cycle. Some insiders took advantage of oversights in the requirements and design phases of the SDLC to carry out their attacks. Others were software engineers or system administrators who actually injected malicious code into the source code in order to commit IT sabotage or fraud.

This chapter was intended to raise awareness of this type of insider threat so that you realize that you need to involve your software engineering teams in your mitigation strategies.

In the next chapter, Best Practices for the Prevention and Detection of Insider Threats, we present an entire collection of best practices that we have accumulated based on the actual crimes in the CERT database. That chapter includes best practices that are applicable to the SDLC-related crimes described in this chapter, as well as all insider threats covered in this book.

Chapter 6

# Best Practices for the Prevention and Detection of Insider Threats

This chapter describes 16 practices, based on existing industry-accepted best practices, providing you with defensive measures that could prevent or facilitate early detection of many of the insider incidents other organizations experienced in the hundreds of cases in the CERT insider threat database.[1]

This chapter was written for a diverse audience. Decision makers across your organization will benefit from reading it. Insider threats are influenced by a combination of technical, behavioral, and organizational issues, and must be addressed by policies, procedures, and technologies. Therefore, it is important that personnel from your management, human resources, information technology, software engineering, legal, and security teams,

---

1. This chapter includes portions from "Common Sense Guide to Prevention and Detection of Insider Threats 3rd Edition–Version 3.1, " by Dawn Cappelli, Andrew Moore, Randall Trzeciak, and Timothy J. Shimeall.

along with your data owners, understand the overall scope of the problem and communicate it to all employees in your organization.

We briefly describe each practice, explain what you should do, and provide a few actual case examples illustrating what could happen if the practice is not implemented. Finally, we describe how the practice could have prevented an attack or facilitated early detection.

While you read, please remember everything else you have read so far in this book regarding contractors and trusted business partners. Although we usually use the term *employee* in this chapter, much of this chapter also applies to contractors and trusted business partners. Please keep this in mind, and do not overlook those insiders!

## Summary of Practices

Each of the 16 practices is summarized here and then expanded on in the following sections.

- *Practice 1: Consider threats from insiders and business partners in enterprise-wide risk assessments.*

   It is difficult for you to balance trusting your employees, providing them access to achieve your mission, and protecting your assets from potential compromise by those same employees. Insiders' access, combined with their knowledge of your technical vulnerabilities and vulnerabilities introduced by gaps in business processes, gives them the ability and opportunity to carry out malicious activity against you if properly motivated. The problem is becoming even more difficult as the scope of insider threats expands due to organizations' growing reliance on business partners with whom they contract and collaborate. It is important for you to take an enterprise-wide view of information security, first determining your critical assets, and then defining a risk management strategy for protecting those assets from both insiders and outsiders.

- *Practice 2: Clearly document and consistently enforce policies and controls.*

   Clear documentation and communication of technical and organizational policies and controls could have mitigated some of the insider incidents, theft, fraud, and IT sabotage, in the CERT database. Specific policies are discussed in this practice. In addition, consistent policy enforcement is important. Some employees in our cases felt they were being treated differently than other employees, and retaliated against this perceived unfairness by attacking their employer's IT systems. Other insiders were able to steal or modify information due to inconsistent or unenforced policies.

- *Practice 3: Institute periodic security awareness training for all employees.*

  A culture of security awareness must be instilled in your organization so that all employees understand the need for policies, procedures, and technical controls. All employees in your organization must be aware that security policies and procedures exist, that there is a good reason why they exist, that they must be enforced, and that there can be serious consequences for infractions. They also need to be aware that individuals, either inside or outside the organization, may try to co-opt them into activities counter to your mission. Each employee needs to understand your security policies and the process for reporting policy violations.

- *Practice 4: Monitor and respond to suspicious or disruptive behavior, beginning with the hiring process.*

  You should attempt to identify suspicious or disruptive behavior by individuals before they are hired, and closely monitor employee behavior in the workplace, including repeated policy violations that may indicate or escalate into more serious criminal activity. The effect of personal and professional stressors should also be considered.

- *Practice 5: Anticipate and manage negative workplace issues.*

  This practice describes suggestions beginning with preemployment issues, continuing through employment, and including termination issues. For example, you need to clearly formulate employment agreements and conditions of employment. Responsibilities and constraints of the employee and consequences for violations need to be clearly communicated and consistently enforced. In addition, workplace disputes or inappropriate relationships between coworkers can serve to undermine a healthy and productive working environment. Employees should feel encouraged to discuss work-related issues with a member of management or human resources without fear of reprisal or negative consequences. Managers need to address these issues when discovered or reported, before they escalate out of control. Finally, contentious employee terminations must be handled with utmost care, as most insider IT sabotage attacks occur following termination.

- *Practice 6: Track and secure the physical environment.*

  While employees and contractors obviously must have access to your facilities and equipment, most do not need access to all areas of the workplace. Controlling physical access for each employee is fundamental to insider threat risk management. Access attempts should be logged and regularly audited to identify violations or attempted violations of the physical space and equipment access policies. Of course, terminated employees, contractors, and trusted business partners should not have physical access to nonpublic areas of your facilities. This practice details lessons learned from cases in the CERT database in which physical access vulnerabilities allowed an insider to attack.

- *Practice 7: Implement strict password and account management policies and practices.*

  No matter how vigilant you are in trying to prevent insider attacks, if your computer accounts can be compromised, insiders have an opportunity to circumvent both manual and automated controls. Password- and account-management policies and practices should apply to employees, contractors, and business partners. They should ensure that all activity from any account is attributable to the person who performed it. An anonymous reporting mechanism should be available and used by employees to report attempts at unauthorized account access, including potential attempts at social engineering. Audits should be performed regularly to identify and disable unnecessary or expired accounts.

- *Practice 8: Enforce separation of duties and least privilege.*

  If employees are adequately trained in security awareness, and responsibility for critical functions is divided among employees, the possibility that one individual could commit fraud or sabotage without the cooperation of another individual within the organization is reduced. Effective separation of duties requires the implementation of **least privilege;** that is, authorizing insiders only for the resources they need to do their jobs, particularly when they take on different positions or responsibilities within the organization.

- *Practice 9: Consider insider threats in the Software Development Life Cycle.*

  Many insider incidents can be tied either directly or indirectly to defects introduced during the Software Development Life Cycle (SDLC). Some cases, such as those involving malicious code inserted into source code, have an obvious tie to the SDLC. Others, such as those involving insiders who took advantage of inadequate separation of duties, have an indirect tie. This practice details the types of oversights throughout the SDLC that enabled insiders to carry out their attacks.

- *Practice 10: Use extra caution with system administrators and technical or privileged users.*

System administrators and privileged users such as database administrators (DBAs) have the technical ability and access to commit and conceal malicious activity. Technically adept individuals are more likely to resort to technical means to exact revenge for perceived wrongs. Techniques such as separation of duties or the two-person rule for critical system administrator functions, nonrepudiation of technical actions, encryption, and disabling accounts upon termination can limit the damage and promote the detection of malicious system administrator and privileged user actions.

- *Practice 11: Implement system change controls.*

A wide variety of insider compromises relied on unauthorized modifications to the organization's systems, which argues for stronger change controls as a mitigation strategy. System administrators or privileged users can deploy backdoor accounts, unauthorized hardware, logic bombs, or other malicious programs on the system or network. These types of attacks are stealthy and therefore difficult to detect, but technical controls can be implemented for early detection. Once baseline software and hardware configurations are characterized, comparison to the current configuration can detect discrepancies and alert managers for action.

- *Practice 12: Log, monitor, and audit employee online actions.*

If account and password policies and procedures are enforced, you can associate online actions with the employee who performed them. Logging, periodic monitoring, and auditing provide an organization the opportunity to discover and investigate suspicious insider actions before more serious consequences ensue. In addition to unauthorized changes to the systems, download of confidential or sensitive information such as intellectual property (IP), customer or client information, and Personally Identifiable Information (PII) can be detected via data-leakage tools.

- *Practice 13: Use layered defense against remote attacks.*

If employees are trained and vigilant, accounts are protected from compromise, and employees know that their actions are being logged and monitored, disgruntled insiders will think twice about attacking systems or networks at work. Insiders tend to feel more confident and less inhibited when they have little fear of scrutiny by coworkers; therefore, remote access policies and procedures must be designed and implemented very carefully. When remote access to critical systems is deemed necessary, you should consider offsetting the added risk with requiring connections only via organization-owned machines and closer logging and frequent auditing of remote transactions. Disabling remote access and collection of your equipment is particularly important for terminated employees.

- *Practice 14: Deactivate computer access following termination.*

When an employee or contractor terminates employment, whether the circumstances were favorable or not, it is important that you have in place a rigorous termination procedure that disables all of the employee's access points to your physical locations, networks, systems, applications, and data. Fast action to disable all access paths available to a terminated employee requires ongoing and strict tracking and management practices for all employee avenues of access including computer system accounts, shared passwords, and card-control systems.

- *Practice 15: Implement secure backup and recovery processes.*

No organization can completely eliminate its risk of insider attack; risk is inherent in the operation of all organizations. However, with a goal of organizational resiliency, risks must be acceptable to the stakeholders, and as such, impacts of potential insider attacks must be minimized. Therefore, it is important for you to prepare for the possibility of insider attack and minimize response time by implementing secure backup and recovery processes that avoid single points of failure and are tested periodically. This practice contains descriptions of insider threat cases in which the organization's lack of attention to incident response and organizational resiliency resulted in serious disruption of service to its customers.

- *Practice 16: Develop an insider incident response plan.*

You need to develop an insider incident response plan to control the damage due to malicious insiders. This is challenging because the same people assigned to a response team may be the insiders who can use their technical skills against you. Only those responsible for carrying out the plan need to understand and be trained on its execution. Should an insider attack, it is important that you have evidence in hand to identify the insider and follow up appropriately. Lessons learned should be used to continually improve the plan.

## Practice 1: Consider Threats from Insiders and Business Partners in Enterprise-Wide Risk Assessments

You need to develop a comprehensive risk-based security strategy to protect your critical assets against threats from inside and outside, as well as trusted business partners who are given authorized insider access.

### What Can You Do?

It is not practical for most organizations to implement 100% protection against every threat to every organizational resource. Therefore, it is important to focus on protecting your critical information and resources and not direct significant effort toward protecting relatively unimportant data and resources. A realistic and achievable security goal is to protect those assets deemed critical to your mission from both external and internal threats.

Risk is the combination of threat, vulnerability, and mission impact. Enterprise-wide risk assessments help identify critical assets, potential threats to those assets, and mission impact if the assets are compromised. You should use the results of the assessment to develop or refine your overall strategy for securing your systems, striking the proper balance between countering the threat and accomplishing your mission.[2]

You need to understand the threat environment under which your systems operate in order to accurately assess enterprise risk. Characterization of the threat environment can proceed in parallel with evaluation of the vulnerability and its impact. However, the sooner the threat environment can be characterized, the better. The purpose of this practice is to assist you in correctly assessing the insider threat environment, your vulnerabilities that enable that threat, and potential impacts that could result from insider incidents, including financial, operational, and reputational.

Unfortunately, many organizations focus on protecting information from access or sabotage by those external to the organization and overlook insiders. Moreover, an information technology and security solution designed without consciously acknowledging and accounting for potential insider threats often leaves the role of protection in the hands of some of the potential threats—the insiders themselves. It is imperative that you recognize the potential danger posed by the knowledge and access of your employees, contractors, and business partners, and specifically address that threat as part of an enterprise risk assessment.

---

2. See www.cert.org/resilience/.

Understanding your vulnerability to a threat is also important, but organizations often focus on low-level technical vulnerabilities, for example, by relying on automated computer and network vulnerability scanners. While such techniques are important, our studies of insider threat have indicated that vulnerabilities in an organization's business processes are at least as important as technical vulnerabilities. You need to manage the impact of threats rather than chase individual technical vulnerabilities.

In addition, new areas of concern have become apparent in recent cases, including legal and contracting issues. Organizations are increasingly outsourcing critical business functions. As a result, people external to your organization sometimes have full access to your policies, processes, information, and systems; access and knowledge previously only provided to your employees. You need to recognize the increased risk; your enterprise boundary includes all people who have an understanding of and privileged access to your organization, information, and information systems.

Insider threats may impact the integrity, availability, or confidentiality of information critical to your mission. Insiders have affected the integrity of their organizations' information in various ways; for example, by manipulating customer financial information or defacing their employers' Web sites. They have also violated confidentiality of information by stealing trade secrets or customer information. Still others have inappropriately disseminated confidential information, including private customer information as well as sensitive email messages between the organization's management. Finally, insiders have affected the availability of their organization's information by deleting data, sabotaging entire systems and networks, destroying backups, and committing other types of denial-of-service attacks.

In those types of insider incidents, current or former employees, contractors, or business partners were able to compromise their organizations' critical assets. It is important that protection strategies are designed focusing on those assets: financial data, confidential or proprietary information, and other mission-critical systems and data.

## Case Studies: What Could Happen if I Don't Do It?

An insider was the sole system administrator for his organization. One day, he quit with no prior notice. His organization refused to pay him for his last two days of work, and he subsequently refused to give the organization the passwords for its system administrator accounts. Over a period of three days, the insider modified the systems so that employees could not access them, defaced the company Web site, and deleted files.

It is critical that you consider the risk you assume when you place all system administration power into the hands of a single employee. Even if you are part of a large organization, do not overlook small development teams, stand-alone machines, and other independently maintained systems in your organization that are not a part of your enterprise infrastructure. We know from doing insider threat assessments that even the largest organizations have these types of systems, which can be a part of critical projects and development or even production systems. Worst of all, there likely has been no formal risk assessment performed that accounts for potential insider threats.

> One case involved an employee of a company that obtained a contract to set up a new wireless network for a major manufacturer. The insider was on the installation team and therefore had detailed knowledge of the manufacturer's systems. He was removed from the team by his employer, apparently under negative circumstances. However, he was able to enter the manufacturing plant and access a computer kiosk in the visitors' lobby. Based on his familiarity with the manufacturer's computer system and security, he was able to use the kiosk to delete files and passwords from wireless devices used by the manufacturer across the country. The manufacturer was forced to remove and repair the devices, causing wide-scale shutdown of facilities and disruption of its processes.

This case highlights several new insider threat issues. First, an enterprise-wide risk assessment should have identified the ability to override security and obtain privileged access to the manufacturer's network from a publicly accessible kiosk. Second, the manufacturer's contract with the insider's organization should have instituted strict controls over employees added to or removed from the project. Specifically, you should consider provisions in your contracts that require advance notification by the contracted organization of any negative employment actions being planned against any employees who have physical and/or electronic access to your facilities or systems. You could require notification a specified amount of time before the action is taken against the contractor, in order to perform your own risk assessment for the potential threat posed to your network, systems, or information.

> A computer help desk attendant employed by a government contractor created fake government email addresses on the government systems for which he was responsible. He then used those email addresses to request replacement parts for equipment recalled by a major supplier. The supplier sent the replacement parts to the address specified in the emails, with the expectation that the original recalled products would be returned after the replacements had been received. The insider provided his home address for the shipments, and never intended to return the original equipment.

> He received almost 100 shipments with a retail value of almost $5 million and sold the equipment on the Internet.

This incident indicates the need to have transaction verification built into supplier agreements. Even though operations might be outsourced, you still need to include those operations in your enterprise risk assessment so that you can ensure that your trusted business partners implement adequate controls against insider threat in their organizations.

> A system administrator had authorized access to sanitized databases of customer information on an FTP server hosted by one of his organization's business partners. The business partner was contracted by financial institutions and phone companies to perform services using customer data. He located an unsanitized version of these customer databases when looking around on the FTP server. The databases were protected with passwords and encryption. The insider ran a password cracking utility and obtained more than 300 passwords he could use to access the protected information. He found original and complete phone records, billing information, and other PII for millions of Americans. He proceeded to download millions of customer records from the databases, including Social Security numbers, birthdates, and other personal information. The insider bragged in online IRC channels about his access to confidential and personal data, and was asked at one point by another individual in the chat room to provide data on an FBI agent who was actively investigating him. The insider provided the information within minutes. The ongoing FBI investigation of that individual led back to the insider, who was found with dozens of CDs and other media containing millions of customer records in his apartment.

In this case, proprietary information from the original organizations' customers was inadequately protected from access by a third organization that was subcontracted by a second organization, the trusted business partner. Legal controls to ensure contractor compliance with your data-handling policies could be employed to protect against the extended pool of insiders created by working with vendors and other external partners. These measures would allow contractors to perform their work, while protecting your sensitive information.

## Practice 2: Clearly Document and Consistently Enforce Policies and Controls

A consistent, clear message on organizational policies and controls will help reduce the chance that employees will commit a crime or lash out at the organization for a perceived injustice.

### What Can You Do?

Policies or controls that are misunderstood, not communicated, or inconsistently enforced can breed resentment among employees and can potentially result in harmful insider actions. For example, multiple insiders in cases in the CERT database took intellectual property they had created to a new job, not realizing that they did not own it. They were quite surprised when they were arrested for a crime they did not realize they had committed.

You should ensure the following with regard to your policies and controls:

- Concise and coherent documentation, including reasoning behind the policy, where applicable
- Fairness for all employees
- Consistent enforcement
- Periodic employee training on the policies, justification, implementation, and enforcement

You should be particularly clear on policies regarding

- Acceptable use of your systems, information, and resources
- Ownership of information created as a paid employee or contractor
- Evaluation of employee performance, including requirements for promotion and financial bonuses
- Processes and procedures for addressing employee grievances

As individuals join your organization, they should receive a copy of your policies that clearly lays out what is expected of them, together with the consequences of violations. You should retain evidence that each individual has read and agreed to your policies.

Employee disgruntlement was a recurring factor in insider incidents; particularly in insider IT sabotage cases. As explained in Chapter 2, Insider IT Sabotage, disgruntlement is usually caused by some unmet expectation on the part of the insider. Examples of unmet expectations observed in cases include

- Insufficient salary increase or bonus
- Limitations on use of company resources
- Diminished authority or responsibilities
- Perception of unfair work requirements
- Poor coworker relations

Clear documentation of policies and controls can help prevent employee misunderstandings that can lead to unmet expectations. Consistent enforcement can ensure that employees don't feel they are being treated differently from or worse than other employees. In one case, employees had become accustomed to lax policy enforcement over a long period of time. New management dictated immediate strict policy enforcement, which caused one employee to become embittered and strike out against the organization. In other words, policies should be enforced consistently across all employees, as well as consistently enforced over time.

Of course, organizations are not static entities; change in organizational policies and controls is inevitable. Employee constraints, privileges, and responsibilities change as well. You need to recognize times of change as particularly stressful times for employees, recognize the increased risk that comes along with these stress points, and mitigate it with clear communication regarding what employees can expect in the future.

## Case Studies: What Could Happen if I Don't Do It?

Two contractors were formerly employed as software developers for a company that provided news filtering and distribution services to Web sites. In response to their termination, their legal counsel faxed a letter to the company. The letter insisted that the insiders owned the software they had created during their employment, and demanded that the company stop using the software and return all copies to them. On the evening before a holiday, the insiders used a home computer and their own credentials, which were still active, to remotely access the company's network and download the proprietary software and business plans. The insiders were arrested after the company discovered the unauthorized access, and connected them to the theft using their usernames and system logs.

In this case, it is clear that there was confusion regarding who owned the software the contractors had created for the company. Intellectual property ownership should be documented in formal policies that are clearly communicated to all employees and contractually enforced for all contractors and trusted business partners. In addition, you should have your employees re-sign the agreements periodically. We have discussed this with several organizations who instituted IP agreements for all employees more than 20 years ago. All employees signed them at that time, and all new employees now sign them. However, some employees have not signed again since they originally signed more than 20 years ago! It is debatable whether those aged agreements would stand up in a court of law!

You might also consider incorporating a new angle into your IP agreements to protect yourself from being the unknowing recipient of stolen IP from *another* organization. As part of your IP agreement that you make new employees sign, you might want to include a statement attesting to the fact that they have not brought any IP from any previous employer with them to your organization.

> An insider accepted a promotion, leaving a system administrator position in one department for a position as a systems analyst in another department of the same organization. In his new position, he was responsible for information sharing and collaboration between his old department and the new one. The following events ensued.
>
> - The original department terminated his system administrator account and issued him an ordinary user account to support the access required in his new position.
> - Shortly thereafter, the system security manager at the original department noticed that the former employee's new account had been granted unauthorized system administration rights.
> - The security manager reset the account back to ordinary access rights, but a day later found that administrative rights had been granted to it once again.
> - The security manager closed the account, but over the next few weeks other accounts exhibited unauthorized access and usage patterns.
>
> An investigation of these events led to charges against the analyst for misuse of the organization's computing systems. These charges were eventually dropped, in part because there was no clear policy regarding account sharing or exploitation of vulnerabilities to elevate account privileges.

This case illustrates the importance of clearly established policies that are consistent across departments, groups, and subsidiaries of the organization.

There are many cases in the CERT database where an employee compromised an organization's information or system in order to address some perceived injustice.

- An insider planted a logic bomb in an organization's system because he felt that he was required to follow stricter work standards than his fellow employees.
- In reaction to a lower bonus than expected, an insider planted a logic bomb that would, he expected, cause the organization's stock value to go down, thus causing stock options he owned to increase in value.
- A network administrator who designed and controlled an organization's manufacturing support systems detonated a logic bomb to destroy his creation because of his perceived loss of status and control.
- A quality-control inspector, who believed his employer insufficiently addressed the quality requirements of its product, supplied confidential company information to the media to force the company to deal with the problem.
- An insider, who was upset about his company's practice of canceling insurance policies for policy holders who paid late, provided sensitive company information to the opposing lawyers engaged in a lawsuit against the company.

What these insiders did is wrong and against the law. Nevertheless, more clearly defined policies and grievance procedures for perceived policy violations might have avoided the serious insider attacks experienced by these organizations.

## Practice 3: Institute Periodic Security Awareness Training for All Employees

Without broad understanding and buy-in from the organization, technical or managerial controls will be short-lived.

### What Can You Do?

All employees need to understand that insider crimes do occur, and there are severe consequences. In addition, it is important for them to understand that malicious insiders can be highly technical people or those with minimal technical ability. Ages of perpetrators in the CERT database range from late teens to retirement. Both men and women have been malicious insiders, including introverted "loners," aggressive "get it done" people, and extroverted "star players." Positions have included low-wage data entry clerks, cashiers, programmers, artists, system and network administrators, salespersons, managers, and executives. They have been new hires, long-term employees, currently employed, recently terminated, contractors, temporary employees, and employees of trusted business partners. There is not one demographic profile for a malicious insider.

Security awareness training should encourage observation of behavior in the workplace to identify employees who may be at higher risk of malicious activity, not by stereotypical characteristics. Behaviors of concern include

- Threats against the organization or bragging about the damage one could do to the organization
- Association with known criminals or suspicious people outside the workplace
- Large downloads close to resignation
- Use of organization resources for a side business, or discussions regarding starting a competing business with coworkers
- Attempts to gain employees' passwords or to obtain access through trickery or exploitation of a trusted relationship (often called social engineering)

Your managers and employees need to be trained to recognize recruitment in which an insider engages other employees to join his schemes, particularly to steal or modify information for financial gain. Warning employees of this possibility and the consequences may help to keep them on the watch for such manipulation and to report it to management.

Social engineering is often associated with attempts to gain either physical access or electronic access via accounts and passwords. Some of the CERT database cases reveal social engineering of a different type, however. In one case, a disgruntled employee placed a hardware keystroke logger on a computer at work to capture confidential company information. After being fired unexpectedly, the now-former employee tried to co-opt a nontechnical employee still at the company to recover the device for him. Although the employee had no idea the device was a keystroke logger, she was smart enough to recognize the risk of providing it to him and notified management instead. Forensics revealed that he had transferred the keystrokes file to his computer at work at least once before being fired.

Training programs should create a culture of security appropriate for your organization and include all personnel. For effectiveness and longevity, the measures used to secure your organization against insider threat need to be tied to the organization's mission, values, and critical assets, as determined by an enterprise-wide risk assessment. For example, if your organization places a high value on customer service quality, you may view customer information as its most critical asset and focus security on protection of your data. Your organization could train your employees to be vigilant against malicious employee actions, focusing on a number of key issues, including

- Detecting and reporting disruptive behavior by employees (see Practice 4)
- Monitoring adherence to organizational policies and controls (see Practices 2 and 11)
- Monitoring and controlling changes to organizational systems—for example, to prevent the installation of malicious code (see Practices 9 and 11)
- Requiring separation of duties between employees who modify customer accounts and those who approve modifications or issue payments (see Practice 8)
- Detecting and reporting violations of the security of the organization's facilities and physical assets (see Practice 6)
- Planning for potential incident response proactively (see Practice 16)

Training on reducing risks to customer service processes would focus on

- Protecting computer accounts used in these processes (see Practice 7)
- Auditing access to customer records (see Practice 12)

- Ensuring consistent enforcement of defined security policies and controls (see Practice 2)
- Implementing proper system administration safeguards for critical servers (see Practices 10, 11, 12, and 13)
- Using secure backup and recovery methods to ensure availability of customer service data (see Practice 15)

Training content should be based on documented policies, and include a confidential means of reporting security issues. Confidential reporting allows reporting of suspicious events without fear of repercussions, thereby overcoming the cultural barrier of whistle-blowing. Your employees need to understand your organization's policies and procedures, and be aware that your managers will respond to security issues in a fair and prompt manner.

Your employees should be notified that system activity is monitored, especially system administration and privileged activity. All employees should be trained in their personal responsibility, such as protection of their own passwords and work products. Finally, the training should communicate IT acceptable use policies.

As described in Chapter 4, Insider Fraud, in many of the insider fraud incidents the insider was recruited to steal by someone outside the organization. In many of these cases, the insider was taking most of the risk while receiving relatively small financial compensation. The outsider was often a relative of the insider or an acquaintance who realized the value of exploiting the insider's access to information. One manager of a hospital's billing records gave patients' credit card information to her brother, who used it for online purchases shipped to his home address. Another insider in the human resources department for a federal government organization gave employee PII to her boyfriend, who used it to open and make purchases on fraudulent credit card accounts.

You should educate your employees on their responsibilities for protecting the information with which they are entrusted, and the possibility that unscrupulous individuals could try to take advantage of their access to that information. Such individuals may be inside or outside the organization. In many of the fraud cases where insiders modified information for financial gain, the insider recruited at least one other employee in the organization to participate in the scheme, possibly as a means to bypass separation of duty restrictions, or to ensure that coworkers wouldn't report suspicious behavior. In one case, several bank janitorial employees stole customer information while working, changed the customer addresses online, opened credit cards in their names, purchased expensive items using the cards, and drained their bank accounts. Your employees should be regularly reminded about procedures the company has in place for anonymously reporting suspicious coworker behavior, or attempts of recruitment by individuals inside or outside the organization.

In Chapter 3, Insider Theft of Intellectual Property, we indicated that many cases involve technical employees who stole their organization's intellectual property because of dissatisfaction. Signs of disgruntlement in cases like those often appear well before the actual compromise. Such attacks can be prevented if managers and coworkers are educated to recognize and report behavioral precursors indicating potential attacks.

Finally, your employees need to be educated about the confidentiality and integrity of your company's information, and that compromises will be dealt with immediately. Some insiders in the CERT database did not understand this, viewing information as being their own property rather than the organization's; for example, customer information developed by a salesperson or software developed by a programmer.

## Case Studies: What Could Happen if I Don't Do It?

> A contractor was employed as a programmer by a high-technology company. He requested to work remotely from home, his request was denied, and he informed the organization that he would be resigning. He actually had obtained employment with a competitor. On the evening before his last day of work, he returned to the facility, outside of normal work hours. He entered a building which was not his normal work location and removed the name plate from an engineer's office. He then asked a janitor to let him in, claiming it was his office and he'd been accidentally locked out. The janitor complied with the request; the insider now had physical access to all of the computers in the engineer's office.

You probably think you know the ending to this case, right? He stole the information and left the office. Not quite; read on...

> The engineer who occupied that office happened to walk in—and caught the insider in the act of stealing his proprietary source code from his computer. The insider quickly made up a false explanation as to why he was there, and promptly left. The following day, the insider reported for his last day of work, and was observed leaving with a CD. The organization reported him to law enforcement, thinking he might have stolen

its intellectual property on the CD. An investigation confirmed the theft, specifically of proprietary source code. The contractor was arrested, convicted, and sentenced to one year of work furlough.

This case demonstrates many interesting security awareness issues. First, would your custodial staff or security guards fall for that scheme? Don't forget them when preparing and delivering your security awareness training! Second, do you educate your employees to report suspicious activity in their offices? Would they fall for this ploy? What would your employees do if they caught someone in their office after hours? Finally, there is good news at the end of this case: The organization was suspicious enough to notify law enforcement of the departing contractor carrying a CD out with him.

> The lead developer of a mission-critical safety-related application had extensive control over the application source code. The only copy of the source code was on his laptop, there were no backups performed, and very little documentation existed, even though management had repeatedly requested it. The insider told coworkers he had no intention of documenting the source code and any documentation he did write would be obscure.

> A month after learning of a pending demotion, he erased the hard drive of his laptop, deleting the only copy of the source code the organization possessed, and quit his job. It took more than two months to recover the source code after it was located by law enforcement in encrypted form at the insider's home. Another four months elapsed before the insider provided the password to decrypt the source code. During this time the organization had to rely on the executable version of the application, with no ability to make any modifications.

This case could have had dire consequences due to the critical nature of the application. How could the problem have been avoided? We could say that management should have had more direct oversight of the development process, but the malicious insider was the lead developer, so you can't necessarily blame management completely. However, the insider's team members were aware of the insider's deliberate inaction; they could have informed management of his statements and actions in time to prevent the attack. This case demonstrates the importance of educating all of your employees that the security and survivability of the system is everyone's responsibility, as well as clear procedures for reporting concerning behavior.

## Practice 4: Monitor and Respond to Suspicious or Disruptive Behavior, Beginning with the Hiring Process

One method of reducing the threat of malicious insiders is to proactively deal with suspicious or disruptive employees.

### What Can You Do?

Your approach to reducing the insider threat should start in the hiring process by performing background checks and evaluating prospective employees based on the information received. Background checks should investigate previous criminal convictions, include a credit check, verify credentials and past employment, and include discussions with prior employers regarding the individual's competence and approach to dealing with workplace issues. When creating a preemployment screening policy or other policies recommended in this practice, it is important to keep in mind privacy and legal requirements (e.g., notification of the candidate).

Recall from Chapter 2 that 30% of the insiders who committed IT sabotage in our original study with the Secret Service had a previous arrest history, including arrests for violent offenses (18%), alcohol- or drug-related offenses (11%), and nonfinancial/fraud-related theft offenses (11%).[3] In fact, some of those insiders had been arrested for multiple offenses. The relatively high frequency of previous criminal arrests underscores the need for background checks. These proactive measures should not be punitive in nature; rather, the individual should be indoctrinated into the organization with appropriate care. In addition, this information should be used as part of a risk-based decision process in determining whether it is appropriate to give the new employee access to critical, confidential, or proprietary information or systems.

In addition to screening for potential red flags during the hiring process, you also should invest time and resources in training your supervisors to recognize and respond to inappropriate or concerning behavior in employees. In some cases, less serious but inappropriate behavior was noticed in the workplace but not acted on because it did not rise to the level of a policy violation. However, failure to define or enforce security policies in some cases emboldened the employees to commit repeated violations that escalated in severity, with increasing risk of significant harm to the organization.

---

3. See [Keeney 2005].

It is important that you consistently investigate and respond to all rule violations committed by your employees and contractors.

Given that financial gain is a primary motive for much insider fraud, you should monitor indications by employees of possible financial problems or unexplained financial gain. Sudden changes in an employee's financial situation, including increasing debt or expensive purchases, may be indicators of potential financial need. In addition, recall from Chapter 4 that fraud may involve theft or modification of small amounts of data (e.g., Social Security numbers) repeatedly over long periods of time. This suggests that for fraud crimes there is ample time to catch the insider in the act while still employed by you. In addition, some of the insiders had personal stressors that may have influenced their actions, including family medical problems, substance abuse, financial difficulties, and physical threats by outsiders. These crimes also had a high rate of collusion with both insiders and outsiders. Secretive meetings among employees and obvious attempts to deceive the organization about outside relationships are of concern.

In Chapter 3, Insider Theft of Intellectual Property, we described that these crimes tend to involve larger amounts of data (e.g., proprietary source code) and often occur within one month of the insider's resignation. However, many of the incidents involve significant planning well before the theft in which the insider becomes more curious about aspects of the information (e.g., software modules) outside of his area of responsibility. In some of those incidents, the insider had already created or was planning to start his own business while still working for the victim organization. Many were deceptive about their reasons for leaving the organization, even while working out the details with competing organizations for the transfer of stolen information. As with insider fraud, suspicious interactions among employees and obvious attempts to deceive the organization about outside business relationships are of concern.

As we described in Chapter 2, Insider IT Sabotage, insiders have also become disgruntled due to professional stressors, including financial compensation issues, problems with a supervisor, hostile working environments, and layoffs. Often, the first sign of disgruntlement is the onset of concerning behaviors in the workplace. Unfortunately in many of our cases, the concerning behaviors were not recognized by management prior to the incidents, or the organization failed to take action to address the behaviors.

Policies and procedures should exist for your employees to report concerning or disruptive behavior by coworkers. While frivolous reports need to be screened, all reports should be investigated. If one of your employees exhibits suspicious behavior, you should respond with due care. Disruptive employees should not be allowed to migrate from one position to another within your organization, evading documentation of disruptive or concerning activity. Threats, boasting about malicious acts or abilities ("You wouldn't believe how easily I could trash this net!"), and other negative sentiments should also be treated as concerning behaviors. Many employees will have concerns and grievances from time to time, and a formal and accountable process for addressing those grievances may satisfy those who might otherwise resort to malicious activity. In general, any employee experiencing difficulties in the workplace should be aided in the resolution of those difficulties.

Once concerning behavior is identified, several steps may assist you in managing risks of malicious activity. First, the employee's access to critical information assets should be evaluated. His or her level of network access should also be considered. Logs should be reviewed to carefully examine recent online activity by the employee or contractor. While this is done, you should provide options to the individual for coping with the behavior, perhaps including access to a confidential employee-assistance program.

Suspicious behaviors, if detected, provide you an opportunity to recognize a higher risk of insider threat and act accordingly. Often, coworkers are aware of issues; anonymous means for reporting coworker suspicions should be in place and communicated to your employees.

Keep in mind that legal and employee privacy issues must be considered when implementing this practice. It is very important that you work with your legal department in developing these types of policies and procedures!

## Case Studies: What Could Happen if I Don't Do It?

A subcontractor worked for an organization that handled state government employee health insurance claims. Using the medical identity number of an unsuspecting psychologist, the insider changed the name and address associated with the psychologist to a coconspirator's name and address. He proceeded to file fake claims and send the payments to the bogus addresses. Auditors discovered the scheme when they began questioning why a psychologist was submitting payment claims for treating broken bones and open wounds, and administering chemotherapy. They also noticed that the name associated with the psychologist was the name of one of their subcontractors. During the investigation it was determined that the insider had a criminal history for fraud and that the subcontracting organization probably did not perform a background check prior to hiring.

Background checks should be required for all potential employees, including contractors and subcontractors.

> A former system administrator at a university's cancer institute deleted 18 months of cancer research after quitting because of personality and work ethic differences between himself, his supervisor, and his coworkers. He had been the sole system administrator on the cancer research project team. On numerous occasions he had displayed aggressive and malicious (nontechnical) behaviors before quitting his job. He was not liked by his coworkers, but was seen as a "necessary evil" for his skills. He was described as very lazy—slacking on the job—but they didn't know how to get rid of him. A few days after quitting, he returned to the lab. His badge had been disabled, so he could not enter on his own; therefore, he asked an employee who recognized him to let him in. Once inside the building, he used a key that had not been confiscated to enter the office and delete the cancer research.

In this case, the employee obviously exhibited concerning behaviors in the workplace. As stated earlier, it is important to have established policies and procedures for dealing with concerning behaviors in the workplace.

## Practice 5: Anticipate and Manage Negative Workplace Issues

Clearly defined and communicated organizational policies for dealing with employee issues will ensure consistent enforcement and reduce risk when negative workplace issues arise.

### What Can You Do?

Beginning with the first day of employment, an employee needs to be made aware of organizational practices and policies for acceptable workplace behavior, dress code, acceptable usage policies, work hours, career development, conflict resolution, and myriad other workplace issues. The existence of such policies alone is not enough. New employees and veteran employees alike all need to be aware of the existence of such policies and the consequences for violations. Consistent enforcement of the policies is essential to maintain the harmonious environment of the organization. When employees see inconsistent enforcement of policies, it may lead to animosity within the workplace. In many of our cases, inconsistent enforcement or perceived injustices within organizations led to insider disgruntlement. Coworkers often felt that "star performers" were above the rules and received special treatment. Many times that disgruntlement led the insiders to commit IT sabotage or theft of information.

When your employees have issues, whether they are justified or not, they need an avenue to seek assistance. Employees need to be able to openly discuss work-related issues with a member of management or human resources without the fear of reprisal or negative consequences. When employee issues arise because of outside issues, including financial and personal stressors, it can be helpful to use a service such as an employee assistance program. These programs offer confidential counseling to assist employees, allowing them to restore their work performance, health, or general well-being. If insiders who committed fraud had access to employee assistance programs, they may have found an alternative way to deal with the financial and personal stressors that appear to be a motivating factor in the crimes.

It is imperative that your employees are aware of and sign intellectual property agreements and noncompete agreements. It is important that they are reminded of those agreements at the time of termination. There should be no ambiguity over who owns intellectual property developed as an employee of your organization. Many of the insiders who committed theft of information claimed to not know it was a violation of company policy when they took customer lists, pricing sheets, and even source code with them upon termination.

Finally, your termination process should include a step to retrieve all organization property from terminating employees. They should be required to return all property, including computers and accessories, software and hardware, confidential information, source code and compiled code, mobile devices, removable media, and any other items that contain sensitive, confidential, or intellectual property owned by you. You should consider showing employees the signed copy of the intellectual property agreement and noncompete agreement and explaining the consequences for violating those policies as part of the employee termination process.

## Case Studies: What Could Happen if I Don't Do It?

A female employee who was a DBA and project manager became increasingly disgruntled when her male coworkers began to override her technical decisions where she was the expert. She filed complaints with HR over what she considered a hostile work environment, but nothing was done about it. After she filed a complaint against her supervisor, her performance reviews, which had been stellar, went downhill. Her supervisor then demoted her by removing her project management responsibilities. Again she complained, but her supervisor started filing complaints against her for failure to follow instructions. She next filed a complaint with the EEOC for discrimination based on her national origin (India), race (Asian, Indian), and gender (female). She eventually resigned because she was frustrated by the organization's lack of responsiveness to her complaints. After resignation, she found out her grievance against the organization had been denied. The last straw was when she found out that the organization only forwarded her negative performance reviews to the new organization where she was now employed. She connected from her computer at home to her previous organization. She used another employee's username and password to log in to the system. Next she entered a critical system using a DBA account, which had not been changed since she resigned, and deleted critical data from the system. She deleted two weeks' worth of data used to determine promotions, transfers, and disability claims, and caused the system to crash.

In this case, the organization did attempt to manage the negative workplace issues. Obviously, the human resources department was involved and progressive disciplinary actions were taken. Unfortunately, the problems were not resolved when she left the organization. In some cases, it is worth considering alternatives to sanctions in dealing with employee issues. This particular insider had been a stellar employee, but unfortunately her

performance was affected by the team with which she worked. A transfer
to another part of the organization might have been considered, in order to
improve a negative situation for a historically excellent employee.

> A vice president for engineering who was responsible for oversight of all
> software development in the company was engaged in a long-running
> dispute with upper management. This dispute was characterized as ver-
> bal attacks by the insider and statements to colleagues about how much
> he had upset management. He engaged in personal attacks once or twice
> a week and on one occasion, in a restaurant, screamed personal attacks at
> the CEO of the company. A final explosive disagreement prompted him
> to quit. When no severance package was offered, he copied a portion of
> the company's product under development to removable media, deleted
> it from the company's server, and removed the recent backup tapes.
> He then offered to restore the software in exchange for $50,000. He was
> charged and convicted of extortion, misappropriation of trade secrets, and
> grand theft. However, the most recent version of the software was never
> recovered.

If the company in this case had recognized that the warning signs—the
disruptive behavior—could signal a potential insider attack, it could
have secured its assets and substantial losses could have been avoided.
It is critical that managers recognize, manage, and realize the potential
consequences of negative workplace issues.

## Practice 6: Track and Secure the Physical Environment

Although organizations are becoming more reliant on electronic communication and online transactions to do business, it is still essential that you track and secure the physical environment against internal and external threats.

### What Can You Do?

First and foremost, you must protect your most critical asset: your employees. This process begins by ensuring your office environment is free from occupational hazards and threats to employees from outsiders. While planning for the security of the physical environment, you should take into consideration the space inside the office walls as well as the perimeter of the building, including lobbies, elevators, stairwells, and parking areas. If you can keep unauthorized people out of your facility, you will add an extra layer to the desired security in-depth model.

Likewise, physical security can lend another layer of defense against terminated insiders who wish to regain physical access to attack. Just as with electronic security, however, former employees have been successful in working around their organization's physical security measures. Employee privacy and related laws should be considered when developing a secure physical environment. Commonly used physical security mechanisms, some that were effective and others that were inadequate, in our cases include the following.

- Maintaining a physical security presence on the facilities at all times. Some of the former employees in the CERT database had to go to extra lengths to carry out their crime due to security guards on duty around the clock. For example, at least one terminated insider lied to the night-shift security guard, who had not been told of the termination, about forgetting his badge. However, it is likely that other former insiders were deterred from malicious actions by those same guards.

- Requiring all employees, contractors, customers, and vendors to have an organization-issued badge and requiring the use of that badge to navigate throughout the facility. One employee in the CERT database had to obtain a badge from a former contractor, used that badge to obtain physical access to an area of the facility for which he was not authorized after hours, and then sabotaged the computers in the network operations center. Another former employee "piggybacked" behind another employee who had a badge to obtain after-hours access to the facility. However, once again, these measures probably would deter a less motivated insider from carrying out a crime.

- Using alarms to deter and alert when unauthorized individuals enter your facility.
- Using closed-circuit cameras to record entry, exit, and critical operations at the facility. Some of the insiders in the CERT database were successfully identified and convicted through use of closed-circuit cameras or video surveillance.

Once the physical perimeter is as secure as possible, you should devote adequate resources to protecting the critical infrastructure, ensuring resiliency of operation. An infrastructure security strategy should begin by defining which assets are critical to the operation of your organization. These assets should be consolidated into a central computing facility with limited access to the physical space. Access control to the facility should be clearly defined and changes made as employees are hired and terminated. Access to the facility should be tracked via an automated logging mechanism or, at a minimum, signing in and out of the facility using a sign-in sheet.

Physical protection of the backup media is also of critical importance. In some cases, malicious insiders were able to steal or sabotage the backups so that they were unusable, slowing down or crippling the organization when it attempted to recover from the insider attack.

In addition to securing the critical assets housed in your computer facility, careful attention should be paid to the computers, workstations, laptops, printers, and fax machines located in all areas, both secured and not secured. The security of the computing infrastructure begins with the protection of the perimeter of the organization and moves down to the protection of office space, by locking doors and windows.

The next layer of physical defense entails securing computing resources—for example, using password-protected screen savers, and securing mobile devices and removable media (such as laptops, memory sticks, and smartphones) by requiring encryption and/or a multifactor authentication method.

To the greatest extent possible, attempts to access your facilities should be logged. A regular audit of the access logs should be performed to identify violations or attempted violations of the access policy. Automated alerting of those violations could enable you to detect a security violation before major damage is inflicted.

Finally, you need to implement a strategy for tracking and disposing of documents that contain controlled information. In addition, precautions against insider threats must be applied to all employees, even if they apparently have no access to your computing resources. Several cases involved the compromise of sensitive, proprietary, confidential, or secret information due to lax controls involving disposal of materials containing that information. In one case, a night-shift janitor obtained personal information for bank customers by searching through office trash, and then used the information to commit identity theft. In another case, an employee was able to obtain documents containing trade secrets from a hopper containing confidential material to be destroyed, and sold the documents to a foreign competitor.

## Case Studies: What Could Happen if I Don't Do It?

An employee was suspended by his employer, "based on an employee dispute." The employee had been subcontracted by his employer as an IT consultant at an energy management facility. Because he was suspended late Friday afternoon, his employer decided to wait until Monday morning to notify the energy management facility of his suspension. Late Sunday night he went to the energy production facility; he still had authorized access since facility personnel had not been notified of his suspension. He used a hammer to break the glass case enclosing the "Emergency power off button" and hit the button, shutting down some of the computer systems, including computers that regulated the exchange of electricity between power grids. For a period of two hours, the shutdown denied the organization access to the energy trading market, but fortunately didn't affect the transmission grid directly.

This case raises important physical security and legal/contracting issues regarding contractors. These types of contracting issues were already discussed in Practice 1. This case serves as another example of why you should alter your contracting practices to require advance notification of pending employee sanctions by your subcontractors, and requiring immediate notification if one of the contractors is terminated or resigns. It also illustrates the potential damage that could be caused by the cascading effects from a disgruntled insider using physical sabotage to impact mission-critical systems.

## Practice 7: Implement Strict Password- and Account-Management Policies and Practices

If your organization's computer accounts can be compromised, insiders can circumvent manual and automated control mechanisms.

### What Can You Do?

No matter how vigilant you are about mitigating the threats posed by insiders, if your computer accounts can be compromised, insiders have an opportunity to circumvent mechanisms in place to prevent insider attacks. Therefore, computer account- and password-management policies and practices are critical to impede an insider's ability to use your systems for illicit purposes. Fine-grained access control combined with proper computer account management will ensure that access to all of your critical electronic assets is

- Controlled to make unauthorized access difficult
- Logged and monitored so that suspicious access can be detected and investigated
- Traceable from the computer account to the individual associated with that account

Some methods used by malicious insiders to compromise accounts included

- Using password crackers
- Obtaining passwords through social engineering
- Employees openly sharing passwords
- Employees storing passwords in clear-text files on their computers or in email
- Using unattended computers left logged in

Password policies and procedures should ensure that all passwords are strong,[4] employees do not share their passwords with anyone, employees change their passwords regularly, and all computers automatically execute password-protected screen savers after a fixed period of inactivity. As a result, all activity from any account should be attributable to its owner.

---

4. See Choosing and Protecting Passwords: www.us-cert.gov/cas/tips/ST04-002.html.

In addition, an anonymous reporting mechanism should be available and its use encouraged for employees to report all attempts at unauthorized account access.

Some insiders created backdoor accounts that provided them with system administrator or privileged access following termination. Other insiders found that shared accounts were overlooked in the termination process and were still available to them. System administrator accounts were commonly used. Other shared accounts included DBA accounts. Some insiders used other types of shared accounts, such as those set up for access by external partners like contractors and vendors. One insider also used training accounts that were repeatedly reused over time without ever changing the password.

Periodic account audits combined with technical controls enable identification of the following:

- Backdoor accounts that could be used later for malicious actions by an insider, whether those accounts were specifically set up by the insider or were left over from a previous employee
- Shared accounts whose password was known by the insider and not changed after termination
- Accounts created for access by external partners such as contractors and vendors whose passwords were known by multiple employees, and were not changed when one of those employees was terminated

The need for every account in your organization should be evaluated regularly. Limiting accounts to those that are necessary, with strict procedures and technical controls that enable auditors or investigators to trace all online activity on those accounts to an individual user, diminishes an insider's ability to conduct malicious activity without being identified. Account-management policies that include strict documentation of all access privileges for all users enable a straightforward termination procedure that reduces the risk of attack by terminated employees.

It is important that your organization's password- and account-management policies are also applied to all contractors, subcontractors, vendors, and other trusted business partners that have access to your information systems or networks. These policies should be written into your contracting agreements, requiring the same level of accountability in tracking who has access to your organization's systems. Contractors, subcontractors, and vendors should not be granted group accounts for access to your information systems. They should not be permitted to share passwords, and when employees are terminated at the external organization, you should be notified in advance so that account passwords can be changed. Finally, be sure to include all shared accounts, including contractor, subcontractor, and vendor accounts, in the regularly scheduled password-change process.

The prevalence of outsourcing, supply-chain management, and the globalization of the marketplace has blurred the line between your boundary and the external world. It is increasingly difficult to tell the difference between insiders and outsiders when it comes to managing access to your data and information systems. Contractors, subcontractors, and vendors are now critical components to an organization that is trying to compete in a global marketplace. When dealing with your contractor, subcontractor, and vendor relationships, you must recognize that insiders are no longer just employees within your four walls. Careful attention must be paid to ensure that the insiders employed by trusted business partners are managed diligently, only allowing them access to the information they need to fulfill their contractual obligations, and terminating their access when it is no longer needed.

## Case Studies: What Could Happen if I Don't Do It?

> A computer administrator for an Internet service provider (ISP) quit his job after becoming dissatisfied, and began to write threatening emails to the ISP. He was able to retain partial access to the organization as a paying customer, and then exploited his knowledge of a company tool to elevate his privileges on the system to that of an employee. The ISP detected his unauthorized access in the log files, and disabled the insider's customer account. The insider, however, was able to continue attacking the organization using two other backdoor accounts he had created. He changed all administrative passwords, altered the billing system, and deleted two internal billing databases. It took an entire weekend to recover from the attack.

This case might not seem applicable to you if you are not an ISP, but take a moment to really think about whether you have any accounts for accessing your systems from outside by customers, vendors, partners, and so on. Remember that your insiders know your vulnerabilities and technical gaps!

> A disgruntled software developer downloaded the password file from his organization's UNIX server to his desktop. Next, he downloaded a password cracker from the Internet and proceeded to "break" approximately forty passwords, including the root password. Fortunately, he did no damage, but he did access parts of the organization's network for which he was

not authorized. The insider was discovered when he bragged to the system administrator that he knew the root password. As a result, his organization modified its policies and procedures to implement countermeasures to prevent such attacks in the future. System administrators were permitted to run password crackers and notify users with weak passwords, and the organization improved security training for employees on how and why to choose strong passwords.

This case ends up being a "good-news" case when you consider how the organization responded to the incident!

## Practice 8: Enforce Separation of Duties and Least Privilege

Separation of duties and least privilege must be implemented in business processes and for technical modifications to critical systems or information to limit the damage that malicious insiders can inflict.

### What Can You Do?

Separation of duties requires dividing functions among people to limit the possibility that one employee could steal information, commit fraud, or commit sabotage without the cooperation of another. One type of separation of duties, called the two-person rule, is often used. It requires two people to participate in a task for it to be executed successfully. The separation of duties may be enforced via technical or nontechnical controls. Examples include requiring two bank officials to sign large cashier's checks, or requiring verification and validation of source code before the code is released operationally. In general, employees are less likely to engage in malicious acts if they must collaborate with another employee.

Effective separation of duties requires implementation of least privilege, authorizing people only for the resources needed to do their job. Least privilege reduces your risk of theft of confidential or proprietary information by your employees, since access is limited to only those employees who need access to do their jobs. Some cases of theft of intellectual property involved salespeople, for instance, who had unnecessary access to strategic products under development.

It is important that management of least privilege be an ongoing process, particularly when employees move throughout the organization for reasons including promotions, transfers, relocations, and demotions. As employees change jobs, organizations often fail to review the employees' required access to information and information systems. All too often, employees are given access to new systems and/or information required for their new job without revoking their access to information and systems required to perform their previous job duties. Unless an employee maintains responsibility for tasks from his or her previous job that require access to information and information systems, the employee's access should be disabled when he or she assumes the new position.

Typically, organizations define roles that characterize the responsibilities of each job, as well as the access to organizational resources required to fulfill those responsibilities. Insider risk can be mitigated by defining and separating roles responsible for key business processes and functions. Here are some examples:

- Requiring online management authorization for critical data entry transactions
- Instituting code reviews for the software development and maintenance process
- Using configuration-management processes and technology to control software distributions and system modification
- Designing auditing procedures to protect against collusion among auditors

Physical, administrative, and technical controls can be used to restrict employees' access to only those resources needed to accomplish their jobs. Access-control gaps often facilitated insider crimes. For example, employees circumvented separation of duties enforced via policy rather than through technical controls. Ideally, you should include separation of duties in the design of your business processes and enforce them via a combination of technical and nontechnical means.

These principles have implications in both the physical and the virtual worlds. In the physical world, you need to prevent employees from gaining physical access to resources not required by their work roles. Researchers need to have access to their laboratory space but do not need access to human resources file cabinets. Likewise, human resources personnel need access to personnel records but do not need access to laboratory facilities. There is a direct analogy in the virtual world in which you must prevent employees from gaining online access to information or services that are not required for their job. This kind of control is often called role-based access control. Prohibiting access by personnel in one role from the functions permitted for another role limits the damage they can inflict if they become disgruntled or otherwise decide to exploit the organization for their own purposes.

It is important to understand that separation of duties alone is not always sufficient to protect against insider threats; it is one layer in a multitiered defense. Many of the insiders who committed fraud in the CERT database collaborated with at least one other insider to carry out the crime. A number of reasons could explain the high degree of collusion. For example, internal collusion could be necessary to overcome controls that enforce separation of duties. Given that the enforcement of separation of duties alone will not prevent insider attacks, it is essential that you implement a layered defense to decrease the likelihood of such an attack.

One pattern observed in multiple fraud cases involved insiders who changed the mailing address and/or email address of customers so that they did not receive automated notifications, bills, and other company correspondences regarding fraudulent credit card accounts that the insiders then opened using the customer's identity. Some banks and other organizations have instituted practices for verifying customer address and email address changes before actually making the change in customer databases. This practice provides an additional control on top of the separation of duties that used to be sufficient for protection of such information.

Finally, it is important to design auditing procedures to detect potential collusion among employees, with the assumption that collusion to override separation of duties controls is quite possible.

## Case Studies: What Could Happen if I Don't Do It?

> A currency trader (who also happened to have a college minor in computer science) developed much of the software used by his organization to record, manage, confirm, and audit trades. He implemented obscure functionality in the software that enabled him to conceal illegal trades totaling approximately $700 million over a period of five years. In this case, it was nearly impossible for auditors to detect his activities. The insider, who consented to be interviewed for the CERT Program/Secret Service Insider Threat Study, told the study researchers that problems can arise when "the fox is guarding the henhouse" [Randazzo 2004]. Specifically, his supervisor managed both the insider and the auditing department responsible for ensuring his trades were legal or compliant. When auditing department personnel raised concern about his activities, they were doing so to the insider's supervisor (who happened to be their supervisor as well). The supervisor directed auditing department personnel not to worry about his activities and to cease raising concern, for fear he would become frustrated and quit.

This case illustrates two ways in which separation of duties can prevent an insider attack or detect it earlier.

- End users of your critical systems should not be authorized to modify the system functionality or access the underlying data directly.
- Responsibility for maintaining critical data and responsibility for auditing that same data should never be assigned to the same person.

A supervisor fraudulently altered U.S. immigration asylum decisions using his organization's computer system in return for payments of up to several thousand dollars per case, accumulating $50,000 over a two-year period. He would approve an asylum decision himself, request that one of his subordinates approve the decision, or overturn someone else's denial of an asylum application. Several foreign nationals either admitted in an interview or pleaded guilty in a court of law to lying on their asylum applications and bribing public officials to approve their applications.

The organization had implemented separation of duties via role-based access control by limiting authorization for approving or modifying asylum decisions to supervisors' computer accounts. However, supervisors were able to alter any decisions in the entire database, not just those assigned to their subordinates. An additional layer of defense, least privilege, also could have been implemented to prevent supervisors from approving asylum applications or overturning asylum decisions with which they or their teams were not involved.

## Practice 9: Consider Insider Threats in the Software Development Life Cycle

Technical employees have taken advantage of defects introduced in the Software Development Life Cycle (SDLC) to deliberately perform malicious technical actions; likewise, nontechnical employees have recognized vulnerabilities and used them to carry out their fraudulent activities.

This best practice is described in detail in Chapter 5, Insider Threat Issues in the Software Development Life Cycle. A summary was intentionally left in this chapter to keep all 16 best practices in one location for easy reference.

### What Can You Do?

Impacts from insiders that exploited defects in the SDLC include

- Closing of a business
- Fraud losses of up to $700 million
- Driver's licenses created for individuals who could not get a legitimate license
- Disruption of telecommunications services
- Modification of court records, credit records, and other critical data
- A virus planted on customers' systems

Clearly, the impacts in these cases were significant. It is important that you recognize these threats, and that you consider potential threats and mitigation strategies when developing and maintaining software internally as well as when implementing systems acquired elsewhere.

Insiders exploited defects in all phases of the SDLC in the cases examined. Each phase of the SDLC is now analyzed in more detail.

### Requirements Definition

Many systems automate business and workflow processes. When defining the requirements for such systems, the processes to be automated must be carefully defined. In the cases examined, many of the insiders were able to carry out their illicit activities because they recognized instances in which protection from insider threats was not considered. For example, in some cases, there was no separation of duties required in automated processes. In others, authentication and role-based access controls were not required for system access. System requirements should also include specification of data integrity and consistency checks that should be implemented for all changes made to production data by system end users, as well as automated checks that must be run periodically to detect suspicious modifications, additions, or deletions. In other words, requirements should consider periodic auditing functions, which can be implemented and run automatically on a more frequent basis than manual system audits.

Note that all of the recommendations detailed here for system requirements definition apply to systems you build in-house and to those you acquire. When evaluating new systems for acquisition, the types of requirements detailed here should also be considered. Once requirements have been defined and potential systems are evaluated for purchase, the capability of each system to meet those requirements is an important part of the evaluation process.

## System Design

In some cases, the organization did address protection from insiders in its system requirements definition process. However, inadequate design of those functions in automated workflow processes enabled some insiders to commit malicious activity. For example, improperly designed separation of duties facilitated some insider crimes. In some cases, separation of duties was not designed into the system at all. In others, although separation of duties was implemented, there was no design to "check the checker." Unfortunately, due to the high degree of collusion observed in insider fraud cases, it is necessary for system designers to consider how they might implement yet another layer of defense on top of separation of duties, to discover cases in which two employees are working together to commit a crime. Most of these types of crimes continue over a prolonged period, so although detection might not be immediate, patterns of suspicious activity can be discovered to catch the activity sooner rather than later.

Another key finding related to system design vulnerabilities involved authorized system overrides. Several insiders used special system functions created for exception handling to carry out their crimes. They realized that these functions were created for exceptional situations in which changes had to be made quickly, thus bypassing the usual mandated security checks. This type of functionality provided an easy way for insiders to "get around the rules." It is important to design special data integrity checks for any data modified, added, or deleted using these exception-handling functions.

## Implementation

Very few insiders actually introduced intentional vulnerabilities or malicious code into source code during the initial development process; that type of activity was more often carried out during the maintenance phase of the SDLC. However, one 18-year-old Web developer did use backdoors he had inserted into his source code during system development to access his former company's network, spam its customers, alter its applications, and ultimately put it out of business. Code reviews and strict change control, a part of any solid software development process, could have detected the backdoors and perhaps saved the company.

During the software development process, you are vulnerable to the same types of insider attacks that can occur on production systems. One software development project manager, recognizing there was no way to attribute actions to a single user in the development environment, repeatedly sabotaged his own team's project. The motivation in this case was unique: His team was falling behind in the project schedule, and he used the repeated sabotage as a convenient excuse for missed deadlines. It is important that you consider resiliency during the development process just as on production systems.

## Installation

A variety of oversights in the process of moving a system from development to production provided avenues for attack by insiders. Examples from several different cases follow.

- The same password file was used for the operational system when it was moved into production as had been used in the development environment, enabling one of the developers to access and steal sensitive data after it had been entered into the operational system.
- Unrestricted access to all customers' systems enabled a computer technician to plant a virus directly on customer networks.
- An organization implemented a Web content-management system that managed all changes to its public Web site. Although it used a change-control system to track changes, it had no process for approval of changes before they were released to the Web site. As a result, a college intern, before leaving for the summer, published material intended to be a joke on the organization's Web site, causing quite a scandal and damage to the reputation of the government agency.

It is important that you carefully consider these types of issues as you move a system from development to production because employees using those systems on a daily basis will likely notice the vulnerabilities.

## System Maintenance

More insider incidents occurred during the maintenance phase of the SDLC than during initial system implementation. We know from our assessments and workshops that organizations impose more stringent controls during the initial development process, but once a system has been in production and stabilized following initial release, those controls tend to become more lax. Insiders in our cases took advantage of those relaxed controls in a variety of ways.

While many organizations institute mandatory code reviews for development of new systems or significant new modules for existing systems, several insiders were able to inject malicious code into stable, fairly static systems without detection. Ineffective configuration or change-control processes contributed to their ability to do so. A few organizations in the cases examined implemented configuration-management systems that recorded a detailed log of the malicious insider activity. However, there was no proactive process for actually controlling system releases using those systems or reviewing the logs to detect malicious activity after the fact.

Insiders were also able to sabotage backup systems that were left unprotected to amplify their attack. Also, known system vulnerabilities were exploited on unpatched systems by a few knowledgeable insiders. Risk management of critical systems needs to extend beyond the system itself to surrounding support systems, such as the operating system and backups.

User authorization is another area that tends to become more lax over time. When a system is initially released, system authorizations and access methods tend to be carefully implemented. Once the system is in production, user access controls tend to slip. Access to the system and to the source code itself must be carefully managed over time.

## Case Studies: What Could Happen if I Don't Do It?

A programmer at a telecommunications company was angry when it was announced that there would be no bonuses. He used the computer used by his project leader, who sat in a cubicle and often left the computer logged in and unattended, to modify his company's premier product, an inter-network communication interface. His modification, consisting of two lines of code, inserted the character *i* at random places in the transmission stream and during protocol initialization. The malicious code was inserted as a logic bomb, recorded in the company's configuration management system, and attributed to the project leader. Six months later, the insider left the company to take another job. Six months thereafter, the logic bomb finally detonated, causing immense confusion and disruption to the company's services to its customers.

This case exemplifies many of the issues discussed in this section. The next case illustrates a more low-tech incident that was enabled by oversights in the SDLC, with serious consequences.

The primary responsibility of a police communications operator was to communicate information regarding driver's licenses to police officers in the field. This case began when the operator was approached by an acquaintance and asked if she would be willing to look up information for three people for him, and she agreed. Over time, she proceeded to look up information on people in return for payment by her acquaintance. At some point she discovered that she not only could read information from the database, but also could use other system functions. At that point, at the request of her accomplice, she began to generate, in return for payment, illegal driver's licenses for people who were unable to gain legitimate licenses. Fortunately, a confidential informant led to her arrest for fraudulently creating approximately 195 illegal driver's licenses.

This case shows the dangers of overlooking role-based access control requirements when defining system requirements, designing the system, and during implementation.

# Practice 10: Use Extra Caution with System Administrators and Technical or Privileged Users

System administrators and technical or privileged users have the technical ability, access, and oversight responsibility to commit and conceal malicious activity.

## What Can You Do?

Recall that the majority of the insiders who committed IT sabotage held technical positions such as system administrator, DBA, or programmer. Technically sophisticated methods of carrying out and concealing malicious activity included writing or downloading of scripts or programs (including logic bombs), creation of backdoor accounts, installation of remote system administration tools, modification of system logs, planting of viruses, and use of password crackers.

System administrators and **privileged users**[5] by definition have a higher system, network, or application access level than other users. This higher access level comes with higher risk due to the following.

- They have the technical ability and access to perform actions that ordinary users cannot.
- They can usually conceal their actions, since their privileged access typically provides them the ability to log in as other users, to modify system log files, or to falsify audit logs and monitoring reports.

Even if you enforce technical separation of duties, system administrators are typically the individuals with oversight and approval responsibility when application or system changes are requested.

Techniques that promote nonrepudiation of action ensure that online actions taken by users, including system administrators and privileged users, can be attributed to the person who performed them. Therefore, should malicious insider activity occur, nonrepudiation techniques allow each and every activity to be attributed to a single employee. Policies, practices, and technologies exist for configuring systems and networks to facilitate nonrepudiation. However, keep in mind that system administrators and

---

5. *Privileged users:* users who have an elevated level of access to a network, computer system, or application that is short of full system administrator access. For example, database administrators (DBAs) are privileged users because they have the ability to create new user accounts and control the access rights of users within their domain.

other privileged users will be the ones responsible for designing, creating, and implementing those policies, practices, and technologies. Therefore, separation of duties is also very important: Network, system, and application security designs should be created, implemented, and enforced by multiple privileged users.

Even if online actions can be traced to the person who engaged in the action, it is unreasonable to expect that all user actions can be monitored proactively. Therefore, while the practices discussed here ensure identification of users following detection of suspicious activity, additional steps must be taken to defend against malicious actions before they occur. For instance, system administrators and privileged users have access to all computer files within their domains. Technologies such as encryption can be implemented to prevent such users from reading or modifying sensitive files to which they should not have access.

As we described in Practice 6, policies, procedures, and technical controls should enforce separation of duties and require actions by multiple users for releasing all modifications to critical systems, networks, applications, and data. In other words, no single user should be permitted or be technically able to release changes to the production environment without online action by a second user. These controls would prevent an insider from releasing a logic bomb without detection by another employee. They would also have been effective against a foreign investment trader, who manipulated source code to carry out his crime. He happened to have a degree in computer science, and was therefore given access to the source code for the trading system. He used that access to build in backdoor functionality, which enabled him to hide trading losses without detection totaling approximately $700 million over a five-year period.

Note that in order to enforce separation of duties for system administration functions, you must employ at least two system administrators. There are a few cases in this book in which the organization was victimized by its sole system administrator. Although many small organizations may not be able to hire more than one system administrator, it is important that they recognize the increased risk that accompanies that situation.

Finally, many of the insiders studied, especially those engaged in IT sabotage, were former employees. You must be particularly careful in disabling access, particularly for former system administrators and technical or privileged users. Thoroughly documented procedures for disabling access can help ensure that stray access paths are not overlooked. In addition, the two-person rule should be considered for the critical functions performed by these users to reduce the risk of extortion after they leave the organization.

## Case Studies: What Could Happen if I Don't Do It?

A system administrator at an international financial organization heard rumors that the annual bonuses were going to be lower than expected. He began constructing a logic bomb at home and used authorized remote access to move the logic bomb to the company's servers as part of the typical server upgrade procedure over a period of two and a half months. When he was informed by his supervisor that his bonus would be significantly lower than he had expected, he terminated his employment immediately. Less than two weeks later, the logic bomb went off at 9:30 a.m., deleting 10 billion files on approximately 1,000 servers throughout the United States. The victim organization estimated that it would cost more than $3 million to repair its network, and the loss affected 1.24 billion shares of its stock.

In this case, the disgruntled insider planted his logic bomb in the script that propagated software to all of the company's servers nightly as part of its configuration-management process. This is an example of a file that should be carefully monitored for changes, as the repercussions of illicit modifications will impact every server in the organization.

An employee was promoted from one position to another within the same organization. Both positions used the same application for entering, approving, and authorizing payments for medical and disability claims. The application used role-based access to enforce separation of duties for each system function. However, when this particular employee was promoted, she was authorized for her new access level, but administrators neglected to rescind her prior access level (separation of duties was inadequately enforced). As a result, she ended up having full access to the application, with no one else required to authorize transactions (payments) from the system. She entered and approved claims and authorized monthly payments for her fiancé, resulting in payments of more than $615,000 over almost two years.

This case illustrates what we mean by "privileged user." The "erosion of access controls" when employees move around within an organization presents a definite vulnerability. We know from our assessments and workshops that this is a very difficult problem that most organizations have not solved. Here is a control that one organization we work with has implemented: When an employee transfers within the organization, the organization sets the transfer date in a database. It has an automated script that sends an email to the manager of the team that the employee transferred *from* three months after the transfer. The script reminds the manager that the employee left, and lists all of the email aliases the employee is still on, all internal Web sites the employee still has access to, all shared folders the employee still has access to, and so on. The organization has found that a three-month transition period is typically the right amount of time in which employees need legitimate access to both their new and old team's information. After three months, the organization has found that most managers are ready to rescind access for their team's former employee.

The following case demonstrates how organizational failures in dealing with disgruntled system administrators and other privileged users can eventually result in IT sabotage.

> A developer of e-commerce software for an organization decided to move his family to a different state, and therefore he could no longer work for the organization. The organization hired him as a consultant and he traveled across state lines to work two days a week, and telecommuted three days a week from home. He was disgruntled because the organization would not provide him the benefits he felt he deserved once he became a contractor, and the relationship continued to deteriorate. Finally, the organization told him his employment would be terminated in approximately one month. After a week and a half, he logged in remotely from home, deleted the software he was developing, as well as software being developed by others, modified the system logs to conceal his actions, and then changed the root password. He then joined a telephone conference, never mentioning what he had done. After the telephone conference ended he reported that he was having problems logging in, again to conceal his actions. At the end of the day he announced his resignation. This action cost the organization more than $25,000, including 230 staff hours and associated costs.

In much of the text in this book we use the word *employees* when we really mean *employees and contractors*. This case points out that you cannot overlook contractors who have system administrator or privileged access to your systems, networks, and information.

# Practice 11: Implement System Change Controls

Changes to systems and applications must be controlled to prevent insertion of backdoors, keystroke loggers, logic bombs, and other malicious code or programs.

## What Can You Do?

**Change controls** are formal processes used to ensure that changes to a product or system are introduced in a controlled and coordinated manner.[6] The wide variety of insider compromises that relied on unauthorized modifications to the organization systems suggests the need for stronger change controls. To support this, you should identify baseline software and hardware configurations. You may have several baseline configurations, given the different computing and information needs of different users (e.g., accountant, manager, programmer, and receptionist). But as configurations are identified, you should characterize the hardware and software that make up those configurations.

Characterization can be a basic catalog of information, tracking information such as versions of installed software, hardware devices, and disk utilization. However, such basic characterizations can be easily defeated, so more comprehensive characterizations are often required. These characterizations include

- Cryptographic checksums (using SHA-1 or MD5, for example)
- Interface characterization (such as memory mappings, device options, and serial numbers)
- Recorded configuration files

Once this information is captured, computers implementing each configuration can be validated by comparing the information against the baseline copy. Discrepancies can then be investigated to determine whether they are benign or malicious. Using these techniques, changes to system files or the addition of malicious code will be flagged for investigation. There are tools called **file integrity checkers**[7] that partially automate this process and provide for scheduled sweeps through computer systems.

Computer configurations do not remain unchanged for long. Therefore, characterization and validation should be part of your change-management

---

6. Wikipedia

7. **File integrity checker:** a tool that partially automates the process of identifying changes to system files or the addition of malicious code and flagging them for investigation. See www.sans.org/resources/idfaq/integrity_checker.php for a discussion of file integrity checkers.

process. Different roles should be defined within this process and conducted by different individuals so that no one person can make a change unnoticed by others within your organization. For example, validation of a configuration should be done by a person other than the one who made changes so that there is an opportunity to detect and correct malicious changes (including planting of logic bombs).

Change logs and backups need to be protected so that unauthorized changes can be detected and, if necessary, the system rolled back to a previous valid state. In addition, some insiders in cases in the CERT database modified change logs to conceal their activity or frame someone else for their actions. Other insiders sabotaged backups to further amplify the impact of their attack.

Many organizations defend against malicious code using anti-virus software and host or network firewalls. While these defenses are useful against external compromises, their value is limited in preventing attacks by malicious insiders in two important respects: They do not work against new or novel malicious code (including logic bombs planted by insiders) and they are concerned primarily with material spread through networking interfaces rather than installed directly on a machine. Change controls help address the limitations of these perimeter defenses.

Just as tools can be implemented for detecting and controlling system changes, configuration-management tools should be implemented for detecting and controlling changes to source code and other application files. As described in Practice 9, some insiders modified source code in order to carry out their attack. Note that these modifications were typically done during the maintenance phase of the SDLC, not during initial implementation. It appears that some organizations institute much more stringent configuration-management controls during initial development of a new system, including code reviews and use of a configuration-management system. However, once the system is in production and development stabilizes, those controls do not seem to be as strictly enforced. It appears that organizations tend to relax the controls, leaving open a vulnerability for exploit by technical insiders with the proper motivation and lack of ethics.

## Case Studies: What Could Happen if I Don't Do It?

A manufacturing firm's system administrator began employment as a machinist. Over a ten-year period, the insider created the company's network supporting the critical manufacturing processes and had sole authority for system administration over that network. The company eventually expanded, opening additional offices and plants nationally and internationally. The insider did the following.

- He began to feel disgruntled at his diminishing importance to the company.
- He launched verbal and physical assaults on coworkers.
- He sabotaged projects of which he was not in charge.
- He loaded faulty programs to make coworkers look bad.

He received a verbal warning and two written reprimands, was demoted, and finally was fired as a result of his actions. A few weeks later, a logic bomb executed on the company's network, deleting 1,000 critical manufacturing programs from the company's servers. The estimated cost of the damage exceeded $10 million, leading to the layoff of approximately eighty employees. The investigation revealed that the insider had actually tested the logic bomb three times on the company's network after hours prior to his termination.

In this case, practices for detection of malicious code would have detected that a new program had been released with timed execution. Change-control procedures with a two-person rule for release of system-level programs, and characterization procedures, could have detected the release of a new system file that was not part of the original system baseline.

An organization built automated monitoring into its software that sent automatic notification to the security officer anytime a highly restricted screen was used to modify information stored in the database. Role-based access control restricted access to this screen to a few privileged users; the automated notification provided a second layer of defense against illegal data modification using that function. However, an IT manager who had access to the source code modified it so that the automated notification was no longer sent; he simply commented out a single line of code. He then proceeded to use the function to steal a large sum of money from his employer.

Interestingly, this organization had a configuration-management system in place for software changes. When a program was compiled, a report was produced listing which files were compiled, by which computer account, and when. It also listed modules added, modified, or deleted. Unfortunately, this report was not monitored, and therefore the application changes were not detected during the year and a half over which the fraud was committed. Had it been monitored, or had the configuration-control system enforced a two-person rule for releasing new versions of software, the removal of the security notification would have been detected and the insider could not have committed the fraud.

Although this insider committed fraud, stop to ask yourself if you have any mission-critical systems that could be modified in this way. What if this had been a safety system, or a security system? What potential damage could one of your employees or contractors inflict by commenting out a few lines of source code?

Some cases in the CERT database involved theft of information using a **keystroke logger**—a hardware or software device that records the exact keystrokes entered into a computer system. Keystroke loggers can be used maliciously to obtain an organization's confidential information or an individual's private information, and in the worst case can be used to obtain passwords or encryption keys.

> A claims manager at an insurance company, who was upset with the company's practice of canceling policies after late payment, installed a hardware keystroke logger on the computer of the secretary to a chief executive. Although he did not have access to the executive's office, he realized that an abundance of confidential information passed from the secretary to and from the executive. Furthermore, her desk was not physically secured, like the executive's office was. The insider used the keystroke logger to gather confidential information from the secretary's computer, which he then sent to the legal team assembling the case against the organization.

Other cases involved software keystroke loggers.

> Two insiders colluded with an external person to collect their company's intellectual property and relay it to a competitor. The external collaborator sent an email message containing an attachment infected with a virus to one of the insiders. The insider deliberately double-clicked on the infected attachment, and it proceeded to install a keystroke logger on machines on the company's network. The keystroke logger periodically sent confidential information to a competitor, who used it to lure customers away from the victim organization.

The software keystroke logger could have been detected by a change-control process as described in this section.

# Practice 12: Log, Monitor, and Audit Employee Online Actions

Logging, monitoring, and auditing can lead to early discovery and investigation of suspicious insider actions.

## What Can You Do?

If account and password policies and procedures are in place and enforced, your organization has a good chance of clearly associating online actions with the employee who performed them. Logging, monitoring, and auditing provide you the opportunity to discover and investigate suspicious insider actions before more serious consequences ensue.

Auditing in the financial community refers to examination and verification of financial information. In the technical security domain, it refers to examination and verification of various network, system, and application logs or data. To prevent or detect insider threats, it is important that auditing involve the review and verification of changes to any of your critical assets.[8] Furthermore, auditing must examine and verify the integrity as well as the legitimacy of logged access.

Automated integrity checking should be considered for flagging a required manual review of suspicious transactions that do not adhere to predefined business rules. Insider threats are most often detected by a combination of automated logging and manual monitoring or auditing. For example, integrity checking of computer account creation logs involves automated logging combined with manual verification that every new account has been associated with a legitimate system user and that the user is aware of the account's existence.

Automated tools could detect creation of the typical backdoor account—a system administrator account not associated with a current employee. Unfortunately, detection of backdoor accounts cannot be totally automated. For example, one insider created virtual private network (VPN) accounts for three legitimate, current employees, and simply did not tell them the accounts had been created. After being fired, he used those backdoor accounts to obtain remote access at night for two weeks. He set up his attack during those two weeks right under the nose

---

8. Many risk management methodologies are based on protection of critical assets—for example, the OCTAVE (Operationally Critical Threat, Asset, and Vulnerability Evaluation) risk-based strategic assessment and planning technique for security [Alberts 2003]. See also www.cert.org/octave/.

of a contractor, who was hired specifically to monitor the network for remote access by him.

Likewise, data audits typically involve manual processes, such as comparing electronic data modification history to paper records or examining electronic records for suspicious discrepancies.

A common reaction to our suggestions for monitoring and auditing for potential insider threats is this: There is an abundance of monitoring tools on the market, and they produce so much information overload that it is impossible to review the data; it's like trying to find a needle in a haystack. The good news is that if you design monitoring strategies based on the patterns in insider threat cases we describe in this book, you will minimize information overload by using a risk-based approach to prioritizing alerts.

Auditing should be both ongoing and random. If employees are aware that monitoring and auditing is a regular, ongoing process and that it is a high priority for the individuals who are responsible for it, it can serve as a deterrent to insider threats. For example, if a disgruntled system administrator is aware that all new computer accounts are reviewed frequently, it is less likely that he or she will create backdoor accounts for later malicious use.

On the other hand, it probably is not practical to institute daily monitoring of every financial transaction in a financial institution. Monthly and quarterly auditing provides one layer of defense against insiders, but it also provides a predictable cycle on which insiders could design a fraud scheme that could go undetected over a long period of time. Random auditing of all transactions for a given employee, for example, could add just enough unpredictability to the process to deter an insider from launching a contemplated attack.

It is also worth mentioning that multiple insiders in cases in the CERT database attacked other external organizations from their computers at work. The forensics and investigation activities that the employees' organizations had to endure as a result were very disruptive to their staff and operations.

As we described in Chapter 3, in almost all of the insider theft of IP cases the insider resigned before or after the theft. The majority of the thefts took place within one month of the insider's resignation, and most stole all of the information at once. Most of those insiders made no effort to conceal their technical actions. This suggests that monitoring of online actions, particularly downloads within one month before and after resignation, could be particularly beneficial for preventing or detecting the theft of proprietary information.

A wide variety of technical means were used in the theft cases to transfer information, including email, phone, fax, downloading to or from home over the Internet, collection and transmission by malicious code, and printing out material on the organizations' printers. If you are monitoring for theft of information, you need to consider the wide variety of ways that information is purloined and customize your detection strategy accordingly. Data leakage tools may help with this task. Many tools are available that enable you to perform functions such as the following:

- Alerting administrators to emails with unusually large attachments
- Tagging documents that should not be permitted to leave the network
- Tracking or preventing printing, copying, or downloading of certain information, such as PII or documents containing certain words like new-product codenames
- Tracking of all documents copied to removable media
- Preventing or detecting emails to competitors, to governments and organizations outside the United States, to Gmail or Hotmail accounts, and so on

Central logging appliances and event correlation engines may help craft automated queries that reduce an analyst's workload for routinely inspecting this type of data.

Some theft cases involved insiders downloading information outside their area of expertise or responsibility. This may provide a means for you to detect suspicious activity, provided you track what information each employee needs in order to accomplish his or her job. Role-based access control may provide a basis for such tracking.

Finally, you must be aware of the possibility that insiders will attack another organization, possibly a previous employer, using your systems. While not common, such crimes can and do happen—there are a few such cases in the CERT database. You need to consider the liability and disruption that such a case could cause.

The bottom line is that you need to have clearly defined employee-monitoring policies, and they must be consistently enforced. Policies must define very clear thresholds for when a specific employee will be audited and monitored. In addition, you cannot monitor some employees who exceed those thresholds and not others. Employee privacy laws must be considered when developing a monitoring policy; employee monitoring policies and procedures should be developed in conjunction with your legal staff.

## Case Studies: What Could Happen if I Don't Do It?

A research chemist was responsible for various research and development projects. His organization offered him a position in a foreign country, but his family did not want to move to that location. Consequently, he sought employment with a competitor; the competing company offered him a position, but the start date was not for a few months. The insider did not notify his current organization of his plan to resign until two weeks prior to starting his new job with the competitor. Over that four-month period, from when he received the job offer to when he left the victim organization, he downloaded nearly 17,000 PDF files and 22,000 abstracts containing trade secrets from his employer's server. The downloads took place on-site, during work hours, over several 15- to 20-hour periods. The amount of data he downloaded was 15 times higher than that of the next highest user and the data was not related to his research. His activities went unnoticed until he left, and the victim organization detected his substantial number of downloads.

After starting his job at the competitor, he transferred the information to a company-assigned laptop. The victim organization notified the competitor that it had discovered the high-volume downloads. The competitor seized the insider's laptop and turned it over to the victim organization, which turned it over to the FBI. Agents discovered documents from the victim organization marked "Confidential," shredded technical documents, and numerous other documents in the insider's apartment and in a storage unit. When the search was conducted, the insider was attempting to erase an external hard drive. He was arrested, convicted, sentenced to 18 months of imprisonment, and ordered to pay $14,500 in restitution and a $30,000 fine.

Consider whether this could happen to you. If so, you should consider use of technical detection methods for alerting when an employee or contractor downloads a significant amount of information. This should not result in "information overload" as one would think this should not happen very often!

A large international company, while performing remote access monitoring, noticed that a former consultant had obtained unauthorized access to its network and created an administrator account. This prompted an investigation of the former insider's previous online activity, revealing he had run several different password-cracking programs on the company's network five different times over a ten-month period. Initially, he stored the cracked passwords in a file on the company's server. Later he installed a more sophisticated password-cracking program on the company's system. This program enabled him to automatically transfer all accounts and passwords that could be cracked to a remote computer on a periodic basis. Five thousand passwords for company employees were successfully transferred.

This case illustrates the importance of logging and proactive monitoring. Because of those practices, this insider's actions were detected before any malicious activity was committed using the accounts and passwords or the backdoor account. The next case provides a contrasting example—one in which lack of auditing permitted the insider to conduct an attack that was less technically sophisticated but that enabled him to steal almost $260,000 from his employer over a two-year period.

> The insider, who was the manager of a warehouse, convinced his supervisor that he needed privileged access to the entire purchasing system for the warehouse. He then added a fake vendor to the list of authorized suppliers for the warehouse. Over the next two years, he entered 78 purchase orders for the fake vendor, and, although no supplies were ever received, he also authorized payment to the vendor. He was aware of approval procedures, and all of his fraudulent purchases fell beneath the threshold for independent approval. The bank account for the vendor happened to be owned by his wife. The fraud was accidentally detected by a finance clerk who noticed irregularities in the paperwork accompanying one of the purchase orders.

This fraud could have been detected earlier by closer monitoring of online activities by privileged users, particularly since this user possessed unusually extensive privileged access. In addition, normal auditing procedures could have validated the new vendor, and automated integrity checking could have detected discrepancies between the warehouse inventory and purchasing records.

## Practice 13: Use Layered Defense against Remote Attacks

Remote access provides a tempting opportunity for insiders to attack with less risk.

### What Can You Do?

Insiders often attack organizations remotely, either using legitimate access or following termination. While remote access can greatly enhance employee productivity, caution is advised when remote access is provided to critical data, processes, or information systems. Insiders have admitted to us in interviews that it is easier to conduct malicious activities from home because it eliminates the concern that someone could be physically observing the malicious acts.

The vulnerabilities inherent in allowing remote access suggest that multiple layers of defense should be built against remote attack. You may provide remote access to email and noncritical data but should consider limiting remote access to the most critical data and functions and only from machines that are administered by your organization. Access to data or functions that could inflict major damage to you should be limited to employees physically located inside the workplace as much as possible. Remote system administrator access should be limited to the smallest group practicable, if not prohibited altogether.

When remote access to critical data, processes, and information systems is deemed necessary, you should offset the added risk with closer logging and frequent auditing of remote transactions. Allowing remote access only from organization-owned machines will enhance your ability to control access to information and networks and monitor the activity of remote employees. Information such as login account, date/time connected and disconnected, and IP address should be logged for all remote logins. It also is useful to monitor failed remote logins, including the reason the login failed. If authorization for remote access to critical data is kept to a minimum, monitoring can become more manageable and effective.

Disabling remote access is a sometimes overlooked but critical part of the employee termination process. It is critical that employee termination procedures include

- Retrieving any organization-owned equipment
- Disabling remote access accounts (such as VPN and dial-in accounts)

- Disabling firewall access
- Changing the passwords of all shared accounts (including system administrator, DBA, and other privileged shared accounts)
- Closing all open connections

A combination of remote access logs and source IP addresses usually helps to identify insiders who launch remote attacks. Identification can be straightforward because the username of the intruder points directly to the insider. Of course, corroboration of this information is required, because the intruders might have been trying to frame other users, cast attention away from their own misdeeds by using other users' accounts, or otherwise manipulate the monitoring process.

## Case Studies: What Could Happen if I Don't Do It?

The chief technology officer (CTO) announced his resignation following a salary dispute with the CEO. He left one month later, and went to work as a temporary employee for an unrelated organization. Three weeks after he left, his former company's voice-mail service started sending some customers to a pornographic telephone service. One week after that incident, unusual traffic on the company's network caused the network to fail. A short time later, its email servers were flooded with thousands of messages containing pornographic images, and auto-reply messages were sent from its email server disparaging the company and its services. The CEO began to receive strange and threatening email messages, some claiming to be from a cremation society. Threatening emails, phone calls, and forum postings continued until law enforcement was able to identify the source of the threatening messages: a computer associated with the former CTO's new employer.

This case highlights an important issue for you to consider: Who has the access and credentials to modify your voice-mail system? This is not an access path one ordinarily thinks of in the employee termination process, but one that could cause you severe embarrassment if modified as in this case!

A government organization notified one of its contract programmers that his access to a system under development was being eliminated and that his further responsibilities would be limited to testing activities. After his protests were denied, the programmer quit his job. Then, three times over a two-week period, he used a backdoor into the system with administrator privilege (which he presumably installed before leaving) to download source code and password files from the developmental system. The unusually large size of the remote downloads raised red flags in the organization, which resulted in an investigation that traced the downloads to his residence and led to his arrest, prosecution, and imprisonment.

This case demonstrates the value of vigilant monitoring of remote access logs and reaction to suspicious behavior in limiting damage to your interests.

# Practice 14: Deactivate Computer Access Following Termination

It is important to follow rigorous procedures that disable all access paths into your networks and systems for terminated employees.

## What Can You Do?

While employed, insiders have legitimate, authorized access to your network, system, applications, and data. Once employment is terminated, it is important that you have in place and execute rigorous termination procedures that disable all access points available to the terminated employee. Otherwise, your network is vulnerable to access by a now-illegitimate, unauthorized user. Some organizations choose to permit continued access by former employees for some time period under favorable termination circumstances; it is important that those organizations have a formal policy in place for these circumstances and carefully consider the potential consequences. In addition, it is important to manage the access of employees who change their status with your organization (e.g., change from an employee to a contractor; change from a full-time to a part-time employee; or take a leave of absence).

If formal termination policies and procedures are not in place, the termination process tends to be ad hoc, posing significant risk that one or more access paths will be overlooked. Our research shows that insiders can be quite resourceful in exploiting obscure access mechanisms neglected in the termination process. If a formal process exists, it must be consistently followed. It is also critical that you remain alert to new insider threat research and periodically review and update these processes. If at the time of termination you have not been diligently following strict account-management practices, it may be too late to perform an account audit for the terminating employee. A backdoor account could have been created months before, and verification of the legitimacy of all accounts of all types—system login accounts, VPN accounts, database or application accounts, email accounts, and so on—can be a very time-consuming process, depending on the size of your organization. When an employee leaves, you should be able to confidently say all access paths available to that employee have been disabled.

Some aspects of the termination process are quite obvious, such as disabling the terminated employee's computer account. However, organizations that have been victims of insider attacks were often vulnerable because of poor, nonexistent, or noncomprehensive account-management procedures. Many employees have access to multiple accounts; all account creations should be tracked and periodically reviewed to ensure that all access can be quickly disabled when an employee is terminated.

Accounts sometimes overlooked in the termination process are shared accounts, such as system administrator accounts, DBA accounts, and testing, training, development, and external organizational accounts, such as vendor or customer accounts. In addition, some applications require administrative accounts that are frequently shared among multiple users. It is important that you meticulously maintain a record of every shared account and every user authorized to have the password to each, and change the passwords for those accounts when employees are terminated.

Remote access is frequently exploited by former insiders. Remote access or VPN accounts must be disabled, as well as firewall access, in order to prevent future remote access by the terminated employee. In addition, any remote connections already open by that employee at the time of termination must be closed immediately.

If an employee is terminated under adverse circumstances, you might consider reviewing the employee's desktop computer, laptop, and system logs to ensure no software or applications have been installed that may permit the employee back into your systems. In one case, a terminated employee left software on his desktop that allowed him to access it, control it remotely, and use it to attack his next employer. In addition, a few insiders who stole intellectual property immediately before leaving the organization were caught when their desktop computer activity logs were analyzed.

In summary, a layered defense that accounts for all access methods should be implemented. Remote access should be disabled, but if an obscure remote access method is overlooked, the next layer of defense is accounts. All accounts should be disabled for use by the former employee so that even if remote access is established, the insider is prevented from proceeding further. Therefore, it is important that intranet accounts, application-specific accounts, and all other accounts for which the user was authorized be disabled or the passwords changed. Also, keep in mind that if the terminated insider was responsible for establishing accounts for others, such as employees, customers, or external Web site users, those accounts could also be accessible to the terminated insider.

Finally, termination procedures must include steps to prevent physical access. Insiders have exploited physical access to gain access to their former employer's systems. Careful attention should be paid to disable access by collecting keys, badges, and parking permits, and disabling access to facilities in card-control systems. When employees are fired, it is important that other employees are aware that the person was terminated. Multiple insider attacks were facilitated when terminated employees were able to obtain physical access to the organization by piggybacking through doors, using the excuse that they forgot their badge.

## Case Studies: What Could Happen if I Don't Do It?

A software engineer at a high-technology company that developed and manufactured computer chips was terminated due to poor performance. He was responsible for managing an automated manufacturing system, and during the work week he maintained a constant remote access connection from his home to the company's network. Prior to informing him of his termination, the company terminated his network access, but failed to detect his remote access connection that was active from home. The day after his termination, outside of work hours and under the influence of alcohol, he used the open remote access connection to completely shut down the company's manufacturing system by deleting critical files. Due to his actions, the company lost four hours of manufacturing time and had to load backup data to restart the manufacturing process. The incident cost the company $20,000 to remedy. Connection and activity logs connected the insider to the incident. He was arrested and convicted, but sentencing details were unavailable.

This case points out one easy step that you should add to your employee termination process, if it's not in there already: Check for any active remote connections by the employee.

A financial organization's system administrator was terminated suddenly with no advanced notice that his employer was dissatisfied with his work. That night he suspected that his replacement, who he felt was technically inferior, had not disabled his access. He attempted to access the system from home and found that he was right—his replacement had failed to disable his access through the company firewall. In addition, although his account had been disabled, she had failed to change the password of the system administrator account. The insider used that account to shut down the company's primary server, one that had been having problems and had in fact crashed the previous weekend (and had taken the organization an entire weekend to bring up again). It took the financial institution three days to bring the server back into service; during that time none of its customers were able to access any of their accounts in any way.

This case illustrates the necessity of thoroughly disabling access, as well as the consequences when you have no competent backup for a single system administrator.

A system administrator logged in one morning and was notified by her custom-written login software that her last login was one hour earlier. This set off immediate alarms, as she had in fact not logged in for several days. She had previously taken steps to redirect logging of actions by her account to a unique file rather than the standard shell history file. Therefore, she was able to trace the intruder's steps and saw that he had read another employee's email using her account, and then deleted the standard history file for her account so that there would be no log of his actions. The login was traced to a computer at a subsidiary of the company. Further investigation showed that the same computer had logged in to the company's system periodically for the past month, and that a former employee had accessed up to 16 of his former employer's systems on a daily basis during work hours. The insider had done the following:

- Gained access to at least 24 user accounts
- Read email
- Reviewed source code for his previous project
- Deleted two software modification notices for the project

The former employee had been terminated for nonperformance and then went to work for the subsidiary.

This case illustrates the importance of terminating access completely for former employees, careful monitoring for post-termination access, and paying particular attention to terminated technical employees.

## Practice 15: Implement Secure Backup and Recovery Processes

Despite all of the precautions you take, it is still possible that an insider will successfully attack. Therefore, it is important that you prepare for that possibility and enhance your resiliency by implementing secure backup and recovery processes that are tested periodically.

### What Can You Do?

Prevention of insider attacks is the first line of defense. However, experience has taught us that there will always be avenues for determined insiders to successfully compromise a system. Effective backup and recovery processes need to be in place and operational so that if compromises do occur business operations can be sustained with minimal interruption. Our research has shown that effective backup and recovery mechanisms affected the outcomes in actual cases, and can mean the difference between

- Several hours of downtime to restore systems from backups
- Weeks of manual data entry when current backups are not available
- Months or years to reconstruct information for which no backup copies existed

Backup and recovery strategies should consider the following:

- Controlled access to the facility where the backups are stored
- Controlled access to the physical media (e.g., no one individual should have access to both online data and the physical backup media)
- Separation of duties and the two-person rule when changes are made to the backup process

In addition, accountability and full disclosure should be legally and contractually required of any third-party vendors responsible for providing backup services, including off-site storage of backup media. It should be clearly stated in service level agreements the required recovery period, who has access to physical media while it is being transported off-site, as well as who has access to the media in storage. Furthermore, case examples throughout this book have demonstrated the threat presented by employees of trusted partners; the mitigation strategies presented for those threats should also be applied to backup service providers.

When possible, multiple copies of backups should exist, with redundant copies stored off-site in a secure facility. Different people should be responsible for the safekeeping of each copy so that it would require the cooperation of multiple individuals to fully compromise the means to recovery. An additional level of protection for the backups can include encryption, particularly when the redundant copies are managed by a third-party vendor at the off-site secure facility. Encryption provides an additional level of protection, but it does come with additional risk. The two-person rule should always be followed when managing the encryption keys so that you are always in control of the decryption process in the event the employees responsible for backing up your information leave your organization.

You should ensure that the physical media on which backups are stored are also protected from insider corruption or destruction. Insider cases in our research have involved attackers who did the following:

- Deleted backups
- Stole backup media (including off-site backups in one case)
- Performed actions that could not be undone due to faulty backup systems

Some system administrators neglected to perform backups in the first place, while others sabotaged established backup mechanisms. Such actions can amplify the negative impact of an attack on an organization by eliminating the only means of recovery. To guard against insider attack, you should

- Perform and periodically test backups
- Protect media and content from modification, theft, or destruction
- Apply separation of duties and configuration-management procedures to backup systems just as you do for other system modifications
- Apply the two-person rule for protecting the backup process and physical media so that one person cannot take action without the knowledge and approval of another employee

Make sure you account for pockets of development systems, or production systems that are maintained independently instead of being managed as part of your IT enterprise. These systems can be just as critical to you as your enterprise systems are, and they are not necessarily managed using the same rigor as your centrally maintained IT systems.

Unfortunately, some attacks against networks could interfere with common methods of communication, thereby increasing uncertainty and disruption in organizational activities, including recovery from the attack. This is especially true of insider attacks, since insiders are quite familiar with your communication methods and, during an attack, may interfere with communications essential to your data-recovery process. You can mitigate this effect by maintaining trusted communication paths outside of the network with sufficient capacity to ensure critical operations in the event of a network outage. This kind of protection would have two benefits: The cost of strikes against the network would be mitigated, and insiders would be less likely to strike against connectivity because of the reduced impact.

## Case Studies: What Could Happen if I Don't Do It?

> An organization was responsible for running the 911 phone-number-to-address lookup system for emergency services. An insider deleted the entire database and software from three servers in the organization's network operations center (NOC) by gaining physical access using a contractor's badge. The NOC, which was left unattended, was solely protected via physical security; all machines in the room were left logged in with system administrator access. Although the NOC system administrators were immediately notified of the system failure via an automatic paging system, there were no automated failover mechanisms. The organization's recovery plan relied solely on backup tapes, which were also stored in the NOC. Unfortunately, the insider, realizing that the systems could be easily recovered, took all of the backup tapes with him when he left the facility. In addition, the same contractor's badge was authorized for access to the off-site backup storage facility, from which he next stole more than 50 off-site backup tapes.

This case illustrates the risk of storing your backups in the same physical location as your critical systems. In addition, there was no layered defense to protect the backups—they were accessible by anyone who had physical access to the NOC. As a result, this very critical system and its backups were totally vulnerable to an insider IT sabotage attack.

> An insider was terminated because of his employer's reorganization. The company followed proper procedure by escorting him to his office to collect his belongings and then out of the building. The IT staff also followed the company's security policy by disabling the insider's remote access and changing passwords. However, they overlooked one password that was known to three people in the organization. The terminated insider used that account to gain access to the system the night of his termination and to delete the programs he had created while working there. Some of

these programs supported the company's critical applications. Restoration of the deleted files from backup failed. Although the insider had been responsible for backups, company personnel believe that the backups were not maliciously corrupted. The backups had simply not been tested to ensure that they were properly recording the critical data. As a result, the organization's operations in North and South America were shut down for two days, resulting in more than $80,000 in losses.

This case illustrates the delay that can be caused in recovery following an insider attack if backups are not tested periodically.

# Practice 16: Develop an Insider Incident Response Plan

Procedures for investigating and dealing with malicious insiders present unique challenges; response must be planned, clearly documented, and agreed to by your managers and attorneys.

## What Can You Do?

An incident response plan for insider incidents differs from a response plan for incidents caused by an external attacker. You need to minimize the chances that the internal perpetrator is assigned to the response team or is aware of its progress. This is challenging since the technical people assigned to the response team may be among the employees with the most knowledge and ability to use their technical skills against the organization. Another challenge of insider incident response is the hesitation or resistance that managers may have to participating in an investigation. This hesitation could have several causes: It could divert the team's resources from mission-critical activities, expose a team member to investigation, or expose shortcomings by management or oversights in system security, opening the managers up to embarrassment or liability for losses.

You need to develop an insider incident response plan with the rights of everyone involved in mind. Specific actions to control damage by malicious insiders should be identified, together with the circumstances under which those efforts are appropriate. The plan should describe the general process to be followed and the responsibilities of the members of the response team. A mediator for communication between the departments of your organization needs to be assigned that is trusted by all department heads. Your department heads need to understand the plan and what information can and cannot be shared in the investigation of the incident.

The details of the insider incident response plan probably would not be shared with all of your employees. Only those responsible for carrying out the plan need to understand it and be trained on its content and execution. Your employees may know of its existence and should be trained on how to (anonymously) report suspicious behavior, as well as specific types of suspicious behaviors that should be reported. Your managers need to understand how to handle personal and professional problems and when they might indicate increased risk of insider compromise. If your organization experiences damage due to a malicious insider or as your risks evolve—for instance, due to new internal or external attack vectors—your employee training should be updated. Lessons learned from insider incidents should be fed back into your insider incident response plan to ensure its continual improvement.

## Case Studies: What Could Happen if I Don't Do It?

> The IT manager in a lottery agency turned losing lottery tickets into winners to steal nearly $63,000 over a year and a half. To carry out the scam, he purchased a ticket as usual, and then modified it to be a winner in the lottery agency's database. When the agency discovered the fraudulent tickets, it started an investigation. Fortunately, the insider was on vacation or he would have been chosen to investigate the incident. Upon his return, when confronted with the fraudulent tickets, he behaved suspiciously, and therefore was put on administrative leave and his physical access was disabled. Management neglected to inform his subordinates of the action, so he still had managerial control of his personnel. Before he left on administrative leave, he deleted a history log that may have proven his criminal acts. He also instructed one of his subordinates to erase four weeks of backup tapes, claiming that they wouldn't be useful under a new backup data format that was being implemented. She complied with this request, and the organization lost much of the evidence of his tampering with system security controls. Once his alleged crime did come to light, he asked a different subordinate to retrieve some additional backup tapes for him that would help him prove his innocence. He complied, and the organization never recovered those tapes.

While the organization took the right actions to remove the suspect from the organization, it neglected to inform his subordinates of the action, so he still had managerial control of organization personnel. If the organization had a formal insider incident response plan in place, and its employees were educated on their responsibilities for responding to the insider's requests, the organization may have been better able to respond to the insider's fraud.

> An assembly inspector at a manufacturing plant complained to management about the lack of support given to inspectors to do their job, saying that inspectors are pressured to approve work regardless of quality. Despite the fact that an independent evaluator determined that his claims were unfounded he threatened to sue the company and offered his silence for a cash settlement. This extortion attempt was declined by the company and no further action was taken until years later when newspaper articles began appearing that divulged some of the company's proprietary information. After receiving an anonymous tip that the insider was responsible for the leaks, the company started an investigation. Working with law enforcement, the organization found evidence that he had been downloading the organization's confidential information, which was outside his area of responsibility, for more than two years. He had downloaded massive amounts of information using a USB drive and stored it at his residence. The investigation also found evidence of the insider's email

correspondence with reporters discussing the proprietary documents, articles, and meetings.

While hindsight is 20/20, if the organization had executed an incident response plan at the time of the attempted extortion, it may have prevented the insider's follow-on actions and have been able to prevent the flow of its confidential information to the media.

## Summary

The best practices presented in this chapter provide a framework for establishing an insider threat program in your organization. Start by including insider threats in your enterprise-wide risk assessment. Next, conduct a security awareness campaign to ensure that insider threat is understood across your organization so that responsibility for the identification of and response to insiders who pose an elevated risk can be distributed enterprise-wide. Develop clearly defined policies, as described throughout this chapter, and enforce them consistently and fairly. Management needs to understand how to recognize and respond to concerning behavior in the workplace, and needs to understand the potential ramifications of negative workplace events. A well-defined employee termination process is essential in preventing attacks following termination. You need to secure both the physical and electronic environment, including account and password management, separation of duties, controls for your software development process, change controls, and extra vigilance for system administrators, other privileged users, and remote access.

You need to apply a consistent monitoring strategy for online actions; your employee monitoring practices should be developed in conjunction with your legal counsel to ensure that they are compliant with employee privacy laws. If monitoring identifies suspicious activity, a well-defined response plan should be enacted to minimize the impact to your organization.

Despite all of the precautions you implement, it is still possible that an insider will successfully attack. Therefore, it is important that your last step in preparing for an insider threat is to prepare for that possibility and enhance your organizational resiliency by implementing secure backup and recovery processes that are tested periodically.

Remember: It is very important not to overlook contractors and trusted business partners that have access to your information systems, information, or networks. Much of what you read in this chapter applies equally well to those types of insider threats!

This chapter presented a framework that you can use across your organization. The "Common Sense Guide" (referenced at the beginning of this chapter) has been one of the most popular documents we have created, so we stand behind its usefulness and strongly encourage you to measure your organization's practices against it to identify gaps that should be addressed.

When we were writing this book, the National Institute of Standards and Technology (NIST) was working on the next version of *Special Publication 800-53: Recommended Security Controls for Federal Information Systems and Organizations.*[9] The special publication is aimed at providing federal agencies, state and local governments, and private-sector organizations a set of security and privacy controls to safeguard their critical assets. This new version will include new guidance in the form of controls to address privacy, mobility, cloud computing, industrial controls, application security, Web applications, and insider threats. The CERT Insider Threat Center contributed input on insider threat controls to the Joint Task Force, a group of civilian-, defense-, and intelligence-agency information security experts working to produce a unified, federal IT security framework. Please refer to that publication[10] for more information on specific controls.

## References/Sources of Best Practices

This chapter described 16 practices, based on existing industry-accepted best practices, providing you with defensive measures that could prevent or facilitate early detection of many of the insider incidents other organizations experienced in the hundreds of cases in the CERT insider threat database. If you would like more detail on implementing any of the practices we described, you should consult the following resources:

- CERT RMM (www.cert.org/resilience/)
- ISO 27002 (www.27000.org/iso-27002.htm)
- NIST 800-53 (http://csrc.nist.gov/publications/PubsSPs.html)
- SANS Top 20 Security Controls (www.sans.org/critical-security-controls/)

---

9. http://csrc.nist.gov/publications/nistpubs/800-53-Rev3/sp800-53-rev3-final.pdf

10. NIST 800-53: http://csrc.nist.gov/publications/PubsSPs.html

# Chapter 7

---

# Technical Insider Threat Controls

Chapter 6, Best Practices for the Prevention and Detection of Insider Threats, covered the broader range of insider threat controls, including both administrative and technical controls. This chapter will be of interest to the more technical readers among you, as it contains suggestions for new technical controls you can implement to prevent and detect insider threats. These controls are the output of the insider threat lab. First, we describe the lab at a high level, then we explain how we developed these controls, and then we describe each control. Note that the controls become increasingly sophisticated as you progress through the chapter, since we present them in the order they were developed. They progress from straightforward controls that many organizations do not seem to implement, to actual signatures that you can import into existing tools in your organization.

Since we anticipate technical experts reading this chapter, you might care about the details behind the lab. However, if you don't care about the lab or how we created the controls you can skip right to the discussion of controls later in the chapter.

We do not include definitions of technical terminology in this chapter, since there would be far too many definitions! We assume that if you are reading this chapter you are technical enough to understand it without that level of assistance.

Also, all of the signatures, rules, and queries contained in this chapter are also available on our Web site: www.cert.org/insider_threat. Please go to the Web site so that you can copy and paste or import them directly into your tools. In addition, we will continue to release improvements for these controls as more organizations implement them, and as we receive feedback from practitioners on how to make them even more useful in an operational environment. These controls have been presented at large conferences such as RSA and have received very positive feedback, but we realize that they will need to be tailored and optimized depending on each organization's specific requirements. Therefore, these controls are not intended to be implemented blindly, but rather should be used as a general template that you can customize for your own use.

> These controls are not intended to be implemented blindly, but rather should be used as a general template that you can customize for your own use.

The insider threat lab is the newest addition to our body of work on insider threat.[1] In 2008 we decided that after studying the insider threat problem for seven years it was time to shift our focus to solutions. We felt that we understood insider threat as well as anyone could: who does it, how, when, why, where, and so on. We also had added technical security experts to our team at that time who had the ability and vision to embark on innovative new work for us. Therefore, in 2009 we started the CERT insider threat lab.

Integrating the insider threat lab into our research has resulted in tremendous advances in helping the community to better understand insider threat. The lab has a variety of purposes, including the following:

- Performing live testing of commercial and open source tools and tool configurations that aim to combat insider threats against re-creations of actual insider events from the CERT database
- Developing new insider threat controls using existing technology

---

1. Material from this chapter includes portions from previously published works. Specifically, Michael Hanley, Tyler Dean, Will Schroeder, Matt Houy, Randy Trzeciak, and Joji Montelibano published information about the lab in "An Analysis of Technical Observations in Insider Theft of Intellectual Property Cases" [Hanley 2011b]. Joji Montelibano also published information about Control 3 in "Insider Threat Control: Using a SIEM Signature to Detect Potential Precursors to IT Sabotage" [Montelibano 2011]. Finally, Michael Hanley published information about Control 4 in "Candidate Technical Controls and Indicators of Insider Attack from Socio-Technical Models and Data," in the Proceedings of the 2010 NSA Center of Academic Excellence (CAE) Workshop on Insider Threat, and in a later refinement of that control [Hanley 2010, Hanley 2011a].

- Creating demonstrational videos for conferences and workshops that illustrate those new controls
- Developing online exercises to give cyberdefenders hands-on experience to better prepare them for insider threats within their organizations

Over the years, our ongoing analysis of insider cases yielded best practices, models of insider behavior, training materials, and other useful results. The insider threat lab enables us to put this body of knowledge into practice, testing our results in a realistic environment. We can determine the effectiveness of various controls and tools against the threat of malicious insiders and are now in a better position to make concrete, technical recommendations for prevention and mitigation.

Our lab team continually reviews the ever-changing commercial and open source tool space to ensure that we understand the available technology, and leverages our case studies of real incidents to draw conclusions about gap areas that exist in the industry. We also factor in knowledge gained by our insider threat assessment teams and workshop instructors regarding feedback from practitioners on what's working and not working for them. When we discover a new control that someone in the community is using successfully, we transition that via our blog, workshops, conference presentations, and reports. We then focus our work in the lab on gap areas for which we have not found a proven solution.

In this chapter we briefly describe the infrastructure of the lab, and the process we use in creating demonstrational videos, new controls, and exercises. Next, we describe the solutions we have developed so far in the lab. Note that demonstrational videos, signatures, and rules are available on our Web site, and we will continue to add new ones even after publication of this book. Keep checking our Web site periodically to ensure that you are picking up the latest releases from the CERT insider threat lab!

## Infrastructure of the Lab

The lab consists of two virtual environments that are capable of simulating very detailed network architectures and system configurations, running from the network perimeter to the end-user workstation. We use one virtual environment to test micro-scale scenarios, and another larger-scale platform to simulate the behavior of a "real" network. In other words, the "micro-lab" provides us with a small network of fewer than ten servers, workstations, and users in order to stage our scenario. The "macro-lab" can replicate a network topology of several hundred servers and workstations, and we have actually used this lab environment to simulate the behavior of up to 5,000 users.

The micro-lab consists of a few physical systems running various virtual machines to simulate complete networks. This flexibility provides a quick way to reconstruct insider attacks and respective defense mechanisms. It enables us to determine the effectiveness of various controls and tools against the threat of malicious insiders and to test our proposed new countermeasures in a realistic environment. As a result, we can now provide concrete, technical recommendations for prevention and mitigation of insider threats. We create realistic environments to study insider attacks and to evaluate candidate defense mechanisms. Additionally, the lab allows us to rapidly prototype small to medium-sized networks at minimal cost and allows us to integrate physical devices into the simulated topology.

The larger macro-lab uses the XNET[2] environment. XNET is a next-generation cybersecurity training and simulation platform. Its infrastructure consists of several server-grade rack-mounted servers capable of seamlessly running simultaneous instances of virtual machines. The major difference between the micro- and macro-labs is scale. We also deploy controls in the micro-lab prior to testing it in the XNET environment. The reason for this approach is that we try to focus on the attack and defense mechanisms when testing in the micro-lab. Once we confirm that our defense strategy is sound, we then deploy the scenario in XNET, to see how our defensive mechanisms behave in a typical network, with a large amount of traffic or "noise." Only when a control passes both of these tests do we release it for pilot testing in production environments.

## Demonstrational Videos

Since the lab was created, we have developed a series of demonstrational videos that depict scenarios taken from real cases in the CERT database. Each video describes an insider threat case and shows how one or more open source tools could be used to detect such an incident and identify the individual responsible should it happen in your environment. We present these videos in our insider threat workshops. We have also presented them

---

2. XNET CERT Exercise Network: http://xnet.cert.org

at various conferences, including the RSA Conference, the U.S. Department of Defense Cyber Crime Conference (DC3), the Government Forum of Incident Response and Security Teams (GFIRST), the Forum of Incident Response and Security Teams (FIRST), and MIS Training Institute InfoSec World.

The demos can be watched at the following URL: www.cert.org/insider_ threat. We release additional demos every few months, so we recommend that you watch that site for new releases. In this chapter we will describe the insider threat mitigation strategies depicted in the demos.

## High-Priority Mitigation Strategies

The first step in creating a new control is case selection. We have a prioritized list of issues we feel need to be addressed, based on our cases, assessments, and feedback from workshop participants. We use that list to select the type of case—sabotage, fraud, or theft of IP—as well as the technical method we wish to address. We then pull the applicable cases from the CERT database, review the details for each case, and eliminate those without much technical detail. The final candidate cases are analyzed once more, and three to four cases are chosen that are interesting, are representative, and have sufficient technical detail for a demonstration. The case that is the most interesting to both a technical and nontechnical audience is the final selection. This ensures that not only is the chosen case optimal for a technical demonstration, but it will also be interesting for the widest audience possible.

Once the case is chosen, tools that could have detected or mitigated the insider attack are selected. As a Federally Funded Research and Development Center (FFRDC), the Software Engineering Institute is unable to endorse or promote specific vendors. Therefore, we try to use open source tools as much as possible in our demos. However, the mitigation strategies we highlight in our demos can be implemented using whatever technologies you already have in place in your organization. Our goal is to teach you the strategy and basic functionality that can be implemented using tools that you likely already have in place, or provide an open source alternative.

Next, we construct the demonstration. We usually have to fill in some gaps in the cases with plausible details as we rarely have complete technical information needed to re-create the case exactly. This results in a product based largely on a factual case with enough technical detail to make it interesting.

Finally, we create the environment for the demo in the insider threat lab. Once the machines are built and the scenario is working correctly, the virtual network is moved into the CERT Program's XNET environment and the demonstrations are recorded.

These demonstrations are not meant to be critical of the victim organizations. We only use these cases as opportunities to point out where a typical organization could be able to intervene, and how, in given scenarios.

In the rest of this chapter we will describe the controls we have created at time of publication. We will describe the case examples used in the corresponding demos, and then explain the countermeasures we suggest you consider to protect you from being a victim of a similar attack. You do not need to watch the videos in order to understand this chapter, but they are available on our Web site in order to reinforce these lessons.

## Control 1: Use of Snort to Detect Exfiltration of Credentials Using IRC

Our first control was modeled after an insider IT sabotage case that occurred at an Internet Service Provider (ISP). We chose this case because it enabled us to illustrate a fundamental concept in insider threat mitigation: You should consider using your intrusion detection system (IDS) to detect not only intrusions, as the name suggests, but also exfiltration of sensitive information. Snort is a popular open source IDS tool that could easily be tuned to examine inbound as well as outbound traffic.

> A technical support employee at an Internet service provider (ISP) had extensive ties to hacker groups, used several online aliases, attended organized hacker meetings, and communicated with hackers from work in online IRC chat sessions. A coworker of the insider discovered that the insider was attending organized hacker meetings.
>
> The employee's Internet access was suspended because his supervisor discovered unauthorized programs on his machine, specifically a credit card number verification program and a network sniffer. Since free Internet access was an employee benefit, this sanction resulted in extreme disgruntlement. In order to exact revenge, the employee connected with an outside hacker via IRC chat and gave him the usernames and passwords for customer accounts that were expired but not disabled. The hacker then used those credentials to deface the ISP's Web site and steal large amounts of customer information.

## Suggested Solution

Our suggested solution focuses on how a known and often rogue channel of communication, IRC chat, could be detected. Assuming that IRC chat is prohibited, a Snort rule could have been alerted on the insider/hacker IRC communication, and an administrator could use the Basic Analysis and Security Engine (BASE) user interface to investigate.

Responding to that alert, the administrator could have investigated further using a packet sniffing application such as Wireshark to rebuild the communication stream. Using Wireshark he could completely reconstruct the full communication stream between the insider and the hacker. He would have immediately seen the exfiltration of credentials for the dormant customer accounts, as well as the hacker's plan to attack the organization. Using open source tools, he could have prevented the attack from occurring.

The lesson to be learned from this case is that many organizations use an IDS to detect attempted intrusions from outside their network. However, you can also tune it to detect unauthorized communications from *within* your network. If communications mechanisms such as IRC chat are prohibited on your network, this Snort rule should not generate many false-positive alerts, and therefore could be an easy, new control for your insider threat mitigation toolbox.

---

# Control 2: Use of SiLK to Detect Exfiltration of Data Using VPN

Our second control was modeled after a theft of intellectual property case in the CERT database. We chose this case because it exemplifies many theft of IP cases, which involve exfiltration of large amounts of data within a short time period from a remote location using a virtual private network (VPN).

> This insider was employed as a software engineer at a telecommunications company. She took two leaves of absence for a total of a year, claiming that she was suffering from severe medical conditions. Although she had no work assignments during these leaves, her company did not disable her VPN access while she was on leave.
>
> During one leave of absence, she negotiated employment with a competitor outside the United States, ultimately accepting an offer from the company to develop telecommunications software. While at their offices abroad, she used her VPN connection to access her employer's network and download

proprietary documents. Four months later she returned to her original job as a full-time employee.

Over the next three days she purchased a one-way ticket abroad, downloaded more than 200 proprietary documents, and removed physical documents from the office. Then she resigned from her job via email, downloaded more information that night, and attempted to leave the United States with the company laptop.

Fortunately, airport security caught her with the proprietary documents as she was leaving the country with them. The laptop, CDs, thumb drive, and a videotape contained proprietary documents and source code.

## Suggested Solution

Our suggested solution utilizes a CERT open source tool suite known as SiLK,[3] which could be used to detect the exfiltration of proprietary information from a network. The SiLK tool suite is designed to collect, store, and analyze network flow data, providing a valuable platform for network situational awareness.

A SiLK sensor could be configured to watch all traffic at the perimeter of a subnet where VPN connections attach to the network. A standard SiLK configuration can be used to identify large flows of traffic from sensitive file servers to users on VPN connections, indicating potentially suspicious traffic. Especially during an off-peak time, a network administrator could detect an anomaly by doing the following:

- Recognizing a change in the distribution of the port/protocol of network traffic
- Seeing two devices moving a large amount of data in one direction in a short period of time

During an off-peak time when network activity is typically low, movement of a large amount of data over Windows file shares would cause the percentage of traffic passing the flow sensor to rapidly rise beyond other protocols, even HTTP. This would alert the administrator to a concerning behavior exhibited on the network. From here, the analyst could use SiLK to identify the specific flows involved, and thus, the specific host on the VPN, for further inquiry.

---

3. See http://tools.netsa.cert.org/silk/ for more information.

This is a prime example of how open source tools can be repurposed to assist with detection of malicious insider behavior. We are now exploring new alerting mechanisms using additions to the SiLK suite that process flow data in real time, looking for patterns that might be associated with data exfiltration. Keep an eye on our Web site for demonstrations of this new technical control in the coming months.

## Control 3: Use of a SIEM Signature to Detect Potential Precursors to Insider IT Sabotage

After creating the first two demonstrations, we decided it was time to begin documenting our controls in a more formal manner, rather than simply creating demonstrations. The remainder of this section describes each control in more detail, and provides more implementation guidance.

This section describes development and suggested application of a Security Information and Event Management (SIEM) signature to detect possible malicious insider activity that could lead to IT sabotage. Since there is no uniform, standardized event logging format, we present the signature in two of the most visible public formats: Common Event Format (CEF) and Common Event Expression (CEE). Because CEF and CEE are both in draft format at the time of this writing, the SIEM described in this section also employs an operational version of the proposed signature in an ArcSight environment.

Recall that insider IT sabotage is defined as an insider's use of information technology to direct specific harm at an organization or an individual. The purpose of this analysis SIEM signature is to detect the presence of a malicious insider based on key indicators related to IT sabotage activity.

> A former software engineer who had been employed by the victim organization, a huge, high-tech company, was responsible for managing an automated manufacturing system. During the workweek, he maintained a constant remote access connection from his home to the organization's network.

> The insider, who had previously worked in another department at the organization, was terminated due to poor performance. Prior to informing the insider of his termination, the organization terminated the insider's network access, but failed to check if his remote access connection was active. (Most organizations we have talked to about this have admitted that they would not catch this either.)

The malicious incident occurred the day after the insider's termination, outside of work hours. While under the influence of alcohol, he used the open VPN connection he had opened earlier in the week, prior to his termination, to remotely connect to critical systems and shut down the organization's manufacturing system by deleting critical files.

Due to his actions, the organization lost hours of manufacturing time and had to load backup data to restart the manufacturing process. Connection and activity logs connected the insider to the incident, and the insider was arrested and convicted.

In this case, since the insider remotely accessed the organization's information systems outside of work hours using his own account, the signature that follows would have alerted on this questionable activity even before the insider sabotaged the data. The signature would have notified system administrators to the insider's initial VPN connection every Monday evening and every day during the week, since the insider left it connected all day, all week. It would have logged from whose account and from where the connection was coming, and could have potentially detected the insider before he deleted the organization's critical information. The signature would also have alerted on the insider's remote connectivity to the critical systems and his deletion of operational files. Without a signature like this, the insider was able to exploit the vulnerability the organization created by failing to disable the insider's connections upon termination.

## Suggested Solution

The cases in the CERT database reveal that almost all insiders involved in acts of IT sabotage displayed behavioral indicators prior to committing their crimes, as described in Chapter 2, Insider IT Sabotage. The respective organizations could have, and ideally should have, acted on these behavioral precursors to prevent the crimes from taking place. Recall from Chapter 2 that behavioral indicators include, but are not limited to, the following:

- Conflicts with coworkers or supervisors
- Improper use of organization information assets
- Sanctions
- Rule violations and/or security violations

This signature is designed to be applied toward a particular user or group of users who are "on the HR radar" for those types of concerning behaviors.

It is not intended to be applied to all users across your enterprise, as doing so will generate a large number of false positives.

Before applying this signature, you should carefully craft policies and practices for formal communications about employees who exhibit escalating or significant concerning behaviors and coordination among relevant departments across your enterprise. Departments that should be included are information technology, information security, human resources, physical security, and legal. These proactive steps are necessary to ensure that any measures you take to combat insider threat comply with all organizational policies, local and national laws, labor union contracts and other contracts, and regulations.

Policies must be clearly defined and consistently enforced. Thresholds for when concerning behaviors warrant targeted monitoring must be clearly defined. In addition, you cannot choose to follow up on concerning behaviors by some employees, but neglect to do so for other employees who exhibit the same behaviors.

Once users are identified who warrant targeted monitoring via this signature, you will then be able to determine the appropriate usernames, account names, host names, and/or host addresses to enter into the signature to make the alert volume more meaningful and manageable.

## Database Analysis

We conducted a brief analysis on the IT sabotage cases in the CERT database based on the following questions to find what information could be used to develop a SIEM signature.

- What time did they attack? After hours or during business hours?
- How many insiders attacked using VPN versus in the office?
- What protocols do insiders use for remote connection? Secure Shell (SSH), Telnet, Remote Desktop Protocol (RDP)?

We found that 26% of the attacks occurred during work hours and 35% occurred outside of work hours; in 39% of the cases the time of attack was unknown, as shown in Figure 7-1. Breaking this down further, out of the cases for which the time of attack is known, 58% of the attacks occurred outside normal work hours and 42% occurred during work hours.

Another enlightening finding concerned the number of insiders who attacked using VPN versus the number of insiders who attacked while in

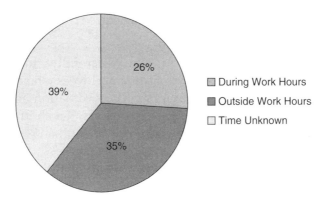

**Figure 7-1** *Time of attack for IT sabotage cases*

the office. We found that 54% of the attacks used remote access and 27% occurred on-site. In only 19% of the cases, the location of the attack was unknown. Therefore, if we discard Unknowns, 66% of the attacks occurred using remote access and 34% occurred on-site. Figure 7-2 presents these findings.

Note that even for employees "on the HR radar" who have been placed under targeted monitoring, the VPN connection alone does not necessarily indicate malicious activity. The insiders in the CERT database most often used a remote connection to the target system *after* they established a VPN connection with the organization's network. For this reason, we do not include VPN traffic as a monitored protocol, but instead we include the VPN *username* in cases where that account may differ from the user's regular username. This will become clearer as you continue reading.

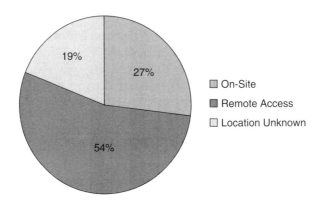

**Figure 7-2** *Location of attack for IT sabotage cases*

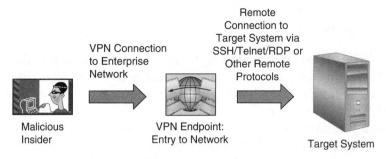

**Figure 7-3**  *Typical remote attack activity via VPN*

Figure 7-3 depicts the typical sequence of events associated with a remote attack via VPN.

The specific protocols insiders use for remote connections are not currently coded in the CERT database. However, through interviews with some of the actual perpetrators, as well as through a more detailed analysis of these cases, we discovered that the most common known ports used for remote attacks are ports 22 (SSH), 23 (Telnet), and 3389 (Terminal Services, or RDP). Since a majority of malicious insiders used remote access for their attacks, we considered instances of connections to these three ports as suspicious in the development of our signature, and pilot testing by practitioners validated this assertion. You will need to account for other protocols used in your own environment to make sure you are monitoring all possible channels of communication.

Based on this analysis of the CERT database, we found that the relevant indicators to be included in this particular control are the location of the attack and the time of the attack. Also, as previously mentioned, since remote access is a common method of attack, it is important to consider the type of protocol the attacker uses (although this information was not specifically coded in the database). This information is the basis for our SIEM signature.

## SIEM Signature

Remember that this signature is to be applied *only* to individuals who warrant increased scrutiny. *This signature should not be applied to all privileged users as it will generate inordinate false positives.*

The characteristics of the attacker involve someone accessing the organization's information systems remotely, outside normal work hours. With these characteristics, we developed the following signature:

```
Detect <username> and/or <VPN account name> and/or <hostname> using
<ssh> and/or <telnet> and/or <RDP> from <5:00 PM> to <9:00 AM>
```

The purpose of the signature is to identify the attacker, the remote connection protocol used, and whether this activity is occurring outside normal work hours. The identity of the attacker can be retrieved through any or all of the following parameters: username, VPN account name, or host name. Similarly, the remote connection protocol can be any or all of the following: SSH, Telnet, or RDP. We have based the signature on the following key fields: username, VPN account name (in case this account name is different from the local username), host name of the attacker, and whether the attacker is using SSH, Telnet, or RDP.

With this basic structure in mind, we used two standards for creating the signature: the Common Event Format, developed by ArcSight, and the Common Event Expression, developed by MITRE. Brief summaries of each standard are provided in the following sections.

## Common Event Format

The Common Event Format is an event interoperability standard developed by ArcSight. The purpose of this standard is to improve the interoperability of infrastructure devices by instituting a common log output format for different technology vendors. It ensures that an event and its semantics contain all necessary information. CEF is an extensible, text-based format designed to support multiple device types in the easiest way possible. It defines syntax for log records consisting of a standard header and a variable extension that is formatted as key-value pairs. This format contains the most relevant information, which makes it easier for event consumers to parse and use them. The format of CEF is (`header/`*`extension`*):

---

```
CEF:Version|Device Vendor|Device Product|Device
Version|Signature ID|Name|Severity|Extension
```

---

The `Version` identifies the version of the CEF format. The `Device Vendor`, `Device Product`, and `Device Version` uniquely identify the type of sending device. The `Signature ID` identifies the type of event reported. The `Name` represents a human-readable and understandable description of the event, and the `Severity` reflects the importance of the event. The `Extension` part of the message is a placeholder for additional fields, which are part of a predetermined set.

Using this standard and the key indicators we identified during the database analysis, we developed the following two CEF-based SIEM signatures to identify suspected attackers. The first signature, for Microsoft products, identifies a suspected attacker by logging his or her username and host name:

```
CEF:0|microsoft|activedirectory|2011|001|username logged
in|10|suser=<username> src=<10.0.0.1> shost=<hostname>
```

With this information, the second signature is for Snort products. It identifies an attacker who initiates a remote connection to TCP port 22, 23, or 3389. It uses the username/IP address/host name of the suspected attacker gathered from the first signature, and alerts on any attempts from this source to the target destination address:

```
CEF:0|sourcefire|snort|2.9|002|remote connection from <suser>
or <src> or <shost> to <dst>|src=<10.0.0.1> or shost=<hostname>
prot=TCP dpt=<22,23,3389> start=<17:00:00> end=<08:00:00>
```

Since a single CEF cannot be used to draw from two separate products, these two signatures are used together to identify a suspected malicious insider.

## Common Event Expression

The Common Event Expression (CEE) architecture defines an open and practical event log standard developed by MITRE. Like CEF, the purpose of CEE is to improve the audit process and users' ability to effectively interpret and analyze event log and audit data. It also enables the creation of useful and efficient log records within applications. It standardizes the event-log relationship by normalizing the way events are recorded, shared, and interpreted.

The basic components of CEE are dictionary and event taxonomy, logging recommendations, log syntax, and log transport. Event records are guided by log recommendations (suggested events to log). Log messages are exchanged via a common log transport (standard communications mechanisms, such as XML, SMTP, Syslog, etc.); log messages are received in common log syntax (consistent data elements and format, such as XML); and the dictionary and event taxonomy specifies the event in a common representation (standard field names, terminology, and event types, such as a user login, service restart, or network connection).

Using the CEE format, we developed a signature based on the key indicators of insider IT sabotage. A sample signature using arbitrary data for `<logTime>`, `<user>`, `<src>`, and `<shost>`, to detect remote access outside normal work hours in XML format, is:

```
<event name="remote connection by suspected malicious insider">
     <logTime>2011-03-17T12:17:32</logtime>
     <suser>maliciousinsider</suser>
     <src>10.0.0.1</src>
     <shost>insider_system</shost>
     <prot>TCP</prot>
     <dpt>{22,23,3389}</dpt>
     <start>17:00:00</start>
     <end>08:00:00</end>
</event>
```

The signature identifies a suspected attacker who is using a remote connection to log on to the organization's internal system using TCP port 22, 23, or 3389 outside normal work hours. It also logs the time the event was recorded.

### Applying the Signature

We ultimately found that translating the signature depends on the SIEM. Initially, we used an open source SIEM for developing the signatures. However, the open source SIEM we used did not have the ability to export the signature in text format. In order to implement and test the signature in a production environment, we deployed it in an ArcSight platform. The ArcSight signature we developed and fully tested using our key indicators to detect remote access outside normal work hours is:

```
((Attacker User Name = <username> OR Attacker Host Name = <host-
name>) AND (Target Port = 3389 OR Target Port = 23 OR Target Port
= 22) AND Manager Receipt Time Between (17:00:00.000,08:00:00.000)
AND Target Address = any)
```

This signature generates an alert if, after normal work hours (i.e., between 5:00 p.m. and 8:00 a.m.), an attacker is connected to any machine via port 3389 (RDP), 23 (Telnet), or 22 (SSH). To identify the attacker, the signature logs the attacker's username or host name.

Note that the major determinant of utility and success of this signature is proper identification of users to whom this signature will be applied. *The SIEM signatures described here should not be applied to a general user population because that will generate a large number of false positives.* Privileged users, such as system administrators, typically connect remotely to various systems outside office hours in the normal course of their daily activities. To determine which users merit more targeted monitoring through this signature, you will have to rely on management and human resources records to properly identify employees who have exhibited concerning behaviors that warrant closer inspection.

> The SIEM signatures described here should not be applied to a general user population because that will generate a large number of false positives.
>
> You will have to rely on management and human resources records to properly identify employees who have exhibited concerning behaviors that warrant closer inspection.

## Conclusion

Ideally, your information security personnel should regularly communicate with different departments across the enterprise, especially with HR and legal. They should be informed when an employee meets the threshold of concerning behavior that warrants targeted monitoring, as explained in Chapter 2. In the CERT database, the vast majority of insiders who committed IT sabotage were guilty of policy violations and ongoing, excessive, concerning behaviors in the workplace prior to the execution of their attack. In most cases, insiders carried out their attack via a VPN connection, from which they launched remote connections to their target systems. Organizations should first identify suspicious insiders and then have their information security staff apply the SIEM signature described in this section to ensure that their actions are closely monitored.

## Control 4: Use of Centralized Logging to Detect Data Exfiltration during an Insider's Last Days of Employment

Next, we selected a set of insider theft of IP cases for deeper study. We know that insiders who steal IP are typically scientists, engineers, or programmers, as described in Chapter 3, Insider Theft of Intellectual Property. They steal assets they created and to which they have authorized access. They usually steal the information within 30 days prior to their termination, whether forced or voluntary. Common exfiltration methods include sending email to competitors or foreign organizations, using personal email accounts from work, and downloading files to removable media or to laptops.

This section describes a control we developed based on those patterns. Using a centralized log storage and indexing engine, such as Splunk,[4] we show an example implementation of this pattern on an enterprise-class system.

> An engineer in a firm that manufactured electronic devices and microprocessors used inside knowledge and privileged access to steal proprietary product information and send it to a competing firm in a country outside the United States.
>
> After communicating back and forth with a high-level official at the competitor, the insider submitted his resignation to his employer with no mention of the competitor. Following his notice of resignation and prior to his last day of work, he proceeded to email several compressed sets of confidential files off the network directly to a contact at the competing firm. The case file also suggests that the insider emailed sensitive information from the corporate network to a personal email address.

## Suggested Solution

Let's start by breaking out key components of the case into technical areas of interest. First, we identify the target asset: stolen trade secrets. Next, we consider the source of the asset, which appears to have been a repository of sensitive documents, likely a file server. Last, the medium used to exfiltrate the data was the corporate network, specifically the standard corporate email environment, from which the insider sent an email directly to an individual at a competitor not based in the United States.

Next, when considering control strategies, we examine what may have prevented the crime, led to earlier detection, or facilitated more efficient and effective incident response after the crime occurred. Of the three strategies, prevention clearly is preferable. However, this is not always possible, especially in global organizations that move millions of email messages across their networks every day. If it is realistic for you to simply block all emails to competitors, and perhaps all emails going to domains outside your country, by all means do so! However, detection is likely to provide the most practical opportunity for success in most organizations.

We know that the insider submitted his resignation, continued working, and stole the proprietary information before his last day of employment. As described in Chapter 3, we also know that most insiders steal intellectual property within a month of termination, whether forced or voluntary.

---

4. www.splunk.com

This compelling pattern from our modeling work provides an interesting opportunity for a technical control.

Our goal was to create a new control using tools already being used by many organizations. We decided to utilize centralized logging, or a centralized log querying mechanism, to detect email sent to a direct competitor's domain, outside the United States, containing an attachment within one month of termination.

---

**CAUTION**

It is important to note that this signature is not intended to be applied to all users across the enterprise, as doing so will generate a large number of false positives. You need to have a policy in place that defines explicit thresholds for monitoring of high-risk insiders, and it must be consistently enforced.

---

Prior to applying this signature, you should facilitate communication and coordination between relevant departments across the enterprise, especially information technology, information security, human resources, physical security, and legal. This cooperation is necessary in part to ensure that any measures you take to combat insider threat comply with all organizational, local, and national laws and regulations.

Once users are identified that warrant targeted monitoring via this signature (which in this case includes employees within the 30-day window of termination), you will be able to determine the corresponding usernames, account names, host names, and/or host addresses to enter into the signature in order to make the alert volume more meaningful and manageable.

## Monitoring Considerations Surrounding Termination

The primary means insiders use for data exfiltration over the network involves the use of either corporate email systems or Web-based personal email services. While no less a threat, monitoring for misuse of personal Web email services is out of scope for this control. We expect to start addressing this challenge in the near future, so keep an eye on our Web site: www.cert.org/insider_threat.

Corporate email accounts running on enterprise-class servers have a wealth of auditing and logging functionality available. This functionality can be used by administrators in an investigation or, in this case, a query to detect suspicious behavior. For example, if you enumerate (but do not blacklist) suspicious transactions, such as data transfers to competitors, those email transactions are recorded in mail server transaction logs in a form that is easily consumed by a log indexing engine. We use these logs to find

- Messages of size, potentially indicating an attachment or large amount of text in the message body
- Messages sent to suspicious domains
- Messages sent within the 30-day window of an employee's termination

Now we have the basic criteria for building a query rule:

> If the email is from a departing insider,
> and the message was sent in the past 30 days,
> and the recipient is not in the organization's domain,
> and the total bytes summed by day are more than a specified threshold,
> then send an alert to the security operator.

This solution first focuses on departing insiders, and then sets a time window of 30 days, representing the window surrounding their termination in which to search for suspicious email traffic. The 30-day window serves as the root of the query. Possible data sources that can be used to instantiate this attribute in a live query include an Active Directory or other LDAP directory service, partial HR records that are consumable by an indexing engine, or other proxies for employee status such as physical badge access status. HR systems do not always provide security staff members with a simple indicator that an employee is leaving the organization. Instead, suitable proxies (preset account expiration, date the account is disabled, etc.) can be used to bound the 30-day window for targeted monitoring.

If you immediately set the account expiration date in your directory service when an employee turns in his or her resignation, this control can determine all employees who will be leaving the organization. Depending on your conventions, some customized logic might be needed to convert the userid (UID) from your directory service into the employee's email address; we simply concatenate the UID to the local domain name.

Next, our query identifies all email traffic from those departing users. From that traffic it focuses on all email traffic that has left your local domain namespace (or other logical boundary in the case of a large federation of disparate namespaces or a wide trust zone with other namespaces). This identifies any possible data exfiltration via email by identifying messages where the intended recipient resides in an untrusted zone or in a namespace you otherwise have no control over. You may choose to significantly pare down this portion of the query based on specific intelligence or threat information. For instance, you could specify sets of "unwanted" recipient addresses by country code top-level domains (ccTLD), known-bad domain names, or other similar criteria.

Because not all mail servers indicate an attachment's presence in the same way, the query next uses byte count to indicate potential data exfiltration. Setting a reasonable per-day byte threshold, starting between 20 and 50 kilobytes, should allow you to detect when several attachments, or large volumes of text in the bodies of email messages, leave your network on any given day.

## An Example Implementation Using Splunk

If you are using Splunk for centralized log indexing and interrogation, you can configure it to raise an alert when it observes the behaviors we described. If you are using a different log correlation engine, you can implement the same functionality by replicating what we demonstrate in this section.

The following is a Splunk rule that you can adjust to your particular environment. The sample rule uses a sample internal namespace to illustrate the implementation. We assume a generic internal namespace of corp. merit.lab, with two servers of interest. MAILHOST is an Exchange server, and DC is an Active Directory domain controller.

The characteristics of the attacker involve someone accessing your information systems remotely, outside normal work hours. With these characteristics, we developed the following Splunk rule:

```
Terms: `host=MAILHOST
    [search host="DC.corp.merit.lab"
        Message="A user account was disabled. *"
        | eval Account_Name=mvindex(Account_Name, -1)
        | fields Account_Name
| strcat Account_Name "@corp.merit.lab" sender_address
        | fields - Account_Name]
    total_bytes > 50000 AND recipient_address!="*corp.merit.lab"
    startdaysago=30
    | fields client_ip, sender_address, recipient_address,
    message_subject, total_bytes`
```

Now we will describe the query by breaking it into manageable segments.

```
Mail from the Departing Insider: `host=MAILHOST []
```

This query is actually a nested query. The outermost bracket refers to a mail server, MAILHOST, and looks for a set of information first pulled from DC, a domain controller in the sample domain. Because the log query tool seeks employees leaving within the 30-day resignation window, the logical place to start looking for employee information is the local directory service. Assuming accounts are set to expire upon resignation, the corresponding alert can be queried for the associated event ID or known text (as in this demonstration) to find all employees leaving the organization. The query then concatenates the account name associated with the disable event to a string that ends with the organization's DNS suffix ("@corp.merit.lab" in this demonstration) to form a string that represents the email sender's address. This ends the first component of the query and provides the potentially malicious insider's email address.

```
Total Bytes Summed by Day More than Specified Threshold: total_bytes
> 50000
```

Not all mail servers provide a readily accessible attribute indicating that an email message included an attachment. Thus, the mail server is configured to filter first for all messages "of size" that might indicate an attachment or a large volume of text in the message body. This part of the query can be tuned as needed; 50,000 bytes is a somewhat arbitrary starting value.

```
Recipient not in Organization's Domain:
recipient_address!="*corp.merit.lab"
```

This portion of the query instructs Splunk to find only transactions where the email was sent to a recipient not in the organization's namespace. This is a vague query term that could generate many unwanted results, but it does provide an example of filtering based on destination. Clearly, not all messages leaving the domain are malicious, and an organization can filter based on more specific criteria such as specific country codes, known bad domain names, Gmail, Hotmail, and so on.

```
Message Sent in the Last 30 Days: startdaysago=30
```

This sets the query time frame to 30 days prior to the date of the account disable alert message. Recall from Chapter 3 that the 30-day window surrounding resignation is actually 60 days total: 30 days before and 30 days after resignation. This can be adjusted as needed, though the data on insider theft of IP exhibits the 30-day pattern discussed previously.

```
Final Section: fields client_ip, sender_address, recipient_address,
message_subject, total_bytes'
```

The final section of the query creates a table with relevant information for a security operator's review. The operator receives a comma-separated values (CSV) file showing the sender, recipient, message subject line, total byte count, and client IP address that sent the message. This information, along with a finite number of messages that match these criteria, should provide sufficient information for further investigation.

## Advanced Targeting and Automation

Originally, this control required manually identifying a user, or users, of interest to populate the query with targets. In fact, we find that there are ways to go a step further using simple tools to identify all users who have accounts set to expire within a 30-day window, and possibly feed these directly into Splunk via a command-line tool.

First, when an employee or contractor resigns, you must set his or her accounts to expire on his or her last day of employment. In Microsoft Active Directory, you can quickly identify the users who have accounts expiring in the next 30 days by using the PowerShell AD administration tools with a simple, one-line query. You can run the following example query by importing the AD PowerShell modules. Depending on privilege delegation in your environment, a privileged user in the directory might be required to run the command.

```
PS C:\Users\ffishbeck_sec> Search-ADAccount -AccountExpiring -TimeSpan
30.00:00:00
AccountExpirationDate : 7/9/2011 12:00:00 AM
DistinguishedName : CN=Brian Smith,OU=Employees,DC=corp,DC=merit,
DC=lab
Enabled : True
LastLogonDate : 7/1/2011 18:40:03 AM
LockedOut : False
Name : Brian Smith
ObjectClass : user
ObjectGUID : a6ed88a4-fab3-494d-9f45-4d9ad11e1069
PasswordExpired : True
PasswordNeverExpires : False
```

```
SamAccountName : Brian Smith
SID : S-1-5-21-2581603451-735610124-1584908375-1108
UserPrincipalName : bsmith@corp.merit.lab
AccountExpirationDate : 7/23/2011 12:00:00 AM
DistinguishedName : CN=Jennifer Burns,OU=Employees,DC=corp,
DC=merit,DC=lab
Enabled : True
LastLogonDate : 6/29/2011 12:18:00 PM
LockedOut : False
Name : Jennifer Burns
ObjectClass : user
ObjectGUID : fdd0b06f-c929-4da9-9f89-4c9415e3d756
PasswordExpired : True
PasswordNeverExpires : False
SamAccountName : Jennifer Burns
SID : S-1-5-21-2581603451-735610124-1584908375-1110
UserPrincipalName : jburns@corp.merit.lab
AccountExpirationDate : 7/2/2011 12:00:00 AM
DistinguishedName : CN=Megan Jordan,OU=Employees,DC=corp,DC=merit,
DC=lab
Enabled : True
LastLogonDate : 6/30/2011 4:30:28 AM
LockedOut : False
Name : Megan Jordan
ObjectClass : user
ObjectGUID : 4f11a5f4-7e49-4ec7-a34b-882fb643e5a3
PasswordExpired : True
PasswordNeverExpires : False
SamAccountName : Megan Jordan
SID : S-1-5-21-2581603451-735610124-1584908375-1117
UserPrincipalName : mjordan@corp.merit.lab
```

Once you know which user accounts are expiring in the near future, you can either manually populate the Splunk query with these LDAP usernames, or experiment with piping them into a command-line Splunk query. There are open source projects, including splunk-powershell, that would support this type of activity with a very simple script.[5] While this project does not appear to work with the newest release of PowerShell 2, it does work with the original PowerShell binaries and will successfully query a current v4.1.x Splunk installation.

---

5. http://code.google.com/p/splunk-powershell/

## Conclusion

According to our research, it is very important that you carefully consider organizational communications during the time frame surrounding an employee's resignation. Many insiders have stolen information within a 30-day window of termination from their organization. Further, many of these thefts occurred via use of standard corporate email servers. A well-constructed rule set can be placed on a centralized logging appliance to identify suspicious mail traffic originating from soon-to-be-departing employees. These well-crafted rules, based on trends observed from actual cases, can reduce analysts' workloads by presenting them with behaviors that are known to be malicious in several actual instances, and therefore merit further investigation.

## Insider Threat Exercises

We recently moved the networks from the insider threat lab into the CERT XNET environment to create realistic training exercises for cyberdefenders. These interactive, team-based exercises re-create complex actual insider threat scenarios and challenge participants to prepare for and respond to insider threat incidents. They include various injects from the teams running the exercise to simulate incidents. These exercises can be conducted within an organization to better equip its defenses against malicious insiders, or can be used in cyberflag exercises to recognize the most sophisticated team among multiple competing organizations. Appendix A, Insider Threat Center Products and Services, contains a description of our insider threat exercises.

## Summary

After spending many years studying the insider threat problem, and fully understanding the patterns in the different types of insider crimes, we created the CERT insider threat lab to test existing technical solutions and begin to create new ones. Many commercial insider threat tools are available; however, we continue to see the same tools, techniques, and procedures (TTPs) that we've been seeing for the past decade. The question is: Why? One answer is that malicious activity by insiders looks very much like their authorized day-to-day online activity. Their behavior does not appear to be anomalous. In addition, many insider threat detection tools result in information overload. The line between malicious and normal behavior is so difficult to discern that these tools end up reporting a multitude of false positives that make the tools unusable. So, what is the answer?

We have discovered that it is possible to create effective insider threat controls using existing technology, even open source tools in many cases. The tools simply need to be configured and integrated based on the patterns of activity observed in our insider threat models.

This chapter presented controls for using

- Snort to detect exfiltration of credentials using IRC
- SiLK to detect exfiltration of data using VPN
- A SIEM signature to detect potential precursors to insider IT sabotage
- Centralized logging to detect data exfiltration during an insider's last days of employment

As you can see, we have used a variety of existing technology to detect insider threats based on the most common behavioral patterns in the CERT database. Keep checking our Web site, www.cert.org/insider_threat, as we continue to release more controls on an ongoing basis!

The next chapter is composed of many case examples from the CERT database. Throughout the years, we have found that these cases are valuable tools in helping practitioners, management, and other leaders to realize the potential threats facing organizations. As you read through the examples, ask yourself once again: Could this happen to me? Unfortunately, in many cases the answer will be *yes*. The good news is that this book can help you to figure out what you need to do to change the answer to *no*.

# Chapter 8

# Case Examples

We've already used many case examples throughout this book. This chapter presents an additional selection of cases from the CERT insider threat database.[1] The descriptions used here were derived from a variety of public sources. While we tried to corroborate the details where we could, it was not always possible. Nevertheless, we believe many lessons can be learned from reviewing these cases—obviously, we have learned a lot from them over the years!

The first section contains IT sabotage cases, followed by cases that were both sabotage and fraud, then theft of IP, fraud, and finally the miscellaneous cases. Within each section, the cases are sorted by the sector of the victim organization. Each section starts with a table describing each case in that section. You might want to use those tables to search for cases that you find particularly interesting, either because of the method used or because of the applicability to your organization.

## Sabotage Cases

Table 8-1 provides an index of sabotage cases in the CERT insider threat database.

---

1. Some of these summaries were pulled from previously published works cited in other chapters. Others were pulled from the CERT insider threat database. We would like to recognize the many staff members on our team who have contributed to these summaries over the past ten years; they are listed by name in the Acknowledgments section of the Preface.

**Table 8-1** *Sabotage Cases*

| Case # | Industry or Government Sector | Description |
|--------|-------------------------------|-------------|
| 1 | Banking and finance | Revenge via framing of another employee |
| 2 | Banking and finance | Logic bomb that covered its tracks |
| 3 | Banking and finance | Logic bomb propagated to server configuration management baseline |
| 4 | Banking and finance | Insider threatens attack from the Internet underground |
| 5 | Commercial facilities | Insider conducts attack with help from the Internet underground |
| 6 | Defense industrial base | Multiple logic bombs |
| 7 | Defense industrial base | Massive leakage of proprietary information to the media by whistle-blower |
| 8 | Defense industrial base | Insider tests logic bomb three times before final attack |
| 9 | Energy | Contractor still has access even after his company suspends him |
| 10 | Food | Consultant steals 5,000 passwords |
| 11 | Government | Contractor plants logic bomb just prior to termination |
| 12 | Government | Former DBA deletes critical information following denied EEOC complaint |
| 13 | Government | Insider changes someone to "deceased" in a government database |
| 14 | Information technology | Consultant attacks after being told contract will end |

| 15 | Information technology | Consultant renders systems inaccessible after being reduced to part-time |
|----|------------------------|-------------------------------------------------------------------------|
| 16 | Information technology | Insider who left ISP prevents customers from accessing Internet for three weeks |
| 17 | Information technology | System administrator, fearing layoffs, plants malicious code |
| 18 | Information technology | Manufacturer suffers widespread shutdown after disgruntled employee of business partner sabotages wireless networks |
| 19 | Information technology | Programmer plants malicious code that disrupts critical operations 12 months after he left |
| 20 | Information technology | Former application developer inserts pornographic images on company Web site |
| 21 | Information technology | IT worker brings down 911 systems so that he can "play the hero" |
| 22 | Information technology | Technical support person works with the Internet underground to compromise his organization and deface its Web site |
| 23 | Information technology | Computer technician with a criminal history posts employees' PII to the Internet |
| 24 | Postal and shipping | Company discovers backups had not been recording critical data after former programmer deletes his software |

## Sabotage Case 1

A disgruntled former employee of a human resources department caused major havoc for the organization over a period of nearly five months. He broke into the organization's systems remotely after he was fired and deleted approximately 1,000 files related to employee compensation. He also modified the payroll records to reflect a large salary increase and substantial bonus for one of his former coworkers. The coworker was a previous romantic interest of his who had rejected him. To further frame the woman for the crime, he sent an email to senior managers from a computer account that contained the female employee's last name. The email had an attachment containing an excerpt of the deleted files. A forensic image of the computer at the insider's new employer revealed that the emails to the senior managers of the victim organization were sent from that computer. The insider was arrested, convicted, ordered to pay more than $90,000 in restitution, and sentenced to 18 months of imprisonment followed by three years of supervised release.

## Sabotage Case 2

A firm's network manager placed a malicious program—a timed logic bomb—on the network to disrupt and damage his employer as revenge for perceived wrongs. He had been advised of adverse employment issues and was placed on a performance improvement plan. The last straw for the organization was his unexcused absence from work several weeks later. The organization immediately terminated him. However, the malicious code he had already placed on the system had been programmed to execute at the end of the month. The malicious software deleted and modified more than 50,000 accounts and disrupted the firm's computer network. The investigation uncovered evidence that the insider had taken steps to conceal his activity: The malicious code actually deleted itself after execution, and the insider had deleted the system logs that had recorded his online activity related to planting the malicious code in the first place. Fortunately, investigators eventually found evidence on a backup tape that confirmed the insider's actions. He was convicted, and sentenced to more than one year of imprisonment, six months of electronic monitoring and home confinement, and three years of supervised release.

## Sabotage Case 3

Rumors spread across an international financial organization that annual bonuses would be smaller than usual. This prompted a system administrator to begin constructing a logic bomb at home, even working on it on Christmas day, and to use authorized remote access to move the logic bomb to the company's network. He then propagated the malicious code to all of the company's servers as part of the standard server upgrade procedure. He resigned when he found out the rumors about low bonuses were true; he had already laid the foundation for his revenge. The logic bomb, which he had set to go off two weeks later, deleted billions of files and disrupted service on thousands of servers throughout the United States. Prior to the logic bomb's detonation, the insider purchased put options of the company stock, expecting the subsequent detonation of the logic bomb to drive the firm's stock price lower. Although the stock price did not drop, the victim organization estimated that the attack would cost more than $3 million in network repairs, and could have affected more than 1 billion shares of its stock. A forensics investigation connected the insider to the incident through virtual private network (VPN) access, and through code snippets both on his home computer and on the organization's network. The insider was convicted and sentenced to more than eight years in prison.

## Sabotage Case 4

A system administrator and several of his colleagues were laid off by a financial firm. Over a period of four days after receiving the bad news, the insider contacted management at the victim organization and threatened them. He stated that if he did not receive a significantly larger severance package and good employment recommendations, he would recruit his friends from an underground Internet hacking ring to attack the victim organization. He also claimed to have opened backdoors throughout the victim organization's systems to facilitate such an attack. The organization contacted law enforcement and consensually recorded phone calls between the insider and the victim, capturing the insider's demands, threats, and intent. He was arrested before the attacks ever came to fruition, was convicted, and was sentenced to 15 months of imprisonment and three years of supervised release.

## Sabotage Case 5

A system administrator for a retail company was terminated over issues with a server for which he was responsible. Following his termination, he recruited members of an online hacking group to help him attack his former employer's systems. He relayed passwords and other access control information to the underground group, and provided detailed instructions on how to use those credentials to break into his former employer's network. Over a period of one week, the insider was able to organize the group and execute a coordinated denial-of-service attack against the retailer that lasted from the day before Thanksgiving until the Sunday after Thanksgiving—commonly recognized as the busiest shopping days of the year. Personnel at the organization detected problems in the network that were obstructing online sales and promptly responded to the incident. The insider was convicted, sentenced to 18 months of imprisonment, and ordered to pay $64,000 in restitution.

## Sabotage Case 6

A self-employed contractor was a system administrator for a military branch, and in that capacity he helped to oversee the daily operation of a computer system used to track and plot the locations of various military vehicles. When the victim organization rejected his proposal for follow-on work and decided to award the work to another firm, he became disgruntled and decided to take action to make the new system administrator "look bad." He sabotaged the organization's systems by planting logic bombs on five servers set to detonate after he left. Three of the five servers were subsequently damaged and went offline. Another system administrator searched for similar malicious code and uncovered the additional logic bombs; the administrator's actions prevented the malicious code from affecting the other two targeted computers. The victim organization then took extensive steps to secure and restore the network and its data. The insider was convicted, ordered to pay $25,000 in restitution and a $10,000 fine, and sentenced to more than a year in prison followed by a period of supervised release.

## Sabotage Case 7

An inspector at a manufacturing plant complained to management about the lack of support given to inspectors to do their job, saying that inspectors were pressured to approve work regardless of quality. Despite the fact that an independent evaluator determined that his claims were unfounded, the insider threatened to sue the company and offered his silence for a cash settlement. This extortion attempt was declined by the company and no further action was taken until years later when newspaper articles began appearing that divulged the company's proprietary information. After receiving an anonymous tip that the insider was responsible for the leaks, the organization started an investigation. Working with law enforcement, the organization found evidence that the insider had been downloading its confidential information, which was outside his area of responsibility, for more than two years. The insider had downloaded massive numbers of proprietary documents using a USB removable storage drive and stored the data at his residence. The investigation also found evidence of the insider's email correspondence with reporters discussing the proprietary documents, articles, and meetings. The entire incident took place over three years and the victim organization estimated its loss at $5 million to $15 million. The trial ended with a continuance agreement between the insider and the victim organization that directed the insider to cooperate with law enforcement to retrieve leaked documents and not leak any further organization information.

## Sabotage Case 8

A manufacturing firm's system administrator began employment as a machinist. Over a ten-year period, the insider created the company's network supporting the critical manufacturing processes and had sole authority for system administration of that network. During this time the insider centralized the only copy of the source code for all of the company's critical production programs on a single server, and convinced management to institute policies mandating this practice. The company eventually expanded, opening additional offices and plants nationally and internationally. The insider began to feel disgruntled at his diminishing importance to the company; launched verbal and physical assaults on coworkers; sabotaged projects of which he was not in charge; and loaded faulty programs to make coworkers look bad. He received a verbal warning and two written reprimands, was demoted, and finally was fired as a result of his actions. A few weeks later, a logic bomb executed on the company's network, deleting 1,000 critical manufacturing programs from the company's server, the one on which the insider had centralized the company's production programs earlier. No other current copy of the software was available to recover from the attack, since he had also requested and received, through intimidation, the only backup tape, violating company policy and amplifying the impact of his attack even further. The estimated cost of the damage exceeded $10 million, leading to the layoff of approximately eighty employees. The investigation revealed that the insider had actually tested the logic bomb three times on the company's network after hours prior to his termination. The insider was convicted and sentenced to 41 months of imprisonment.

## Sabotage Case 9

A contractor was employed in the IT department of an energy-management facility. In response to an employee dispute, the contractor's employer suspended his access to its systems, but failed to notify the energy management facility of the suspension, and his facility access was not disabled. A few days later, on a Sunday evening, he gained access to the energy production facility, used a hammer to break the glass case enclosing the "emergency power off" button, and hit the button. As a result, some of the computer systems were shut down, including computers that regulated the exchange of electricity between power grids. The day following the shutdown, the insider emailed a bomb threat to his supervisor. The email prompted the evacuation of 500 employees for six hours. To restore the system, the victim organization had to transfer control to another facility and utilize 20 computer specialists for approximately seven hours. Employee security access codes, as well as computer access, system, and video surveillance logs, were used to identify the insider. The insider was convicted, ordered to pay $34,000 in restitution, and sentenced to six months of house arrest and five years of probation.

## Sabotage Case 10

An information systems consultant at a large manufacturer ran several different password-cracking programs on the company's network five different times over a ten-month period. Initially, he stored the cracked passwords in a file on the company's server. Later he installed a more sophisticated password-cracking program on the company's system. This program enabled him to automatically transfer all accounts and passwords that could be cracked to a remote computer on a periodic basis. Five thousand passwords for company employees were successfully transferred. The company discovered the unauthorized activity, while performing remote access monitoring after the consultant had been terminated. It noticed that the former consultant had obtained unauthorized access to its network and created an administrator account. This prompted an investigation of the former insider's previous online activity, uncovering his unauthorized activity while employed. The incident-related impact was $10,000, the organization's cost of assessing the damage, verifying system security, and restoring integrity to its computer systems. The insider was convicted, ordered to pay $10,000, and sentenced to three years of probation and 250 hours of community service.

## Sabotage Case 11

A system administrator who worked for a contractor to a government agency was reprimanded by his government supervisor for frequent tardiness, absence, and unavailability for work. After finding out he was about to be terminated, the insider constructed and planted a logic bomb on the government organization's server to delete critical files. He placed the logic bomb in two different scripts. The first was in a Solaris script that rotated log files when a volume reached a certain point; rather than rotating log files it would execute his logic bomb. He placed the second logic bomb in his supervisor's log-in script. This logic bomb was set up to display a threatening and insulting message to his supervisor during login, execute the logic bomb, and remove all traces of itself from the system, including in log files, thus framing his supervisor for the malicious act. The insider was caught after arousing suspicion by comments to a coworker after planting the logic bomb.

The organization heeded warnings by the coworker, shut down the servers, discovered the problem, removed the destructive code, and reestablished system security and integrity before the logic bomb executed. Fortunately, the logic bomb never executed. The insider was sentenced to 15 months in prison, three years of supervised release, and $108,000 in restitution.

## Sabotage Case 12

A database administrator and project manager at a government agency became increasingly disgruntled when her male coworkers began to override her technical decisions where she was the expert. She filed complaints with HR over what she considered a hostile work environment, but she was not satisfied with their response. After she filed a complaint against her supervisor, her performance reviews, which had been stellar, went downhill. Her supervisor then demoted her by removing her project management responsibilities. Again she complained, but her supervisor started filing complaints against her with human resources for failure to follow instructions. She next filed a complaint with the EEOC for discrimination based on her national origin, race, and gender. She eventually resigned and transferred to another government agency because she was frustrated by the organization's lack of responsiveness to her complaints.

Two months following her resignation, she found out her EEOC grievance against the organization had been denied. The last straw was when she found out that the organization only forwarded her negative performance reviews to the new organization where she was now employed. She connected from her computer at home to her previous organization. She used another employee's username and password to log in to the system. Next she accessed a critical system using a database administrator (DBA) account password, which had not been changed since she resigned, and deleted critical data from the system. She dropped critical tables from the database, unaware that the database backups had been failing for two weeks. Recovery efforts required 115 employees working a total of 1,800 hours to reenter the data manually; the systems were down for three days. Remote access, database, and Internet service provider (ISP) logs connected the insider to the incident. The insider was arrested, convicted, ordered to pay $35,000 in restitution, and sentenced to five months of home detention followed by three years of supervised release.

## Sabotage Case 13

A government claims representative had a confrontation in an online chat room that was unrelated to his work. Because he had access to a critical

U.S. government database, he was able to change the chat room moderator's status in the database so that she appeared as deceased. The insider was apparently getting revenge on the moderator for kicking him out of the online forum. The incident was detected when the moderator tried to open a bank account and was informed that she was listed as deceased in the government database. The action caused the moderator enormous inconvenience in financial transactions that were disrupted due to her deceased status. The insider was connected to the incident by the victim, who identified the insider by the picture he used in the chat room. The insider was apologetic and stated he did not realize the extent of the damage he would be causing by his actions. The insider was convicted, sentenced to one year of probation, and fined.

## Sabotage Case 14

An e-commerce developer decided to move his family to a different state. As a matter of organizational policy, he could no longer work as a full-time employee, so he was hired as a consultant. He traveled across state lines to work two days a week and telecommuted three days a week from home. The relationship between the organization and the insider deteriorated due to his disgruntlement over his perceived inadequate benefits after becoming a consultant. Finally, the organization told him his employment would be terminated in approximately one month. After a week and a half, he logged in remotely from home, deleted the software he was developing, as well as software being developed by others, modified the system logs to conceal his actions, and then changed the root password. He then joined a telephone conference, never mentioning what he had done. After the telephone conference ended, he reported that he was having problems logging in, again to conceal his actions. At the end of the day he announced his resignation. The sabotage was detected when the organization noticed the missing software. Forensic audits revealed that the server had been accessed from the insider's ISP's domain. The insider's attack cost the organization more than $25,000, including 230 staff hours and associated costs. The insider was convicted, sentenced to three years of probation, and ordered to pay more than $25,000 in restitution.

## Sabotage Case 15

A consultant for a company that managed client data and business operations for other companies had a verbal contract with the organization and was its principal software developer. He repeatedly made demands over the course of a year for partial ownership of the company. The organization finally informed him that in five months he would be reduced to part-time status, lowering his compensation and benefits. The day after his demotion to part-time status, the insider, during work hours, remotely logged in to the organization's computer system. He removed critical code from the system, preventing employees and authorized users from accessing software he had created that was used to manage client data and business operations. The organization detected the attack when customers reported their inability to access the system. The organization connected the insider to the attack when an employee contacted him for technical support and he revealed that he had taken the program down in order to acquire 20% of the company. The owner of the organization, accompanied by corporate counsel, contacted the insider via telephone. He admitted that he had taken down the computer system, intending to disrupt the organization's business operations, and indicated that he would not cause any more disruptions if the organization met his demands. Three days later, the organization had not met the insider's demands, so he remotely accessed the system and modified passwords, preventing employees and authorized users from accessing the computer system. He was convicted, ordered to pay $10,000 in restitution, and sentenced to six months of home detention followed by two years of probation.

## Sabotage Case 16

The insider worked for an ISP that provided wired and wireless Internet service to residential and business customers. As part of its service, the organization provided communication services in interstate and foreign commerce and communication. The ISP's technology used wireless radio (Wi-Fi) signals between radio towers and its customers' wireless access points. Radio towers and access points were operated by computers at the organization's facilities.

The insider left the ISP over business and financial disputes and went to work for a direct competitor. In his attack on his ex-employer's network, the insider used administrator accounts to take control of the ISP's network. He reprogrammed 110 of the ISP's customers' wireless access points to cut off their Internet service. He executed his written programs and commands on the radio-tower computers. The execution caused the radio-tower computers to send commands to customers' access points, which prevented customers from accessing the Internet. The disconnected services included the service of one customer who was relying on electronic mail for news of an organ donor. Unfortunately, no recovery plan for remote access to customer configurations had ever been conceived. Unable to remotely repair the network, the ISP dispatched technicians to the premises of the subscribers who lost Internet access. Servicing all customers took the ISP three weeks, leaving some customers without Internet access for that entire period. The insider's action also caused the ISP's access points to repeatedly broadcast radio signals that interfered with the signals of another ISP.

In total, more than 170 customers (including individuals, families, and businesses) lost Internet service, some of them for as long as three weeks, and collectively caused more than $65,000 in losses. The insider was convicted, ordered to pay $65,000 in restitution, and sentenced to 24 months of imprisonment followed by periods of supervised release and community service.

## Sabotage Case 17

A system administrator, fearing layoffs, embedded malicious code within scripts on his organization's servers, which were responsible for managing prescription benefit plans. The incident spanned a year and two months from the creation of the malicious code to its detection. The malicious code, a timed logic bomb, was set to execute on his next birthday, approximately six months in the future. Had he been successful, the code would have wiped out critical data on more than 70 servers and caused widespread financial damage. It also would have caused potential health risks to the organization's customers. Even after surviving the layoffs, the insider did not remove the malicious code; in fact, he modified it one month later. The malicious code contained a programming error and failed to execute on his birthday as scheduled. However, he allegedly corrected the programming error six months later, setting the code to execute on his next birthday.

Fortunately, a few months before the intended execution date, another system administrator investigating a system error discovered the malicious code and disabled it. The insider was convicted, ordered to pay $81,200 in restitution, and sentenced to 30 months of imprisonment.

## Sabotage Case 18

An employee of a company that set up a new wireless network for a major manufacturer was on the installation team, and therefore had detailed knowledge of the manufacturer's systems. He was removed from the team by his employer, apparently under negative circumstances. The insider, posing as an authorized technical support provider, used password information obtained from his previous employer to access 60 of the manufacturer's computer kiosks located in the visitors' lobby. Based on his familiarity with the manufacturer's computer system and security, he was able to use the kiosks to delete files and passwords from wireless devices used by the manufacturer across the country. The manufacturer was forced to remove and repair the devices, causing widespread shutdown of facilities and disruption of its processes. The manufacturer sustained nearly $30,000 in damages incurred by removal and repair of the devices and shutting down the facilities for seven and a half hours. The insider was convicted, sentenced to one year of probation, and ordered to pay $30,000 in restitution.

## Sabotage Case 19

A programmer at a telecommunications company was angry when it was announced that there would be no bonuses. He used the computer of the project leader, who sat in a cubicle and often left his computer logged in and unattended, to modify his company's premier product, an inter-network communication interface. His modification, consisting of two lines of code, inserted the character *i* at random places in the supported transmission stream and during protocol initialization. The malicious code was inserted as a logic bomb, recorded in the company's configuration management system, and attributed to the project leader. Six months later, the insider left the company to take another job. Six months after that, the logic bomb finally detonated. The incident was initially detected by customers, who reported that they could not use the company's services. Software developers at the organization discovered the malicious insertion, removed the logic bomb, and reissued the code. The lead developer suspected that the insider was responsible for the incident, and identified the insider as the perpetrator through audit logs. The insider was convicted, ordered to pay $16,000 in restitution, sentenced to six months of home detention, and required to perform community service.

## Sabotage Case 20

A market trend product analysis organization failed to disable a former application developer's accounts or change account passwords upon termination. One month after termination, he remotely logged in to the organization's systems, modified its Web site (including the insertion of pornographic images), changed system passwords, and sent emails to customers saying that their accounts had been hacked and their passwords stolen. The emails included the client's username and password. The incident involved two separate attacks, which were more than a month apart. Web logs showed the IP address used to launch the attack was associated with the insider's wife's ISP account. The organization spent $53,000 and more than 330 hours repairing the damage. The insider was convicted, ordered to pay more than $48,000 in restitution, and sentenced to five months of imprisonment followed by two years of supervised probation.

## Sabotage Case 21

An IT worker was located in the network support department of a telecommunications company that administered an emergency 911 system. One Friday night, the insider deleted the entire database and software from three servers in the organization's network operations center (NOC) by gaining physical access using a contractor's badge, which he later claimed to have found. The NOC, which was left unattended, was solely protected via physical security; all machines in the room were left logged in with system administrator access. The motivation of this particular insider was a bit unusual: A new boss was starting work on Monday, and on Friday night he decided he would "play the hero" to gain favorable attention from the new boss on Monday morning. Obviously, the impacts were huge, since he brought down the 911 systems on a Friday night.

Although the NOC system administrators were immediately notified of the system failure via an automatic paging system, there were no automated failover mechanisms. The organization's recovery plan relied solely on backup tapes, which were also stored in the NOC. Unfortunately, the insider, realizing that the systems could be easily recovered, took all of the backup tapes with him when he left the facility. In addition, the same contractor's badge was authorized for access to the off-site backup storage facility, from which the insider next stole more than 50 additional backup tapes. The insider turned himself in and physical access logs connected him to the incident. He was convicted, ordered to pay more than $200,000 in restitution, and sentenced to five years of probation, including six months of home detention.

## Sabotage Case 22

An employee working in a technical support role at an ISP was caught with unauthorized software on his computer, specifically a credit card number verification program and a **network sniffer.**[2] As a result, the ISP suspended his Internet access. Angered by this, he recruited a friend, an outsider, to help him retaliate. Both the insider and his friend were active members of a hacking group, and regularly attended the organization's meetings. They used **IRC channels**[3] to communicate back and forth with each other and to relay information under assumed hacker names in an attempt to mask their identities. The outsider obtained root access to the organization's system via a buffer overflow attack. The outsider accessed company systems, perused email, monitored the network, and ran a sniffer, which emailed him results every morning. The outsider obtained multiple user IDs and passwords, which he used to attack the organization's systems. The two were able to gather enough information about the organization's systems that they successfully defaced the organization's Web site. A coworker of the insider discovered that he was attending organized hacker meetings. The insider responded by threatening his coworker's health via IRC chat. Access logs connected the insider and outsider to the incident. The insider was arrested, convicted, ordered to pay a $4,000 fine, and sentenced to one year of imprisonment.

## Sabotage Case 23

A computer technician with privileged access at a network communications company was fired only a month after starting his job because he refused to give his Social Security number to the human resources department, and he failed to disclose prior criminal convictions. Before leaving the organization, he stole Personally Identifiable Information (PII) for 8,000 employees and posted it to a Web site he had established to smear the organization's image. The Web site threatened to publish more information and link it to underground sites known to facilitate and engage in identity theft and fraud. He also protested outside the organization's offices and used his picketing sign to advertise his Web site.

He sent emails to the organization's executives, directing them to his Web site—using an ISP account that was registered under the name of

---

2. **Network sniffer** (also known as a sniffer): a computer program or a piece of hardware that can intercept and log traffic passing through a network.

3. **Internet Relay Chat (IRC) channel:** functionally similar to a multiuser chat instance.

the organization's chairman. The IP address associated with the action was connected to an ISP account registered to the insider's wife. The organization obtained a temporary restraining order directing the insider to stop publicizing its employees' PII. After a process server attempted to deliver a copy of the restraining order to him, the insider posted a threat to kill the process server on his Web site. He also threatened the organization's assistant general counsel (including posting a detailed map to her home on the site) and the chairman of the victim organization. He was convicted and sentenced to 46 months of imprisonment. After his release, he had severely limited access to computers and was restricted from communication with the victims of his threats as well as witnesses.

### Sabotage Case 24

A programmer in a logistics company was terminated as the result of a reorganization within the company. The company followed proper procedures by escorting him to his office to collect his belongings and then out of the building. The IT staff also followed the company's security policy by disabling his remote access and changing passwords. However, they overlooked one password that was known to only three people in the organization. The terminated insider used that account to gain access to the system the night of his termination and to delete the programs he had created while working there. The organization detected the incident when one of the servers and several financial packages failed. The insider had installed several backdoors and was one of only two people who knew the password to the account used in the attack. Restoration of the deleted files from backup failed. Although the insider had been responsible for backups, company personnel believe that the backups were not maliciously corrupted. The backups had simply not been tested to ensure that they were properly recording the critical data. As a result, the organization's operations in North and South America were shut down for two days, causing more than $80,000 in losses. The insider was convicted, ordered to pay $80,000 in restitution, and sentenced to one year in prison followed by six months of home confinement.

## Sabotage/Fraud Cases

Table 8-2 provides an index of sabotage/fraud cases in the CERT insider threat database.

**Table 8-2** *Sabotage/Fraud Cases*

| Case # | Industry or Government Sector | Description |
|---|---|---|
| 1 | Banking and finance | DBA works with Internet underground for two years to commit fraud using employee data |
| 2 | Information technology | Sole security administrator for small firm holds company hostage for more pay and launches attacks from its network |
| 3 | Information technology | VP of engineering quits, takes source code and backups, and demands $50,000 for its return |

## Sabotage/Fraud Case 1

A DBA responsible for a very large database containing personal employee information for an insurance company became frustrated over time by what he perceived to be unfairly low pay. He took revenge against the organization over a two-year period. He downloaded personal information associated with employees from the database to removable media, resulting in the compromise of 60,000 employee records. He solicited bids for the sale of the information over the Internet by using message boards to advertise the availability of the information to individuals whom he hoped would be able to fraudulently use the information. He also leveraged newsgroups dedicated to credit card fraud to post employee credit card numbers and encouraged the malicious use of these credit cards or others obtained in the names of victim employees. Law enforcement eventually captured the insider when an undercover agent posed as a potential buyer of the insider's stolen information. He was convicted, ordered to pay $3,000 in restitution, and sentenced to three years of probation with required participation in a mental health program.

## Sabotage/Fraud Case 2

The sole security administrator for a small telecommunications firm quit his job with no advance notice. During his tenure with the firm, he had expressed feelings of dissatisfaction due to insufficient gratitude and compensation for his work, and also had a series of conflicts with coworkers. He had a lengthy history of pirating material online and had committed prior electronic crimes related to unauthorized system and network access. Following his termination, a manager at the organization called him at home to request administrative passwords since he had not turned them over to anyone when he quit his job. He refused to disclose the administrative passwords until he received additional pay to which he felt entitled. He turned them over three days later, after locking the organization out of all administrative functions. For a month afterward, he used backdoor accounts he had created previously to remotely access the organization's systems and delete files that he had created during his employment. He also changed the DNS records for the Internet-facing servers to point to another server named to slander the organization, and launched offensive attacks from within the organization's network. For instance, he used the victim's network to run network scanning tools against military networks. He was convicted, ordered to pay a $3,000 fine, and sentenced to two years of supervised probation.

### Sabotage/Fraud Case 3

A vice president of engineering who was responsible for oversight of all software development in his company was engaged in a long-running dispute with upper management. This dispute was characterized by verbal attacks by the insider and statements to colleagues about the degree of upset he had caused to management. He engaged in personal attacks once or twice a week and on one occasion, in a restaurant, screamed personal attacks at the CEO of the company. A final explosive disagreement prompted the insider to quit. When no severance package was offered, he copied a portion of a software product under development to removable media, deleted it from the company's server, and removed the recent backup tapes. He then offered to restore the software in exchange for $50,000. Unfortunately, the most recent version of the software was never recovered. The insider was convicted, sentenced to five years of probation, and ordered to pay restitution.

# Theft of IP Cases

Table 8-3 provides an index of theft of intellectual property cases in the CERT insider threat database.

**Table 8-3** *Theft of IP Cases*

| Case # | Industry or Government Sector | Description |
|--------|------------------------------|-------------|
| 1 | Chemical | Product development director is caught stealing IP when laptop he returned upon termination is examined |
| 2 | Defense industrial base | Former systems engineer modifies the company's software slightly and sells it abroad for new employer |
| 3 | Government | Large downloads from the network trigger investigation that leads to former contract programmer |
| 4 | Information technology | Insiders from multiple high-tech companies steal IP and start company funded by foreign government |
| 5 | Information technology | Company's IP is stolen by nephew of an employee of a trusted business partner's trusted business partner |
| 6 | Information technology | Trio of insiders conspire to steal IP, give it to foreign manufacturer, and receive commissions from that company's sales |

## Theft of IP Case 1

The insider worked as a chemist and later a product development director at a paint manufacturing plant. He made a business trip abroad to work with one of his organization's subsidiaries, and a coworker noticed that he was unusually interested in a competitor based in another country. A few weeks after the trip, the insider resigned abruptly. This raised some suspicion at his organization. They investigated the company laptop he had returned and noticed that he had deleted all of the temporary files. Upon further examination, they discovered a hidden file that contained, among other things, a prohibited data copy program and 44 GB of unauthorized data that included the organization's intellectual property. Upon executing a search warrant, authorities confiscated a USB drive from the insider's luggage as he was attempting to leave the country. The drive contained IP belonging to the organization, including formulas for products that the insider had not worked on and thus had no legitimate reason to possess. The authorities also noticed that his LinkedIn profile stated that he was now employed by a similar company in another country. The duration of the incident was approximately five months, but the majority of the trade secret theft occurred in the two weeks prior to his resignation. He was convicted, sentenced to 15 months of imprisonment and three years of supervised release, and ordered to pay more than $30,000 in restitution.

## Theft of IP Case 2

A senior systems engineer at a visual simulation company resigned; at his exit interview he falsely stated that he had returned all proprietary information as required by the IP agreement he had signed as a precondition to employment. After he moved abroad, a month after his resignation, he agreed to serve as an independent consultant to his former employer and continued to access the company's proprietary information. Over a three-month period while serving as a consultant, he compiled and coerced others to compile proprietary source code in direct violation of company policy. Before terminating his consultancy with the company, he accepted a job with a competitor based outside the United States. For a year after leaving the company, he made several product demonstrations to various foreign agents and customers using the information he stole. During several of the presentations, he slightly modified the stolen intellectual property to make it appear as though his new employer had developed it. He was eventually arrested when an individual at one of his demonstrations noticed that the product he was displaying belonged to his former employer and notified the authorities. He was convicted, but the case material does not state whether the IP was returned to the victim company or recovered from the competitor. The insider was ordered to pay a $10,000 fine and sentenced to two years of imprisonment followed by a period of probation.

## Theft of IP Case 3

The insider was formerly contracted as a programmer by a government organization that maintained an authoritative medical database. The organization notified him that his access to a system under development was being disabled and that his further responsibilities would be limited to testing activities. After his protests were denied, he quit the organization. Then, three times over a two-week period, he used a backdoor into the system with administrator privilege (which he presumably installed before leaving) to download source code and password files from the developmental system. The unusually large size of the remote downloads raised red flags in the organization, which resulted in an investigation that traced the downloads to the former contractor's residence. He was convicted, ordered to pay $10,000 in restitution, and sentenced to five months of imprisonment followed by a period of probation.

## Theft of IP Case 4

The "lead" insider and an accomplice worked as engineers at two different high-technology companies. In addition, the lead insider worked at two other high-technology companies. From the four companies, the individuals stole various IP and started a company funded by a foreign government to sell products based on the stolen information. They attempted to recruit other insiders to steal information and work for their company. The resultant investigation revealed that both insiders possessed IP, including physical documents, in their homes and offices. Unfortunately, reports of the crime do not specify the exact time frame of the insiders' employment in the companies or of the series of thefts. Both individuals were convicted and sentenced to one year in prison. With the insiders' cooperation, authorities seized IP belonging to all four companies that was in the insiders' possession.

## Theft of IP Case 5

The outside legal counsel for a high-tech company was preparing to represent the company in civil litigation. The outside counsel was provided with documents containing the company's trade secrets, which were necessary to prepare the legal case. The legal firm had a contract with a document imaging company for copying documents for its cases. An employee of the document imaging company brought in his nephew to help him copy the company's information, including the trade secret documents, due to the amount of work required. The nephew, a university student not officially on the payroll, converted scanned **TIFF images**[4] of trade secret documentation associated with anti-piracy technology to PDF format and transmitted them to the leader of an online community whose purpose was to pirate telecommunication services. The forum administrator originally refused to post the information, stating it was too sensitive to be released, but eventually did so under pressure from the nephew who had stolen it. The nephew's goal was to help the hacker community crack the high-tech company's premier product. Attorneys for the other organization involved in litigation with the victim organization discovered the information online and notified the victim

---

4. **TIFF images:** Tagged Image File Format (or .tif) is a file type often used in image manipulation programs.

organization. The nephew was convicted, ordered to pay approximately $146,000 in restitution, and sentenced to home confinement and probation.

## Theft of IP Case 6

A senior engineer, his wife, and another accomplice all worked for an auto parts manufacturer. The insider's wife quit her job as a vice president of sales, and conspired with the accomplice inside the organization to set up a new company. The trio intended to steal proprietary information from the auto parts manufacturer in the United States, provide it to a manufacturer based outside the United States, and then receive commissions on sales made by the manufacturer. While still employed by the auto parts manufacturer, the engineer was able to copy hundreds of files to CDs, including proprietary design and manufacturing process information. He then relayed this information to his wife, who proceeded to forward it to the external manufacturer. The theft was detected and reported by the suppliers to the external manufacturer, when they received email about the proprietary manufacturing processes. The primary insider—the senior engineer—was convicted and sentenced to six months of imprisonment followed by periods of house arrest and probation. The conspirators were also convicted and imprisoned.

# Fraud Cases

Table 8-4 provides an index of fraud cases in the CERT insider threat database.

**Table 8-4** *Fraud Cases*

| Case # | Industry or Government Sector | Description |
|---|---|---|
| 1 | Banking and finance | Loan officer is recruited to steal identity information from her customers as part of a six-person identity theft ring |
| 2 | Banking and finance | More than $4 million in risky loans result from ring of coworkers who modify credit histories for pay |

| 3 | Banking and finance | Foreign-currency trader covers up trading losses for five years |
|---|---|---|
| 4 | Commercial facilities | Insider intentionally opens infected email attachment, installing malicious code that sends confidential information to his company's competitor |
| 5 | Defense industrial base | Computer help desk attendant at a military contractor steals more than $8 million worth of equipment using fake email addresses |
| 6 | Emergency services | Police communications operator creates 195 illegal driver's licenses due to lack of role-based access controls |
| 7 | Food | Group shares their passwords so that they can work more efficiently |
| 8 | Government–Federal | Supervisor uses his authority and privileged access to grant asylum to foreign nationals who had been denied asylum in the United States |
| 9 | Government–Federal | After being promoted, insider retains old role and new role in a system, enabling her to enter and approve of fraudulent transactions |
| 10 | Government–State/ Local | Insider with multiple roles is able to authorize payments of more than $250,000 to his wife |
| 11 | Government–State/ Local | Manager instructs subordinate to reformat backup tapes, destroying the evidence against him |
| 12 | Health care | Subcontractor changes address of medical provider and has checks sent to her accomplice |

## Fraud Case 1

The insider was a loan officer in a financial institution. The incident was part of a massive identity theft ring composed of six individuals. They stole identities from at least 25 people, and then used the identities to defraud ten financial institutions and 25 retailers in multiple states for a total of $335,000 over a four-year period. The ringleader, an outsider, carefully recruited participants, each with a specific role in the scheme. This particular insider was recruited to steal personal and financial information of customers applying for a mortgage with her company, and another insider, an employee at an escrow firm, stole financial information of her company's clients. The insider's part in the crime occurred over a ten-month period. The information was used by two members of the crime ring with equipment to create counterfeit driver's licenses. The remaining conspirators used the licenses to open new credit accounts with banks and retailers, purchased goods and services with the new accounts, and drained the cash from existing checking and savings accounts of the victims. The incident was detected by a probation officer, who discovered equipment for creating false identification documents at the home of one of the coconspirators. The insider was convicted, ordered to pay $200,000 in restitution, and sentenced to 18 months of imprisonment.

## Fraud Case 2

The insider maintained the information in the consumer credit database at a consumer credit report organization. In exchange for money from an external collaborator, she conspired with coworkers to artificially inflate the credit scores of specific consumers to enable them to secure loans from credit institutions and lenders. Over four months, she and her internal conspirators modified or deleted credit-history data for 178 consumers. The purpose was to strengthen their creditworthiness and cause lenders to issue loans to these consumers. She received advance payment for the modification and passed the payment on to coworkers to make the alterations in the database. She was experiencing financial difficulties, which motivated her to participate in the scheme. More than $4 million of risky loans resulted in this case. It cost the organization $5,000 to restore the integrity of the information in the database, but the organization also had to pay more than $675,000 to creditors. The insider was arrested, convicted, ordered to pay a $3,000 fine, and sentenced to five months of imprisonment followed by five months of home detention and three years of supervised release. She fully cooperated with authorities, which led to the sentencing of her two coconspirators.

## Fraud Case 3

A foreign-currency trader in a financial institution was responsible for collecting and trading assets for the organization in order to generate profits. His annual bonus was a function of how much profit was produced for the organization by his trades. However, he started losing money on trades. Fearing job-related consequences, he executed a complex fraud scheme that involved convincing other employees not to track his trades or validate them, exploiting the fact that the organization did not record trading phone calls, and using remote access to the organization's computing facilities to continue the fraud. The scheme lasted five years. While initially most of his fraud occurred at work, he increasingly found it easier to conduct his illicit activities from home in the middle of the night because he did not have to worry about anyone in the office or at home looking over his shoulder.

At one point, the insider threatened to quit when managers became suspicious and pressed him regarding his practices. An internal audit, combined with external observation, detected the insider's illicit activities, specifically large transactions he had made. After his arrest, he claimed to have had difficulty keeping the scheme alive, and to have developed a drug abuse problem along the way. He said that group trading (trading by a team of traders), rather than individual trading, can help mitigate an organization's risks, because it is easier to detect illegal or suspicious trading practices when there are multiple team members trading from the same account. He did not directly profit from the scheme, but acquired $650,000 in bonuses by making it appear that the bank was profiting instead of losing vast sums of money. He was convicted, ordered to pay $700 million in restitution, and sentenced to more than seven years of imprisonment followed by five years of probation. The insider was required to pay the victim organization $1,000 a month during probation.

## Fraud Case 4

A salesman for an information analysis provider was recruited by an outsider employed by a competing firm to relay his company's private communications. The outsider sent the insider an email message containing an attachment infected with a virus. The outsider offered the insider $1,000 for each of the company's computers he helped to infect with the virus. The insider deliberately double-clicked on the infected attachment, and as a result installed the malicious program, a keystroke logger, on several machines on his company's network. Over a period of three weeks, the keystroke logger periodically sent confidential information to the outsider, who used it to lure customers away from the victim organization. The insider and an internal accomplice were convicted and ordered to pay $5,000 in restitution.

## Fraud Case 5

A computer help desk attendant employed by a military contractor executed a scheme whereby he would fraudulently request replacement equipment parts from a supplier and then sell them for as much as he could get. The supplier would send replacement parts expecting that the recalled originals would be returned. He used fake email addresses, which he created on the military systems for which he was responsible, to request the replacement parts. He provided his home address for the shipments in the email. The scheme worked perfectly and, of course, the original equipment was never returned to the supplier. Over 20 months, he received shipments of 500 products with a retail value of more than $8 million. He sold 90 of those products through an Internet auction site for more than $500,000. He admitted that he needed money to care for his elderly parents. He was convicted and ordered to pay more than $8 million in restitution, and was sentenced to more than four years in prison followed by two years of supervised release.

## Fraud Case 6

The primary responsibility of the insider, a police communications operator, was to communicate information for driver's licenses, such as license validity and vehicle registration, to law enforcement officers in the field. She was recruited by an outside acquaintance and, for more than two and a half years, she provided driver's license information in return for payment. The fraud escalated when she started using other functions in the system to issue fake driver's licenses to people who were not able to obtain legitimate licenses. Fortunately, a confidential informant led to her arrest and conviction for fraudulently creating approximately 195 illegal driver's licenses. She was convicted and sentenced to 37 months in prison.

## Fraud Case 7

Two temporary data entry clerks and one permanent employee of an agricultural products firm manipulated data to fraudulently issue payments to their relatives. The employees were part of a group that openly shared their passwords to enhance productivity; it was "more efficient" to share passwords to overcome separation of duties constraints in the systems. Over a five-month period, clerks were able to use privileged accounts to subvert the business process governing vendor payment. First, they entered valid data into the database using their own accounts. Then they used the privileged accounts for which they had been given the password to modify the vendor's name and address to that of a friend or relative, issued the check from the system, and then modified the data back to the original, valid vendor information. The fraud was discovered when an accountant in the general ledger department noticed that the number of checks issued was larger than normal and further investigation revealed the irregularities in the handling of the checks. The malicious insiders were identified by the names of their relatives on the account. In the end, the insiders embezzled almost $70,000. The primary insider was convicted and sentenced to eight months of imprisonment followed by three years of supervised release, including community service and fines.

## Fraud Case 8

The insider supervised individuals processing asylum applications for the U.S. government. He fraudulently altered U.S. immigration asylum decisions using his organization's computer system in return for payments of up to several thousand dollars per case. He would approve an asylum decision himself, request that one of his subordinates approve the decision, or overturn someone else's denial of an asylum application. An outsider, who was likely a non-U.S. native, recruited the foreign nationals who wished to acquire political asylum. To conceal his activity, the insider used his subordinates' computers and credentials. Several foreign nationals either admitted in an interview or pleaded guilty in a court of law to lying on their asylum applications and bribing public officials to approve their applications. The insider received $50,000 for granting political asylum for 20 to 30 foreign nationals. The fraud was detected by the director of the insider's office and was reported to law enforcement. The insider was convicted and sentenced to 21 months of imprisonment.

## Fraud Case 9

A supervisor in a department handling disability claims used her own account to modify claims and direct monthly disability payments to her fiancé over almost two years. The organization failed to update her access rights when she changed positions, enabling her to modify data and also to approve the changes. Both positions used the same application but different roles for entering, approving, and authorizing payments for medical and disability claims. When she was promoted, she was authorized for her new access level, but administrators neglected to rescind her prior access level. As a result, she ended up having full access to the application, with no one else required to authorize transactions (payments) from the system. She also recruited a coworker to increase the disability rating on her fiancé's claim, which increased the amount of the monthly checks. The coworker detected the incident when she recognized the insider's fiancé's name and reported that he was not disabled. The insider was convicted, ordered to pay $615,000 in restitution, and sentenced to 33 months of imprisonment followed by two years of supervised release and 50 hours of community service.

## Fraud Case 10

A requisition officer in a city warehouse convinced his supervisor that he needed privileged access to the entire purchasing system. He used his legitimate, but excessive, access privileges to modify the city's database to add a fake vendor, create purchase requisitions, and modify the inventory system. Over a period of two years, he entered 78 purchase orders for the fake vendor, and, although no supplies were ever received, he also authorized payment to the vendor. He was aware of approval procedures, and all of his fraudulent purchases fell beneath the threshold for independent approval. The bank account for the vendor, which was credited more than $250,000 as part of the scheme, was owned by the insider's wife. The fraud was accidentally detected by a finance clerk who noticed irregularities in the paperwork accompanying one of the purchase orders. The insider was convicted, ordered to pay a $600 fine and $10,000 in restitution (the organization's insurance deductible), and sentenced to two consecutive sentences of 36 months of imprisonment followed by five years of probation.

## Fraud Case 11

A computer information resource manager in an organization that operated a state lottery modified computer records and fraudulently claimed prizes for lottery tickets for 18 months. To carry out the scam, he purchased a ticket as usual, and then modified it to be a winner in the lottery agency's database. He purchased regular instant tickets but physically damaged them so that retailers had to use a special program to validate them directly against the corrupted agency database. The incident was detected when a suspicious retailer mailed the mangled tickets to a district manager, who confirmed that they were not winners. The insider was not initially suspected, until he started behaving strangely. Consequently, he was placed on administrative leave. Before he left on administrative leave, he deleted a history log that may have contained evidence of his criminal act. He also instructed one of his subordinates to reformat the backup tapes, claiming that they wouldn't be useful under a new backup data format that was being implemented. The subordinate complied with this request and the organization lost much of the evidence of his tampering with system security controls. He fraudulently won almost $63,000 from the state lottery system (he used 141 tickets and claimed prizes for 126 of them). He was convicted, ordered to pay the $63,000 restitution, fined $25,000, and sentenced to 60 days in jail and three years of probation.

### Fraud Case 12

The primary insider was a subcontractor working for an organization that handled state government employee health insurance claims. Using the medical identity number of an unsuspecting psychologist, she changed the name and address associated with the psychologist to an internal accomplice's name and address. Over two and a half months, she filed 40 fake claims and sent the payments to the bogus medical provider and address. One of her internal accomplices granted her the increased access she needed to perpetrate the fraud. Another accomplice was responsible for cashing the checks and distributing the money. Auditors discovered the scheme when they began questioning why a psychologist was submitting payment claims for treating broken bones and open wounds, and administering chemotherapy. They also noticed that the name associated with the psychologist was the name of one of their subcontractors. During the investigation it was determined that the primary insider had a criminal history for fraud. She was arrested on a separate fraud charge and accepted a plea bargain after one of her accomplices named her as the ringleader of the incident.

## Miscellaneous Cases

Table 8-5 provides an index of miscellaneous cases in the CERT insider threat database.

**Table 8-5** *Miscellaneous Cases*

| Case # | Industry or Government Sector | Description |
|---|---|---|
| 1 | Banking and finance | Former employee "eavesdrops" on executives' emails regarding pending employee terminations three years following termination |
| 2 | Education | Student gains access to his professor's university and personal account and changes his grade |
| 3 | Education | Student installs malicious program that steals personal information for 37,000 students |
| 4 | Government | Contractor "breaks" 40 organization passwords in order to prove his complaints about lack of security |
| 5 | Information technology | Millions of customer records are compromised by a system administrator at a trusted business partner's trusted business partner |
| 6 | Information technology | System administrator's customized login software catches former employee's unauthorized access |

## Miscellaneous Case 1

The vice president of technology at a finance market information publisher was dismissed after five years due to a disagreement with the organization. He oversaw the company's computer network and internal email system. Three years after termination, he went back into his former company's email system to eavesdrop on top executives' emails about employees' job status. He spied on email traffic from his home over a five-month period, curious about which employees were being terminated. He intercepted the emails of the human resources director and high-level executives that discussed employees' termination. He notified those employees of their possible termination. The employees who received the email warning notified their supervisors, who initiated an investigation. The victim organization spent more than $100,000 investigating the case. Remote access log files as well as records from Yahoo and the insider's ISP connected him to the crime. The insider was convicted, sentenced to one year of probation with six months of house arrest, and ordered to pay $30,000 in restitution and a $2,000 fine.

## Miscellaneous Case 2

A university student used several methods for gaining access to unauthorized authentication credentials for one of his professors over a period of about two months. First, he decrypted the password file on a departmental computer system and obtained the password for his professor's account. Using that password, he was able to gain access to the professor's personal account on Yahoo.com. The student also wrote and installed a program in the professor's computer account that would run when he logged in, capturing his user ID and password for the university's administrative computer system. The student obtained personal information, including grades, regarding other students and tried to change his grade for the class he took with the professor. Fortunately, the grade file that he modified was a backup file; the professor stored final grades on his personal laptop. University officials started an investigation when the professor received an email that his account had been compromised. The insider eventually confessed to university officials, and was subsequently convicted and sentenced to four months of imprisonment.

## Miscellaneous Case 3

A computer science major at a university wrote a malicious program to access a database on a server that was used as a portal for enrollment services. The attack allowed the student to steal 8,000 names and Social Security numbers along with 37,000 personal records. The university was alerted of problems when, on several occasions, the malicious program inadvertently shut down the university server. The insider was convicted, ordered to pay $170,000 in restitution, and sentenced to probation with community service.

## Miscellaneous Case 4

A disgruntled software developer complained about the lack of security in the systems of the organization with which he was contracted to provide services. When his complaints went unresolved, he downloaded the password file from one of the organization's UNIX servers to his desktop.

Next, he downloaded a password cracker from the Internet and proceeded to "break" approximately forty passwords, including the root password. Fortunately, he did no damage, but he did access parts of the organization's network for which he was not authorized. The insider was discovered when he bragged to the system administrator that he knew the root password. The insider was convicted, ordered to pay a $5,000 fine, and sentenced to probation and community service.

## Miscellaneous Case 5

A system administrator was employed by a marketing firm that was contracted by another organization, one of the world's largest processors of consumer data. As a result of the contractual relationship, he was given access to the contracting organization's FTP server so that he could periodically download sanitized, aggregated information from the consumer data organization's customers. The customers included banks, credit card companies, and phone companies. He found several unprotected files on the FTP server containing encrypted passwords for the original customer databases. He used a password-cracking program to discover the passwords to the customer databases belonging to the consumer data organization's customers (approximately 200 large companies). He proceeded to copy the personal data for millions of Americans to dozens of CDs. He bragged in online IRC channels about his access to confidential and personal data, and was asked at one point by another individual in the chat room to provide data on an FBI agent who was actively investigating him. He provided the information within minutes. The ongoing FBI investigation of that individual led back to the insider, who was found with dozens of CDs and other media containing millions of customer records in his apartment. There was no evidence of broad-scale distribution of the data; rather he appeared to be stealing the information to brag about it in IRC chat rooms. The insider was convicted, ordered to pay $2.7 million in restitution, and sentenced to 45 months of imprisonment followed by a period of supervised release.

## Miscellaneous Case 6

The insider was formerly employed as a contract software developer and tester by a telecommunications organization. He was terminated for poor performance and was subsequently employed by a subsidiary of the organization. Over a period of about a month, he accessed up to 16 of his former employer's systems on a daily basis during work hours. The insider gained access to at least 24 user accounts, read electronic mail, reviewed source code for his previous project, and deleted two software modification notices for the project. The activity was detected when a system administrator logged in one morning and was notified by her custom-written login software that her last login was one hour earlier. This set off immediate alarms, as she had in fact not logged in for several days. She had previously taken steps to redirect logging of actions by her account to a unique file rather than the standard shell history file. Therefore, she was able to trace the intruder's steps and saw that the intruder had read another employee's email using her account, and then deleted the standard history file for her account so that there would be no log of his actions. The login was traced to a computer at the company subsidiary. The insider was convicted and sentenced to two concurrent terms of probation, as well as unspecified fines and penalties.

## Summary

This chapter presented a variety of cases from the CERT insider threat database. We chose cases that exhibited different characteristics and from which different lessons can be learned. You may wish to refer back to this chapter periodically to test your own organization's countermeasures against these cases by asking the question: Could this happen to us?

# Chapter 9

# Conclusion and Miscellaneous Issues

This chapter wraps up the book by covering two miscellaneous issues that we mentioned briefly but did not cover in detail earlier: insider threats from trusted business partners, and malicious insiders with ties to the Internet underground. We conclude with a final summary, which could serve as a handy reference should you need a "cheat sheet" for future discussions on insider threat.

## Insider Threat from Trusted Business Partners

Trusted business partner (TBP): any external organization or individual an organization has contracted to perform a service for the organization. The nature of this service requires the organization to provide the TBP authorized access to proprietary data, critical files, and/or internal infrastructure. For example, if an organization contracts with a company to perform billing services, it would have to provide access to its customer data, thereby establishing a trusted business partnership. However, the TBP concept does not include cases in which the organization is simply a customer of another company. For example, when an organization uses a bank, it is simply a client of the bank. This customer–vendor relationship would not be considered a TBP relationship.

Trusted business partners can be individuals or other organizations.[1] For example, when an organization outsources its customer help desk support service to an outside company it enters into a TBP relationship with that company. In this case, the organization must grant access to its customer database to the outside company. On the other hand, TBPs also include individual consultants, temporary employees, and contractors, including any former employees of the organization who are then hired as consultants or contractors.

Use of TBPs is common in today's business environment for weathering the ups and downs of the economy without impacting the permanent workforce, and maximizing profits by outsourcing appropriate functions. That is why it is important that you read this section and carefully consider the potential insider threat risk posed by those contractors and business partners that you provide authorized access to for your systems, information, and networks.

A few examples of each type of TBP follow, in order to help you to understand the difference. First, we present a few examples of organizational TBP relationships. The first example is especially important as it is an insider threat from an IT services provider—an emerging threat in today's cloud computing environment.

> A company—the TBP—provided IT and information security solutions for its customers. One of its employees was an information security analyst who used his access to the customers' networks to steal 637,000 credit card numbers. He then advertised the stolen data for sale on an Internet site used for marketing stolen credit card information. Fortunately, he sold the majority of the credit card numbers to two undercover investigators; only 318 credit card numbers were sold to individuals that wanted to perpetrate credit card fraud. The insider was arrested and sentenced to 50 months of imprisonment.

> A financial institution was having problems with its computer system, so it contracted with a company to repair it—the TBP—and supplied the TBP with passwords for its systems. These passwords also provided access to other critical transaction systems. One of the employees at the contracted organization was having financial difficulties, and abused his access to the financial institution's systems to initiate fraudulent transactions. He accessed the Automated Clearing House (ACH) system and performed unauthorized transactions. He then used the money received from the

---

1. Material from this section includes portions from a joint CyLab and CERT Program article titled "Spotlight On: Insider Threat from Trusted Business Partners," authored by Robert Weiland, Andrew Moore, Dawn Cappelli, Randy Trzeciak, and Derrick Spooner [Weiland 2010].

falsified transactions to pay for construction projects on his properties, two mortgages, car loans, overseas vacations, and other debts. The money was transferred to his personal accounts, his wife's accounts, and his business's accounts. Cashier's checks were also purchased with fraudulent funds. The fraud was detected and reported by the insider's business partner at the TBP when he noticed large deposits to the business account. He contacted the victim organization, which then conducted an investigation using ACH data and system logs. The victim organization stated that the fraud would have likely gone undetected had it not been reported by the TBP itself. The insider was sentenced to five years in prison and five years of supervised release, and had to repay more than $1.8 million in restitution.

Next are two examples of individuals who were trusted business partners of the victim organization.

A contractor—the TBP—was formerly employed as a help desk and network technician by the victim organization. While working for the company, he had system administrator and remote access to the network, in order to perform maintenance and to troubleshoot problems from home. He was a temporary employee hoping to be hired into the organization full-time, but his application for full-time employment was rejected because he had received a poor performance review from his supervisor, who characterized him as volatile, angry, inflexible, and not a team player. The insider, who was trying to gain full custody of his daughter, also had financial issues. Due to cutbacks at the organization and rules surrounding temporary employment, he was informed that his employment would be terminated in two months. After learning of his pending termination, he wrote several emails to the organization's human resources department, threatening to sue the organization for unfair labor practices. As a result of the emails, he was immediately terminated. He used backdoors he had previously created to access the organization's network and removed access to systems, changed administrative passwords, deleted system event logging, and modified accounts associated with individuals who were involved with his termination. The insider's actions were discovered the following day when employees could not access the system. Fortunately, the insider had failed to delete all of the logs that connected him to the incident. He admitted responsibility for the incident, acknowledged that he made a mistake, and wanted to help minimize damages.

A contractor was employed as a process controls engineer by a manufacturing organization. He became angry with his supervisor and feared that his job was in jeopardy, so he disclosed the organization's technical drawings to another organization via email and fax over the course of one month. The insider was arrested, convicted, ordered to pay $1.3 million in restitution, and sentenced to 27 months in prison.

## Overview of Insider Threats from Trusted Business Partners

According to a recent study by the security companies RSA and Interactive Data Corporation (IDC), which surveyed C-level executives, "Contractors and temporary staff represent the greatest internal risk [to] organizations."[2] The purpose of this section is to raise awareness to the threat from trusted business partners; however, it is worth noting that contractors account for less than 10% of the cases in the CERT database. We are not saying that you should not be concerned about contractors; on the contrary, we advise you to consider insider threat risk from all individuals and organizations that have authorized access to your systems, networks, and information. It is concerning that C-level executives do not recognize the risk posed by their own employees.

Table 9-1 shows the breakdown of TBP cases by sector, including the percentages of all individual as well as organizational TBP cases.

**Table 9-1** *Breakdown of Trusted Business Partner Cases*

| Sector | Percentage of All Individual TBP Cases | Percentage of All Organizational TBP Cases |
|---|---|---|
| Banking and finance | 11% | 13% |
| Commercial facilities | 11% | 6% |
| Defense industrial base | 3% | 9% |
| Education | 6% | 3% |
| Energy | 3% | 3% |
| Food | 3% | — |
| Government | 19% | 22% |
| IT | 33% | 19% |
| Manufacturing | — | 3% |
| Not a member of a critical sector | — | 6% |
| Public health | 11% | 13% |
| Water | — | 3% |

---

2. See www.rsa.com/solutions/business/insider_risk/wp/10388_219105.pdf.

**Table 9-2** *Breakdown of Trusted Business Partner Cases by Type of Crime*

| Type of Crime | Percentage |
| --- | --- |
| Fraud | 26% |
| IT sabotage | 41% |
| Theft of IP | 20% |
| Miscellaneous | 14% |

We will leave it to each sector to interpret the information in Table 9-1. However, we do recommend that the sectors with the highest percentages seriously consider their business processes and technical measures for contractors and/or trusted business partners.

Table 9-2 shows the breakdown of TBP cases by type of crime. It is important that you understand the meaning of this table in your strategy for mitigating insider threats from TBPs.

## Fraud Committed by Trusted Business Partners

You are at risk of fraud committed by TBPs when you hire contractors for positions requiring access to Personally Identifiable Information (PII), sensitive customer information, or financial information. Likewise, if you outsource business functions requiring that level of access, you put yourself at risk of insider fraud. In addition, any systems that manipulate sensitive information provide an opportunity for TBPs—contractors or employees at outsourced operations—to accept payments from outsiders for illicit transactions. In summary, you need to consider everything you read in Chapter 4, Insider Fraud, when you hire contractors or outsource applicable business functions.

For example, consider the following case:

> A claims processor at a company contracted by an insurance company used authorized access to divert millions of dollars through falsified insurance claims to a personal address. The insider got away with the crime because there was no system in place to double-check the edited claims.

This case is very similar to the types of cases we discussed in Chapter 4. The only difference is that the insider worked for a trusted business partner, rather than at the victim organization. Note how this situation complicates the mitigation strategy for this type of case! If the victim organization performed this function in-house, it could design its business process to mitigate this threat, and implement auditing controls to detect any malfeasance. Since this function was outsourced, the victim organization could consider several countermeasures.

- Review the TBP's business process.
- Implement separation of duties by only outsourcing the data entry process, retaining the approval process in-house.
- Perform auditing functions against the TBP's data.

The bottom line is that while it might appear that outsourcing business functions will result in cost savings, be sure to factor in the insider threat risk from your new "insiders" at the TBP before making your final decision.

## IT Sabotage Committed by Trusted Business Partners

Recall from Chapter 2, Insider IT Sabotage, that this crime is committed by technically privileged users who seek revenge for negative work-related events; the crime often is set up prior to termination, but carried out following termination. You are at risk of insider IT sabotage by contractors who are on your IT staff or those hired as contract programmers. In addition, if you subcontract with a firm for any type of IT support or services, you are exposing yourself to insider threats from the firm's staff. This is particularly important in a cloud type of environment.

Consider the following case:

> A contractor was employed as a programmer and UNIX engineer by the victim organization, a mortgage company. The organization notified the insider that his contract would be terminated for a script error he had made earlier in the month, but the insider was permitted to finish out the day at work. Subsequently, he planted a logic bomb in a script that would have disabled monitoring alerts and logins, deleted the root passwords for 4,000 of the organization's servers, and erased all data, including backup data, on those servers by overwriting it with zeros. The script was designed to remain dormant for three months and to greet administrators with a login message that read, "server graveyard." Five days later, another engineer at the organization detected the malicious code. The insider was subsequently arrested, but details regarding the verdict were unavailable at the time of this writing.[3]

This case is very similar to the IT sabotage cases described in Chapter 2. In fact, the mitigation strategies described in that chapter apply equally well

---

3. Because no verdict was known, the insider's actions described in this case are alleged.

to both contractors and employees. For example, the organization should not have allowed the insider to access the network after being fired. It also could have imposed targeted monitoring of the insider's online activities once it determined it was going to fire him. It is unclear how the organization detected the logic bomb, so it is actually quite possible that it might have had countermeasures like these in place, which is why it was able to detect the logic bomb and prevent its destructive effects.

In our insider threat assessments, we find that contractors are typically not handled with nearly as much care in the termination process as permanent employees. After all, a reason why many of you hire contractors is to avoid dealing with all of the employee issues, right? However, contractors have feelings, too! And as we see in these TBP cases, they have the ability and have been known to retaliate against what they perceive as unfairness just like permanent employees have. Therefore, you need to consider all of the issues discussed in Chapter 2 for contractors as well as employees.

## Theft of Intellectual Property Committed by Trusted Business Partners

In Chapter 3, Insider Theft of Intellectual Property, we noted that IP is usually stolen by scientists, engineers, programmers, and salespeople who use authorized access to steal information as they walk out the door. The same type of pattern applies to contractors hired in those types of positions, as well as subcontractors hired for those types of work. Consider the following case:

> Two engineers worked at an international manufacturing company with locations in the United States and China, among other countries. The company manufactured equipment for the victim organization, and also had a contract with a Chinese company to manufacture a new piece of equipment that it was struggling to design. The victim organization had its own trade-secret version of the equipment that the insiders' organization needed to design to fulfill the contract with the Chinese company. The insiders scheduled a visit to the victim's manufacturing plant under the pretense of inspecting their own equipment for potential repairs. The victim's plant had restricted access behind several secure doors, and signs stating that cameras were prohibited. Visitors were required to sign in and out, and be escorted at all times. The victim organization also asked visitors to sign a nondisclosure agreement; however, the insiders falsely stated that they had already signed one the previous year. While one insider kept a lookout, the other insider proceeded to take several pictures of the trade-secret equipment with the camera on his cell phone. After they left the victim's facility, one insider downloaded the images from his camera

and emailed them from his personal account to his work email. Later, he proceeded to send the images from his work account to other coworkers in another plant who were tasked with actually manufacturing their version of the trade-secret equipment for the Chinese company.

This case is somewhat similar to the cases related in Chapter 3. The insiders used authorized access to steal the trade secrets from their client. The countermeasures described in Chapter 3 apply here as well: It is important to identify your most valuable IP, and target your countermeasures on protecting it. You can't possibly watch everything everyone does on a daily basis; therefore, you need to focus your attention on what's most important. In this case, the organization obviously had extensive controls for protecting its trade secrets; however, it did not recognize the threat posed by its TBPs, and allowed them to access the area unescorted, even though all *visitors* had to be escorted at all times.

## Open Your Mind: Who Are Your Trusted Business Partners?

By now you probably understand that you need to include contractors and companies you do business with when designing countermeasures for insider threat risk. But before you stop reading, are you sure you haven't forgotten anyone? Is there anyone else you provide authorized access to your systems, information, or network?

The reason we ask is because we have two cases involving a different type of trusted business partner: prisoners. This is a perfect example of how you have to open your mind to the expanding complexity of insider threat for your organization.

> An inmate at a prison was incarcerated because he was previously involved in a hacking and phishing scam and had also engaged in credit card fraud. The prison asked him to write a program and create an internal, closed network television station. The inmate was left unsupervised and altered the system passwords and locked everyone out of the prison's network. The prison hired external consultants to repair the damage, and the inmate was put into segregation as punishment. It is unknown whether charges were filed against the inmate in relation to the incident.

This case clearly illustrates a new angle on insider threats! In Chapter 6, Best Practices for the Prevention and Detection of Insider Threats, we indicated that you should consider the increased risk that is posed by potential employees with a criminal history. Providing authorized access to a convicted hacker obviously poses additional risk of insider threat.

The next case also involves a prisoner, but not one with known hacking skills.

> An inmate at a prison was serving time for possession of child pornography. The prison permitted inmates to use computers for legal research. Computers used by the inmates could access only a legal research program, which was updated through CD-ROMs. The computer accessed by the inmate was a **thin client,** meaning that it did not run programs or store data itself, but accessed those programs and data over a network from a central legal research computer server that was stored in another part of the prison. The computer accessed by the inmate was connected through the prison's network to the Internet solely so that it could obtain updates for the operating system. The inmate discovered and exploited an idiosyncrasy in the legal research software, and was able to obtain the username and password to a critical management program. He unsuccessfully attempted to log in to that program and also unsuccessfully attempted to send two emails outside of the prison. He also used the Internet to download two short video files, photographs of two prison employees and two fellow inmates, and a publicly available aerial shot of the prison itself. The inmate was also able to configure the prison's network to provide himself and other inmates access to additional programs and computer files from the prison's network and to obtain PII for 1,100 current and former prison employees. The incident was discovered when prison personnel found a piece of paper containing the username and password for the prison's management computer program. The duration of the incident was five months. The inmate was convicted and sentenced to an additional 18 months of imprisonment followed by three years of supervised release.

This case did not involve an "insider" with known technical skills, but it certainly reinforces the notion that you need to identify potential insider threat risk and impose controls accordingly.

## Recommendations for Mitigation and Detection

This section summarizes a set of recommendations for organizations concerned about malicious acts by trusted business partners.

- *Recommendation 1: Understand the policies and procedures of the trusted business partner.*
  You establish policies and procedures to protect your own systems, information, and network. When you consider enlisting the support of a trusted business partner, you should ensure that the TBP's policies and procedures are at least as effective as

your safeguards. This includes physical security, staff education, personnel background checks, security procedures, termination, and other safeguards.

- *Recommendation 2: Monitor intellectual property to which access is provided.*
  When you establish an agreement with a trusted business partner, you also need assurance that the intellectual property you provide access to is protected. You need to get assurances that access to and distribution of your data is monitored. You should verify there are mechanisms for logging the dissemination of your data. You should also be aware of procedures that the trusted business partner has to investigate possible disclosure of your information.

- *Recommendation 3: Maintain access rights management.*
  When contracting with a trusted business partner to handle sensitive data, it is important for you to know how data is going to be managed. In a number of cases, the trusted business partner could not handle the full workload it took on and subcontracted to another organization or brought in temporary employees in order to be able to process the job. You should be aware of these arrangements and ensure the data will be handled by means acceptable to you.

- *Recommendation 4: Understand the personnel policies and procedures of the trusted business partner.*
  When contracting with a trusted business partner, you should insist that the partner organization's employees are investigated and cleared to handle data in ways similar to your own employees. In a few cases, the trusted business partner employed workers with criminal backgrounds or connections to the Internet underground. You should not compromise your security requirements in order to have a job accomplished faster.

- *Recommendation 5: Anticipate and manage negative workplace issues.*
  When you decide to hire consultants, contractors, or temporary employees, they should be made aware of your policies and practices for acceptable work behavior. Negative workplace issues have been known to trigger illicit insider activity; it is important that policies and procedures for managing such events consider permanent employees, contractors, consultants, and temporary employees. It is also important that you do not provide false hope for these employees regarding likelihood of being hired. If you indicate you might hire a contractor or consultant full-time but then decide not to do so,

you should perform an assessment of the individual's insider risk. You should remove the individual's access and change any shared accounts that access was provided in order to mitigate risks when the individual is informed he or she will not be hired. It has proven risky to retain the services of disappointed or disgruntled temporary workers.

- *Recommendation 6: Deactivate access following termination.*
  When an employee, consultant, or contractor is terminated or suspended, all access that the person had should be disabled. When you are drawing up an agreement with a trusted business partner, you should make certain the trusted business partner performs rigorous termination procedures as well. In a number of cases involving contractors, access was not disabled immediately after termination and the insider was able to exploit that access in the commission of his crime.

- *Recommendation 7: Enforce separation of duties.*
  A number of insiders exploited the fact that certain actions could be performed in such a way that circumvented normal separation of duties controls. Business processes should enforce separation of duties, regardless of the speed or priority required. While different levels of controls may be associated with different priority tasks, no processes should be left without protections against possible exploitation by a disgruntled or greedy insider.

- *Recommendation 8: Create clear contractual agreements that specifically state that the TBP is also responsible for protecting organizational resources.*
  Contracts with a trusted business partner should include restrictions on how the TBP handles and shares your information. This should include restrictions on the TBP's ability to subcontract with other organizations on tasks involving your sensitive information and systems. There should be standard terms and conditions that allow you to apply the same policies and procedures to contractors, subcontracts, and consultants that you apply to your own employees, including mandatory flow-down provisions from prime contractors to subcontractors. Also, contracts should include notification requirements for breaches and termination of key employees. You should make your security requirements clear and also develop consequences that will incentivize the TBP to protect key resources.

# Malicious Insiders with Ties to the Internet Underground

In this section, we focus on insider threat cases in which the insider had relationships with the Internet underground community. Let's start by defining what we mean by the Internet underground.[4]

As we told you in Chapter 4, the FBI defines organized crime as ". . . any group having some manner of a formalized structure and whose primary objective is to obtain money through illegal activities."[5] Whereas the word *underground* ". . . describes an activity that is secret and usually illegal."[6] Initially, we intended to analyze insider crimes involving either the Internet underground or organized crime due to anticipated similarities between the cases. However, after reviewing cases from the CERT database, we realized that organized crime and the Internet underground produce very different types of insider threat. We included malicious insiders with connections to organized crime in Chapter 4 because those cases typically involved fraud. However, as you will see in this section, crimes involving the Internet underground are not limited to fraud.

We use the following definition of Internet underground:

> **Internet underground**: *a collection of individuals with shared goals where there is some degree of hierarchical structure and the primary communication mechanism or agent of electronic crime involves the Internet. Further, it may demonstrate some degree of pseudoanonymity and/or secrecy, which may be useful for organizing and carrying out electronic crimes.*

Both the Internet underground and organized crime are somewhat covert in their operations. Back-room conversations are replaced by short-lived IRC chat servers while crime bosses and an ordered hierarchy of leadership is replaced by a forum administrator and a loosely cohesive set of followers. Interestingly, however, there are tiers of organization in the Internet underground community. While the norm seems to be a looser type of organization, many of the top-tier underground organizations are highly professional, extremely organized, and run in a fashion not very

---

4. Material from this section includes portions from a joint CyLab and CERT Program article titled "Spotlight On: Malicious Insiders with Ties to the Internet Underground Community," authored by Michael Hanley, Andrew Moore, Dawn Cappelli, and Randall Trzeciak [Hanley 2009].

5. See Federal Bureau of Investigation—Organized Crime—Glossary of Terms for more information (www.fbi.gov/about-us/investigate/organizedcrime/glossary).

6. See definition on Cambridge Dictionaries at http://dictionary.cambridge.org/.

different from traditional organized crime. These are interesting facets of the problem to bear in mind as we continue our discussion of the Internet underground community.

The goal of this section is not to recommend detection methods for locating employees and contractors who might be involved with the Internet underground. That would be prohibitively expensive and would likely have a fairly high false-positive detection rate given that several tools and forums in the underground do have legitimate uses. Instead, this section demonstrates how motivated insiders could use the Internet underground community and its resources as a force multiplier to amplify the impact of their attacks against you. Also, the best practices detailed in Chapter 6 might have eliminated the organizational and technical vulnerabilities that the insiders in these cases were able to exploit.

## Snapshot of Malicious Insiders with Ties to the Internet Underground

The majority of these incidents were IT sabotage cases, which follow the patterns we described in Chapter 2. Therefore, the proactive measures we have described throughout this book for prevention and early detection of insider IT sabotage are applicable to many of these cases. As in most IT sabotage cases, the majority of these insiders held technical roles, such as system administrators, database administrators (DBAs), computer technicians, and technology architects; many of them were former employees or contractors at the time of the attack. They were often considered to be among the most technical individuals in their organizations; special care should be used when employing technically skilled individuals with known or suspected connections to Internet underground communities.

Only a few of the insiders were in positions that were purely managerial or nontechnical. In addition, all of these insiders were male; however, recall our caution in Chapter 2 that technical positions are highly male-dominated. Therefore, you should not focus on male employees in your mitigation efforts. Some of these insiders were characterized by fellow employees and their organization's leadership as the most technically valuable employees in the organization.

Most of these insiders were motivated by revenge against their employer, although a few had motivators such as looking for recognition, proving some ideological point, or supporting an underground movement.

## Range of Involvement of the Internet Underground

The case examples in this section reflect varying degrees in which insiders were involved with the Internet underground community. At the low end is a system administrator who worked for a market research firm. He used his legitimate access to steal PII he found on servers that belonged to one of his employer's business partners. There was no evidence that he distributed the stolen data via the Internet underground; rather, he appeared to enjoy the thrill of collecting it and bragging about it in online IRC chat rooms.

Most of the insiders in the CERT database used their ties to the Internet underground to generate support for their attack. One insider had access to trade secrets relating to anti-piracy technology used by an organization to protect its primary business service. He stole the information and actively distributed it throughout the hacker community to promote piracy of the organization's services. In another case, a system administrator for a retail clothing firm was terminated over issues with a server for which he was responsible. He then engaged the Internet underground community for assistance in organizing and executing a **denial-of-service attack**[7] against his former employer using passwords and access mechanisms he provided to them.

## The Crimes

Most attacks targeted the organization directly. For example, insiders deleted critical files, disrupted system operations, and denied access. Others used their organization's systems for their own illicit activities—for example, running sniffers and port scans of governmental systems. One targeted an unsuspecting outsider by changing her status to deceased in a critical government database. Other employees or contractors transmitted proprietary information to hacker sites, collected PII, and broke into systems and defaced Web sites for fun. Some provided information to outsiders who used it to commit cybercrimes, including one person who posted instructions to an online hacker group on how to break into his organization's systems, and another who posted employees' PII to a Web site.

---

7. **Denial-of-service attack:** a type of cyberattack in which a large amount of traffic is directed at a server in an attempt to disable it.

## Attacks Involving the Internet Underground

Attacks involving the Internet underground used some of the following technical methods:

- Exploitation of unpatched vulnerabilities
- Organized distributed denial-of-service (DDoS) attacks by the Internet underground crime
- Change of all administrative passwords
- Modification of DNS server to point to malicious site
- Use of hacking techniques that were accumulated from various underground forums and Web sites
- Downloading of employee PII to removable media and then posting the PII on underground sites
- Downloading of files to a home computer
- Exfiltration of copyrighted source code, which was then sold on the "black market" and eventually made available on underground file sharing sites
- Theft of trade secrets by scanning physical documents and transmitting to the Internet underground
- Unauthorized use of a coworker's account or computer
- Malicious modification of data
- Creation and use of backdoor accounts and unknown access paths

### Use of Unknown Access Paths Following Termination

In the cases that follow, procedures for ensuring secure separation of employees at the conclusion of their employment were not sufficient to prevent an insider attack. Insiders were able to exploit access that was not disabled upon termination, allowed to copy data before leaving the facility for the final time, or able to access previously created privileged backdoor accounts used to attack the organization after termination.

A system administrator for a retail company was terminated over issues with a server for which he was responsible. Following his termination, he recruited members of an online hacking group to help him attack his former employer's systems. He relayed passwords and other access information to the underground group, and provided detailed instructions on how to use those credentials to break into his former employer's network. He was able to organize the group and execute a coordinated denial-of-service attack against the retailer that lasted from the day before Thanksgiving until the Sunday after Thanksgiving—commonly recognized as the busiest shopping days of the year.

A computer technician was fired shortly after starting his job because he refused to give his Social Security number to the human resources department and he failed to disclose prior criminal convictions. Before leaving, he stole PII for 8,000 employees and posted it to a Web site he had established to smear the organization's image. The Web site threatened to publish more information and link it to underground sites known to facilitate and engage in identity theft and fraud. The insider had been with the organization for only a short time but had been given system administrator access to the systems he attacked within his first few weeks at the organization.

A system administrator was fired after a confrontation with his manager over the possibility of being laid off. The manager had suggested that since the systems were performing well, the employee's help may no longer be needed. Outraged by this, he immediately created a set of backdoor accounts with full access to all networked machines within his control and planted a malicious program that would erase hard drives on command. The day after his termination, he remotely triggered the execution of that program and wiped out several devices at the organization. Several months after the initial attack, he attacked the organization a second time by redirecting the organization's domain name for their external-facing Web site to a Web site that hosted pornographic images, racial slurs, and defamatory statements against his former employer. During the investigation, it was discovered that during his employment he had broken into other sites while at work, and had accumulated a wealth of hacking material from various underground forums and Web sites that may have helped him launch his attack against his former employer. In addition, investigators found disk loads of pornography, passwords, hacking tools, credit card information, and music downloads.

The sole security administrator for a small telecommunications firm quit his job with no advance notice. While he was employed he had expressed feelings of dissatisfaction due to insufficient gratitude and compensation for his work, and also had a series of conflicts with coworkers. He had a lengthy history of pirating material online and had committed prior electronic crimes related to unauthorized system and network access. For a month following his departure, he used backdoor accounts he had created previously to remotely access the organization's systems and delete files that he had created during his employment. He also redirected the Internet-facing Web servers to point to another server named to slander the organization, and launched other offensive attacks from within the organization's network, such as using the victim's network to run network scanning tools against government military networks.

As we have mentioned previously in this book, you should develop a formal employee termination process. The process should involve

- Disabling of accounts and access paths
- A debriefing regarding nondisclosure or intellectual property agreements
- Communication to the rest of the organization that the trust relationship with the former employee has been terminated, and that the employee should not be allowed physical or electronic access from that point forward

Please refer to Chapter 6 for more details regarding employee termination procedures.

One additional item of note pertains to the last two cases described in this section, both of which redirected external DNS registrations to sites meant to disrepute and slander the victim organization. Authorization to maintain DNS registration falls under a special category of highly privileged but infrequently used functions that require special documentation. Because these functions are used infrequently, access to them may go unnoticed and be forgotten when an administrator leaves the organization. This leaves a potential access path for a disgruntled insider to exploit for months, if not years, after the separation takes place. A suggested countermeasure is to maintain an inventory of privileged functions and a list of employees who have authorization to execute those functions. A regular review of this inventory for necessary changes based on job function or employment status can help mitigate the risk of items such as this that may slip through the cracks with serious consequences.

> Authorization to maintain DNS registration falls under a special category of highly privileged but infrequently used functions that require special documentation. Because these functions are used infrequently, access to them may go unnoticed and be forgotten when an administrator leaves the organization.

## Insufficient Access Controls and Monitoring

The following incidents demonstrate the consequences of insufficient access controls and monitoring of access to highly sensitive information and materials, especially when trusted business partners are involved.

A document imaging firm was contracted by a law firm that was working for a telecommunications provider as outside counsel. An employee of the document imaging firm brought in his nephew, the insider in this case, to help with a backlog of copying to be completed at night. The nephew scanned images of trade-secret documentation associated with anti-piracy technology and transmitted it to the leader of an online community whose purpose was to pirate the services offered by the telecommunications firm. The forum administrator originally refused to post the information, stating it was too sensitive to be released, but eventually did so anyway under pressure from the insider.

A DBA responsible for a very large database containing PII for an insurance company became frustrated by what he perceived to be unfairly low pay. He lashed out at the organization by downloading PII for more than 60,000 people from the organization's database to removable media. He used message boards to advertise the availability of the information to underground individuals, and solicited bids for the information. He also leveraged newsgroups dedicated to credit card fraud to post credit card numbers, suggesting that the information he was providing be used to obtain additional credit cards in the names of the victims. Law enforcement eventually captured the insider when an undercover agent posed as a potential buyer of his stolen information.

A common theme in these cases is largely unrestricted access to proprietary data by the insiders, due to poor data handling policies and practices and lack of granular access controls. Interestingly, the first case involves a trusted business partner as well as the Internet underground! In the first example, company trade secrets were left largely unsecured in the hands of a third-party organization (the document-imaging company) contracted by the trusted business partner (the law firm). Trade secrets should be protected appropriately, given their value. Contracts should specify physical and electronic security requirements, as well as personnel security requirements for anyone with access to the information.

The second case involves an insider with uncontrolled and unmonitored access to proprietary data. Although it is difficult to control access by DBAs, countermeasures should be considered for critical organizational data. For example, a "two sets of eyes" policy could be implemented and technically enforced, whereby two DBAs together are required to perform sensitive functions. Other possible solutions involve delegation models that use technical measures to limit the control that any one account has over the environment, or cryptographic controls that require the use of specifically trusted devices that cannot be removed from a controlled area to perform sensitive functions. These techniques limit the insider's capacity to misuse access to systems or data without having at least one accomplice.

## Conclusions: Insider Threats Involving the Internet Underground

The threat of insider actions associated with the Internet underground is very real. As shown in the case examples in this chapter, these crimes occur primarily out of revenge that stems from unmet expectations and disgruntlement over salary or other work-related issues. Many of the attacks occur off-site, after termination, using access and prior knowledge the employee or contractor had as part of his job role.

Further, nearly all attacks involved the use of at least one form of compromised account, such as an authorized third-party account or a backdoor account created specifically for the execution of the insider's attack plans. Finally, most of the insiders in the CERT database were considered to be highly technical and were working in some kind of privileged technical role for the organization.

Of course, it is not always readily apparent that employees have connections with the Internet underground. You can institute measures to block certain illicit communication channels at the workplace, or monitor and investigate their use. In addition, it is important that managers of technical employees exercise good management practices, including attempting to maintain a degree of awareness of employees' morale, and suspicious behaviors both at work and outside the workplace.

Since most of these insiders were highly technical, chances are good that they could have attacked alone, without enlisting assistance from the Internet underground. In most cases, their associates simply helped them to amplify their attack. Therefore, implementing the best practices described in Chapter 6 of this book could have corrected many of the vulnerabilities that the insiders in these cases were able to successfully exploit.

## Final Summary

You now should understand what we mean by malicious insider threat. This is not meant to be an authoritative definition, but it is important that you understand that everything you read in this book was grounded by this definition:

> *A malicious insider threat is a current or former employee, contractor, or business partner who has or had authorized access to an organization's network, system, or data and intentionally exceeded or misused that access*

*in a manner that negatively affected the confidentiality, integrity, or availability of the organization's information or information systems.*

Next, we will turn our attention to, among other things, unintentional insider threats. However, everything we presented in this book pertains to intentional malicious insider threats.

We covered three main types of insider threats in the book.

- **IT sabotage:** an insider's use of information technology (IT) to direct specific harm at an organization or an individual.
- **Theft of intellectual property (IP):** an insider's use of IT to steal proprietary information from the organization. This category includes industrial espionage involving insiders.
- **Fraud:** an insider's use of IT for the unauthorized modification, addition, or deletion of an organization's data (not programs or systems) for personal gain, or theft of information that leads to an identity crime (e.g., identity theft, credit card fraud).

We categorized them in this way because each type of crime has a prevalent pattern that is common across the majority of the cases. Every type of insider crime is very different: who, what, where, why, when, and how! Here are specifics regarding those differences.

- Insider IT sabotage is typically committed by technical users with privileged access, such as system administrators, DBAs, and programmers. The motivation in these crimes is usually revenge for a negative workplace event, and the crimes are often set up while the insider is still employed, but are executed following termination.
- Insider theft of IP is usually committed by scientists, engineers, programmers, and salespeople. These insiders usually steal the information they worked on, and take it with them as they leave the organization to either start their own business, take with them to a new job, or give to a foreign government or organization.
- Insider fraud is usually committed by lower-level employees such as help desk, customer service, and data entry clerks. The crimes are motivated by financial need or greed, and they typically continue for a long period of time. Many of these insiders are recruited by outsiders to steal information. Collusion with other insiders is very common in crimes involving modification of information for payment from outside.

> Every type of insider crime is very different: who, what, where, why, when, and how!

You should also now recognize the expanding complexity of insider threat:

- Collusion with outsiders
- Trusted business partners
- Mergers and acquisitions
- Cultural differences
- Foreign allegiances
- The Internet underground

We covered collusion with outsiders in the theft of IP and fraud crimes. We discussed trusted business partners and insiders with ties to the Internet underground at length in the beginning of this chapter. And we explained how insiders stole intellectual property for the benefit of a foreign government or organization in Chapter 3. We did not discuss mergers and acquisitions or cultural differences much at all, however. The reason for that is that we have not done research specifically in those areas yet. We recognize them as being important issues, and therefore want to raise your awareness to them. We are exploring research potentials in both areas, so keep an eye on our Web site for possible future reports on those topics.

The crime profiles and many case examples in this book should have convinced you that malicious insider online activity is very similar to what insiders do every day in the course of their normal jobs. That is why prevention and detection are so complex. However, mitigation strategies rooted in the crime profiles that involve the entire organization working together have a much better chance of success than implementation of broad technical controls alone. If there is one fact you take away from this book, it should be this: IT and information security personnel cannot stop insider threats alone! They need the cooperation of management, human resources, security, legal, data owners, and physical security.

> If there is one fact you take away from this book, it should be this: IT and information security personnel cannot stop insider threats alone! They need the cooperation of management, human resources, security, legal, data owners, and physical security.

We urge you once again to periodically reread the case examples throughout his book, and ask yourself the question: *Could this happen to us?* Learn from the lessons these organizations have learned in painful ways!

We hope that you refer often to Chapter 6. The best practices from that chapter are also repeated on the inside of the book cover for your convenience. But make sure you pay attention to the details! Unfortunately, malicious insiders are aware of every minute flaw in your processes and technologies; therefore, high-level implementation of those practices is not good enough. The devil is in the details—make sure you have taken care of every issue of concern that was exploited by insiders in the CERT database.

We also urge you to offer Chapter 7, Technical Insider Threat Controls, to your technical staff for consideration. These technical controls are based on our cases, and should assist your technical security staff in raising insider threat alerts without excessive information overload. We would love to get feedback on how they work, and better yet, how you tailor them for your environment. You tell us, and we'll spread the word!

We have been doing this work for ten years, and we urge you to take advantage of our expertise if you are extremely concerned about insider threats in your organization. We have various products and services available as described in Appendix A, Insider Threat Center Products and Services. Also, please contact us! Our key to success is being in touch with the community, and we honestly welcome your feedback, questions, and cases. Please contact us at insider-threat-feedback@cert.org.

Keep an eye on our Web site at www.cert.org/insider_threat. We will put new releases there, including an updated best practice guide, scheduled for publication in early 2012. That guide will contain at least four new best practices, as well as updates for most existing practices.

## Let's End on a Positive Note!

We thought it would be nice to end on a positive note, by providing case examples of insiders who were successfully detected in time to prevent their crime from happening. Hopefully this will provide the incentive you need to take action based on what you've read in this book!

### Fraud: Insider Sells Stolen PII to Police Informant and Undercover Agent

A contractor was formerly employed in the human resources department of a government agency. As a function of his job, he had access to a database of PII, including names, dates of birth (DOBs), and Social Security numbers (SSNs).

The insider's employment was terminated for undisclosed reasons. On three occasions over a six-month period, the insider sold 40 individuals' names, DOBs, and SSNs to a law enforcement informant. Subsequently, the insider tried to sell a USB drive with 1,100 SSNs and 1,600 bank account numbers to an undercover agent. When the insider downloaded the information remains undetermined, but the organization believes that the insider downloaded the PII prior to his termination. The insider was arrested, convicted, ordered to pay $50,000 in restitution, and sentenced to 42 months of imprisonment followed by three years of supervised release.

### Theft of IP: Insider Caught before IP Released

Prior to the incident, the insider, a naturalized U.S. citizen who was a programmer at an investment banking firm, submitted his letter of resignation. The duration of the incident was five days; the insider used both on-site and remote access, outside of work hours, to carry out the attack. He used a swipe card to access the building, and used a Bash script that copied, compressed, and merged source code files, then encrypted, renamed, and uploaded them to an external file host. On four separate occasions, he uploaded 32 MB of files to a file host outside the country. He deleted the encryption program and attempted to erase the Bash history, but the organization retained backup copies of the Bash history. The insider claimed that the upload was accidental and that the intent was to transfer only open source information. The information was not passed to any third parties because the organization had safeguards in place, including monitoring outgoing email attachments, disallowing outgoing FTP, monitoring HTTPS, and requiring the insider to sign an intellectual property agreement. The incident was detected through regular auditing of HTTPS traffic. The insider was arrested, but verdict details were unavailable.[8]

### IT Sabotage: Logic Bomb Detected before It Went Off

After hearing he was going to be terminated, the insider planted a logic bomb to delete the root credentials of 4,000 of the organization's servers, disable all monitoring, and erase all of the data. Five days after the insider was terminated, however, one of the organization's engineers detected the malicious script and alerted organization officials before it was able to execute.

---

8. Because no verdict was known, the insider's actions described in this case are alleged.

# Appendix A

# Insider Threat Center Products and Services

The purpose of this book is to raise awareness and assist you in formulating a mitigation strategy for insider threats. Some of you might choose to take advantage of products and services readily available from the CERT Insider Threat Center to jumpstart your efforts. That is the purpose of this appendix. We provide an overview of products and services currently available from the CERT Program. Table A-1 identifies problems that you might have with regard to managing insider threat risks and how our current products and services could help solve those problems.

**Table A-1** *Solutions to Current Problems*

| Your Pain Points | Solutions from the Insider Threat Center | Benefits to Your Organization |
|---|---|---|
| *How can I become more aware of any organizational issues impacting my risk of insider threat?* | Insider threat workshops | Greater understanding of the nature and prevalence of insider threat concerns and candidate countermeasures |

*Continues*

**Table A-1** *Solutions to Current Problems (Continued)*

| Your Pain Points | Solutions from the Insider Threat Center | Benefits to Your Organization |
| --- | --- | --- |
| *How can I get better indications and warnings of malicious behavior and detect warning signs?* | Insider threat assessment | More comprehensive protection, knowing that you are watching for the attack patterns of previous malicious insiders |
| *How do I make the best use of my existing tools?* | Customized, tactical countermeasure guidance based on new operational controls from the CERT insider threat lab<br><br>Insider Threat standards (NIST SP 800-53) | Better situational awareness and improved security posture since tools are configured and properly tailored to the unique systems and concerns found in the mission operating environment<br><br>Cost savings—analysts' time is used more efficiently |
| *Where can I get education and training for my staff to effectively deal with and diagnose insider attacks?* | Insider threat workshops<br><br>Customized insider threat executive workshop<br><br>Cyberdefense exercises conducted on the CERT Exercise Network (XNET) | Technical security workforce more skilled in detecting indications and warnings of insider threat<br><br>More effective incident response, reducing the likelihood that an insider attack will be missed, misdiagnosed, or dealt with inappropriately |

| Are my policies and procedures inhibiting detection and prevention of insider threats? | Insider threat assessment<br><br>Customized insider threat executive workshop<br><br>Strategic action plan and supported execution | Stronger ability to detect and respond to insider attacks, which will protect the organization and avoid compromises of assets, information, and reputation |
|---|---|---|
| Other issues of concern | Sponsored research by the Insider Threat Center | Reduction in international insider threat risk, risk in cloud computing environment, unintentional insider threats, etc. |

The rest of this appendix provides information on the five primary products and services offered:

- Insider threat workshop
- Customized insider threat executive workshop
- Insider threat exercises
- Insider threat assessment
- Insider threat sponsored research

Brochures describing the products and services are also available on our Web site at www.cert.org/insider_threat. Thanks to CERT Business Services, CERT Information Services, and the CERT Insider Threat Center staff for help in preparing these materials.

# Insider Threat Workshop

We have combined all of our work into a two-day workshop on insider threat.[1] The workshop consists of presentations and interactive exercises in which participants are led through portions of the CERT insider threat assessment instrument, which was developed to enable organizations to assess their insider threat risk. The assessment addresses technical,

---

1. We also offer half-day and one-day versions of the workshop.

organizational, personnel, security, and process issues. The purpose of the exercises is to assist participants in assessing their own organization's vulnerability to insider threat in specific areas of concern. To reinforce the principles taught in the workshop, we will also present technical demonstrations of monitoring techniques that could have detected malicious activity in actual insider threat cases. Our goal is that participants leave the workshop with actionable steps that they can take to better manage the risk of insider threat in their organization.

## Who Should Attend?

The target audience is managers, leaders, directors, and chief executives across all facets of the organization including IT, HR, legal, physical security, and operations. The workshop will benefit team leaders, project managers, business managers, finance managers, security officers, risk officers, C-level managers, and anyone else responsible for creating, implementing, enforcing, and auditing practices and procedures throughout the organization.

## Topics

Topics include the following:

- Overview of insider threats
- Insider IT sabotage
- Insider theft of intellectual property
- Insider fraud
- Best practices for prevention and detection

## Objectives

The workshop objectives include the following.

- Attendees will leave the workshop with actionable steps that they can take to better manage the risk of insider threat in their organization.
- Attendees will understand the best practices that can be implemented to prevent insider incidents or detect them as early as possible.
- Attendees will know what "observables" they should be looking for within their organizations that could indicate a pending insider attack.
- Attendees can compare our list of technical methods against their organizations' technical controls to identify gaps.

## Customized Insider Threat Executive Workshop

This workshop is conducted with the executive management team in your organization. It differs from the public workshop in several ways. First, it is streamlined for an executive audience. Second, the workshop materials can be tailored to include actual malicious insider incidents that occurred in your organization. To prepare for the customized workshop, you provide us with a number of insider incidents so that we can understand your threat landscape. For three days prior to the workshop, members of the Insider Threat Center will be on-site at your location, interviewing staff members who are familiar with the set of insider incidents. *We treat all customer data as confidential.*

The actual workshop spans two days. The first day consists of interactive exercises, which help you to assess your vulnerability to insider threat. The second day focuses on providing you with actionable steps to better manage your risk of insider threat. On the second day, we help the executive team in developing a strategic action plan to address the risk of insider threat in your organization. This action plan is useful because it is created and endorsed by senior leadership, addresses the particular problems faced by your organization, and considers your unique corporate culture.

The target audience for the workshop is senior executives and decision makers within an organization. However, the complex nature of the insider threat problem requires a holistic approach. Multiple departments must be involved in the overall strategy. These departments include, but are not limited to, human resources, information technology, legal and contracting, physical security, and software engineering. This inter-departmental cooperation is the key to creating an effective strategy against insider threat.

## Insider Threat Exercises

In our insider threat workshops we spend a significant amount of time exploring our crime profiles, with the goal that attendees can compare our list of technical methods against their organizations' technical controls to identify gaps. To reinforce the principles taught in the workshop, we also present technical demonstrations of monitoring techniques that could have detected malicious activity in actual insider threat cases.

Our insider threat exercises go beyond lectures and demos, providing realistic training exercises for cyberdefenders in insider threat mitigation. We use real examples from their insider threat database to create a training platform using the CERT XNET[2] environment that showcases actual tactics, techniques, and procedures used by insiders to steal critical or sensitive information, or to damage an organization's image or infrastructure. The exercises teach participants how to detect, prevent, and respond to crimes by insiders and helps tune their focus for trends in insider behavior highlighted by the CERT Insider Threat Center's previous body of work.

These interactive, team-based exercises re-create complex actual insider threat scenarios and challenge participants to prepare for and respond to insider threat incidents. They include various injects from the teams running the exercise to simulate incidents. These exercises can be conducted within an organization to better equip its defenses against malicious insiders, or can be used in cyberflag exercises to recognize the most sophisticated team among multiple competing organizations.

To date, we have created two exercises that we have offered at individual customer sites and in conjunction with information security conferences.

The first exercise involves the participants detecting and responding to a malicious code infection on their enterprise network and determining how the machines were infected (by malicious insider or malware). Participants are given the information that there is an infection somewhere on their network, and the exercise progresses via quizzes that guide the participants toward strategies for locating the source of the infection. Participants are provided with familiar network monitoring tools such as Snort, Ntop, and Wireshark, as well as a netflow tool called SiLK. Using these tools, they will need to examine a network that includes simulated user traffic designed to model a small business organization.

The second exercise begins with the participants detecting a large source code exfiltration and determining how the exfiltration was carried out. After investigating that attack, they will encounter several other attacks against internal systems and respond to them accordingly. The exercise is intended to surprise participants by revealing the insider as a system administrator, making it difficult for them to tell whether changes were authorized or not.

## Insider Threat Assessment

The insider threat assessment enables you to gain a better understanding of insider threat and an enhanced ability to assess and manage associated

---

2.  XNET CERT Exercise Network: http://xnet.cert.org

risks. The assessment instrument encompasses information technology, human resources, physical security, business processes, legal, management, and organizational issues. It merges technical, behavioral, process, and policy issues into a single, actionable framework.

For the assessment, members of the Insider Threat Center staff will spend three to five days at your organization. During that time, we will review documents, interview key personnel, and observe key processes and security issues. We sign nondisclosure agreements, and all collaborations will remain confidential. After the on-site visit, we provide you with a confidential report that contains the findings of the assessment and considerations for potential mitigation strategies. Organizations have used this report to do the following:

- Identify and implement short-term tactical countermeasures
- Help guide their ongoing risk management process for implementing long-term, strategic countermeasures
- Justify follow-up actions to key decision makers

Our research has proven that the insider threat problem is quite complex, and you need an instrument that has the following characteristics:

- Encompasses policies, practices, and technologies
- Is empirically based yet adaptable to current trends and technologies
- Focuses on prevention, detection, and response strategies

The CERT insider threat assessment, which is based on psychological expertise as well as technical expertise, helps you to better safeguard your critical infrastructure. The purpose of the assessment is as follows:

- Enable you to gain a better understanding of your vulnerability to insider threat and an enhanced ability to assess and manage associated risks
- Include technical, organizational, personnel, and business security and process issues from all of our past research in a single, actionable framework
- Benefit all individuals involved in the insider threat vulnerability assessment process: information technology, human resources, physical security, data and business process "owners," and all levels of organizational management

## Insider Threat Sponsored Research

All of the products and services offered here have evolved from sponsored research projects we have undertaken in the past. We are always seeking new research and development opportunities to assist government and private industry organizations with their specific areas of concern. For example, we would like to investigate international insider threat risk, insider threat risk in cloud computing environments, and unintentional insider threats. We also are actively developing, pilot-testing, and transitioning new insider threat controls to the community.

If you are interested in discussing potential collaborations, please contact us at insider-threat-feedback@cert.org.

# Appendix B

# Deeper Dive into the Data

We are constantly mining the CERT insider threat database for new and useful information, sometimes to support specific research and development activities, sometimes based on curiosity, and sometimes at the request of someone outside of our team. Frequently when we hold workshops or give conference presentations we are asked new questions that we have not yet explored in the data. We often take those queries back with us, ask our database experts to find the answers, and provide the answers to the person who asked. We also try to incorporate those answers into posts on our blog,[1] in our workshops, and in new publications if applicable. The purpose of this appendix is to provide some of those details to you, because we believe it could be useful to you in designing your insider threat mitigation strategies.

## Breakdown of Cases by Critical Infrastructure Sectors

Figure B-1 shows the breakdown of cases by critical infrastructure sector. As you can see, the banking and finance sector accounts for the highest number of crimes in our database, followed by the information and

---

1. www.cert.org/blogs/insider_threat/

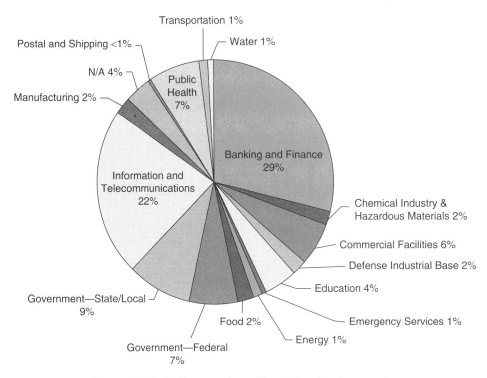

**Figure B-1** *U.S. cases by critical infrastructure sector*

telecommunications sector. Those two sectors together account for more than half of all of the cases in our database! If you are a part of one of those sectors, it is a good thing you are reading this book!

The government sectors are next, followed by public health, and then commercial facilities. This is particularly interesting to us because the public health sector did not even show up in our breakdown until the past few years. However, it is quite possible that those cases were occurring before, but organizations were keeping them quiet. More recently, in light of the data breach laws, organizations no longer have the option of covering up theft of private information.

In Figure B-2 we dig a little deeper into the top six sectors. Now we see that, no surprise, fraud is the most prevalent crime in the banking and finance sector. They are not immune to theft of IP or IT sabotage, however, and therefore still need to focus on protecting assets such as merger and acquisition plans, strategic plans, and earnings. And as mentioned earlier in the book, no sector should ignore the risk of insider IT sabotage.

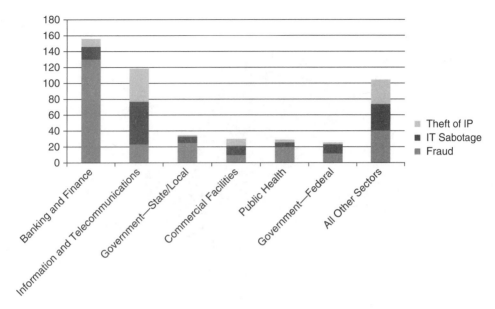

**Figure B-2** *Breakdown of crimes for top six sectors*

The IT sector, on the other hand, has suffered a large number of IT sabotage attacks, as well as theft of intellectual property. Theft of IP is no surprise, due to the highly competitive nature and innovative nature of their business. The prevalence of IT sabotage also deserves attention in that sector; the consequences of those crimes can be highly damaging!

The government sector has suffered most from fraud, followed by IT sabotage. It is important that the government sector protect the PII with which it is entrusted by its citizens. In addition, it should not ignore the risk of IT sabotage, as there were some significant cases in that sector.

## Breakdown of Cases by Type of Crime

Now let's take another look at the data in a different way: by type of crime. Where are the crimes occurring? This type of information could be useful in making risk-based decisions regarding insider threat mitigation.

Figure B-3 shows where the insider IT sabotage cases are occurring. As mentioned earlier, the IT sector seems to be at high risk for insider IT sabotage, accounting for almost half of all of the sabotage crimes in the

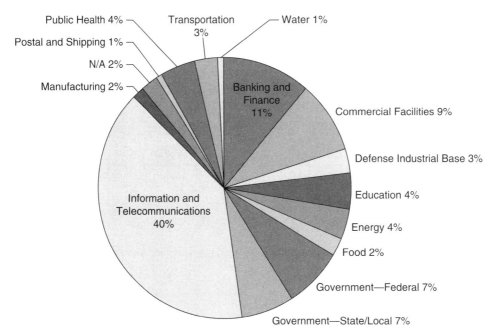

**Figure B-3** *U.S. insider IT sabotage cases by sector*

database! The banking and finance sector is second in terms of prevalence of IT sabotage attacks, followed closely by commercial facilities. It is somewhat reassuring to see that many of the sectors which could result in catastrophic harm to individuals as a result of IT sabotage have had very few incidents: public health, manufacturing, transportation, chemical and hazardous materials, food, energy, and emergency services.

Figure B-4 depicts the theft of IP cases by sector. Again, as mentioned earlier, the IT sector has been hard hit by theft of intellectual property, accounting for nearly half of all theft of IP cases. If a company loses its IP to a competitor, the impacts can be devastating. These impacts are even greater when the IP leaves the United States, which happened in close to one-third of the theft of IP cases in our database. Therefore, we suggest that the IT sector consider increasing risk mitigation efforts for these types of crimes. In addition, the banking and finance, manufacturing, chemical industry and hazardous materials, and commercial facilities sectors should pay close attention to Chapter 3, Insider Theft of Intellectual Property.

Finally, Figure B-5 shows the distribution of all of our fraud cases by critical infrastructure sector. Not surprising, the banking and finance sector has been hardest hit by insider fraud, accounting for almost half of all insider

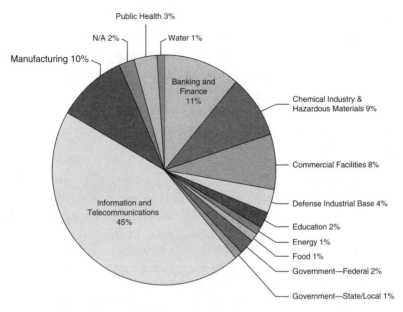

**Figure B-4**  *U.S. insider theft of IP cases by sector*

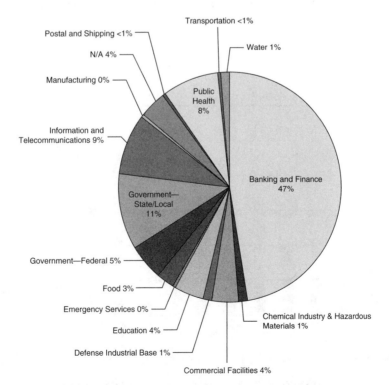

**Figure B-5**  *U.S. insider fraud cases by sector*

fraud cases. Government–state/local is second, followed by information and telecommunications and public health. Some of the sectors had little if any insider fraud cases; however, if you are in any of those sectors mentioned you should pay close attention to Chapter 4, Insider Fraud.

## Trends over Time

We are frequently asked if the insider threat problem is getting better or worse. Figure B-6 breaks down the incidents in our database by the year in which the incident ended. Some of these incidents, primarily fraud, went on over many years. According to this graph, in 2009 more insiders were caught than in any other year. Why the drastic drop in 2010? We can only be cautiously optimistic about 2010 for this reason: Incidents often do not become public knowledge until the case goes to trial, and that can be years following the arrest of the insider. In addition, we generated this graph in mid-2011 when we were writing the book. Therefore, only time will tell what the real number for the 2010 bar is in our graph! However, we would

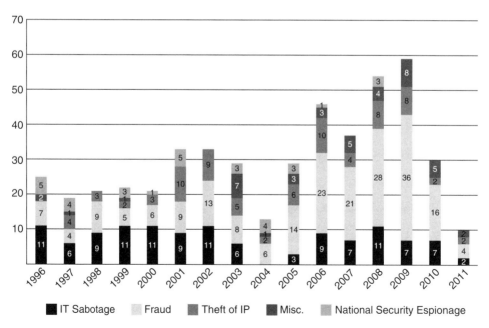

**Figure B-6**  *Insider incident end dates over time*

like to think that the widespread attention our work has gotten in recent years might be helping to increase the success rates for preventing these crimes, or detecting them in the planning or early execution stages, before the damages occur.

## Employees versus Contractors, Current versus Former

Figure B-7 shows the number of cases per year by employee type. Until the past year, the percentage of incidents involving a contractor hovers around 15%. As mentioned previously, our experience has shown that any data for 2010 and 2011 is going to change quite a bit as more and more cases come to light, and therefore we will focus on the previous years in this graph. Whether the number of total incidents for a particular year is higher or lower, the percentages stay roughly the same. What is also interesting is that this ratio has stayed the same over the course of ten years of a fairly tumultuous economic environment. This result may indicate that it isn't likely for contractor crimes to raise or lower significantly. But with almost one in seven of our insider threat crimes being committed by contractors, are you adequately considering the risk posed by this group?

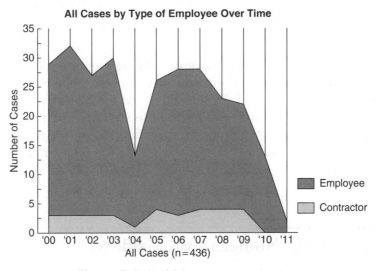

**Figure B-7** *Insiders versus contractors*

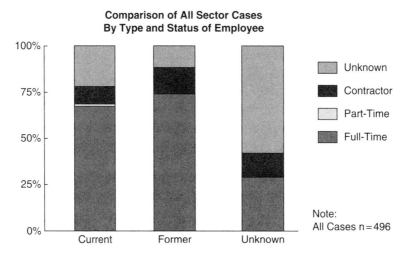

**Figure B-8**  *Comparison by employee type and status*

Figure B-8 shows the percentage of cases perpetrated by current and former employees, as well as employment type (full-time, part-time, or contractor). In some cases, we were not certain whether the incident was committed by a current or former employee, so we indicated those incidents as unknown. Full-time employees account for the greatest percentage for both current and former employees. Part-time employees made up a very small percentage of our cases, and all of them were current employees when they committed their illicit activity. Contractors are somewhat interesting in that more contractors attacked following termination than when employed by the victim organization.

Figures B-7 and B-8 provide some interesting data points for you to consider. Do you use the same prevention and detection controls for all employees and contractors, or are you only worried about the majority—the current, full-time employees you see on a daily basis? What are your procedures when a contractor leaves? Can you be sure that the contractor's access has been fully disabled? Food for thought as you decide on the next steps after reading this book. . . .

# Technical versus Nontechnical Insiders

Figure B-9 shows technical versus nontechnical insiders over the past 11 years. Note that only six months of 2011 are represented in this graph.

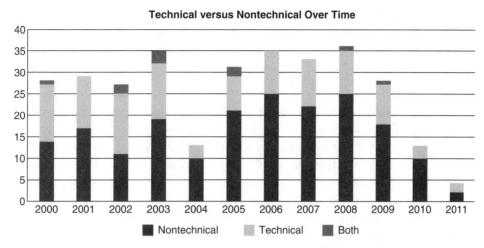

**Figure B-9** *Technical versus nontechnical insider threats*

How have you allocated resources for preventing, detecting, and responding to threats posed by technical and nontechnical employees? Do you focus on one type of employee and not the other? Our observations indicate that you should consider potential insider threats from both technical and nontechnical employees. Insider threats could come from anyone.

## What's Next: Other Threats

We have more than 700 cases in our insider threat database. Most of those cases represent intentional insider incidents that occurred in the United States. However, we also have been collecting cases for other types of threats as well, for future research purposes. Cases include

- Intentional insider incidents that occurred outside the United States
- Unintentional insider incidents
- External intrusions

We have collected very few unintentional insider threat cases. We suspect that most of these cases are handled internally; there is no reason to attract media attention for these cases unless they are part of a more significant event. One such event would be the disclosure of Personally Identifiable

Information (PII), which in most cases would have to be reported under the data breach laws. Another such event would be when an insider unintentionally provides access to an external intruder—for example, by clicking on an infected attachment, clicking on a link in a phishing email, and so forth.

We have been somewhat successful in collecting insider cases that occurred outside the United States, but have not collected enough from any one country to actually perform an empirical analysis. There has been a high degree of interest over the years in having us study the similarities and differences in intentional insider crimes committed in countries outside the United States. It is more difficult to locate international cases because in the United States, when someone is arrested it becomes a matter of public record, likewise when that person goes to trial. However, outside the United States this is not always the case. To perform a thorough insider threat study outside the United States we believe we need a partnership with international law enforcement, other organizations located in the country of interest, or global organizations. Table B-1 shows the breakdown of our 45 international intentional malicious insider threat cases by country of origin.

**Table B-1**  *International Malicious Insider Cases in Our Database*

| Number of Cases | Country |
|---|---|
| 18 | United Kingdom |
| 4 | Australia |
| 3 | India |
| 2 | Japan |
| 4 | Korea |
| 1 | Canada |
| 2 | China |
| 1 | Europe |
| 2 | France |
| 1 | Greece |
| 1 | Italy |

| 1 | Romania |
|---|---|
| 1 | Russia |
| 1 | Singapore |
| 1 | Switzerland |
| 1 | Thailand |
| 1 | United Arab Emirates |

Stay tuned to our Web site, www.cert.org/insider_threat, for new research in these areas!

# Appendix C

# CyberSecurity Watch Survey

To properly allocate information security resources and budgets, organizations need to know the prevalence of insider threat, especially as compared to outsider threat.

In 2004 we decided that we should develop another method for measuring the prevalence of malicious insider incidents across the United States. Therefore, we partnered with *CSO* Magazine and the Secret Service to conduct the first annual CyberSecurity Watch Survey. The survey has been a successful method for gathering information regarding electronic crimes, techniques, best practices, and emerging trends; therefore, we have continued to conduct the survey on an annual basis[1] [CSO 2011a].

The survey is sent out annually to *CSO* Magazine readers and site visitors, as well as members and partners of the Secret Service's Electronic Crimes Task Forces. Results from the 2011 survey are provided in this section to describe the prevalence and current trends of insider threat according to that survey [CSO 2011b].

---

1. Note that in some years Deloitte and Microsoft also participated in the survey.

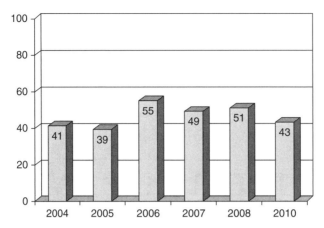

**Figure C-1** *Percentage of survey participants who experienced a malicious insider incident (Source: 2011 CyberSecurity Watch Survey, CSO Magazine, U.S. Secret Service, Software Engineering Institute CERT Program at Carnegie Mellon University, and Deloitte, January 2011.)*

The overarching question we always ponder is how many organizations are actually victims of insider threats. Figure C-1 displays the results of that question throughout the years. As you can see, the number of organizations experiencing a malicious insider incident peaked in 2006, and definitely decreased in 2010. After the number hovered at around 50% for three years, we are greatly encouraged by the drop last year! We know from annual survey results that organizations are implementing the countermeasures recommended by organizations like ours, which might explain the decrease.

Note that the size of organizations was well represented; 38% of the organizations have more than 5,000 employees and 37% of organizations have fewer than 500 employees.

One of the questions we are frequently asked is the breakdown of insiders versus outsiders. The e-crime survey is an opportunity to obtain data to answer that question. Figure C-2 shows the breakdown in our survey results.[2]

---

2. Source: 2011 CyberSecurity Watch Survey, CSO Magazine, U.S. Secret Service, Software Engineering Institute CERT Program at Carnegie Mellon University, and Deloitte, January 2011 [CSO 2011b].

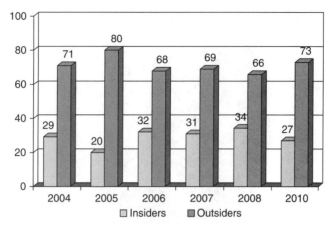

**Figure C-2** *Insiders versus outsiders (Source: 2011 CyberSecurity Watch Survey, CSO Magazine, U.S. Secret Service, Software Engineering Institute CERT Program at Carnegie Mellon University, and Deloitte, January 2011.)*

Again, there was quite a change last year; insiders accounted for about one-third of all incidents for three years, and then last year dropped to slightly more than one-fourth. Again, we are optimistic that our work is having an impact, as we did see more organizations implementing our suggested countermeasures in last year's survey results.

Since insiders only accounted for 27% of all electronic crimes for organizations surveyed in 2011, you might reconsider whether it's really worth your time to continue reading this book. Before making that decision, please consider the following key question from the survey: Which crimes were more costly or damaging, those committed by insiders or by outsiders? Figure C-3 shows the results of that question.[3] If we omit the responses of "Unknown," 43% of respondents indicated that insider crimes were more costly or damaging, and 57% indicated those committed by outsiders. This means that more than 260 of the more than 607 responding organizations believe that insiders were more costly or damaging than outsiders. But many organizations target their security defenses almost exclusively at the malicious outsider rather than the malicious insider. The

---

3. Ibid.

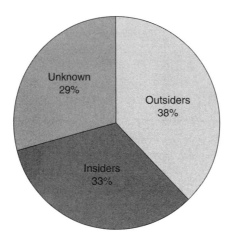

**Figure C-3** *Which crimes were more costly? (Source: 2011 CyberSecurity Watch Survey, CSO Magazine, U.S. Secret Service, Software Engineering Institute CERT Program at Carnegie Mellon University, and Deloitte, January 2011.)*

information contained in this book will help you right-size your defense against the very real insider threat.

One conclusion we can draw from the survey results is that insider threats are obviously prevalent in organizations in the United States. Nearly one out of every two organizations is victimized by at least one malicious insider incident per year. Why, then, have we only been able to collect 700 cases? The answer lies in the next question from the survey.

Since 2004 we have been asking survey respondents how they handled the insider electronic crimes they experienced. The results to this question have been very consistent from year to year.[4] Results from the 2011 survey are shown in Figure C-4. It may or may not surprise you to see that more than three-fourths of all insider crimes are handled internally, with no contact to law enforcement and no legal action.

Two of the top reasons cited for choosing to handle insider incidents internally were that the victim organizations lacked the evidence to be able to prosecute and they could not identify the individual(s) responsible

---

4. Ibid.

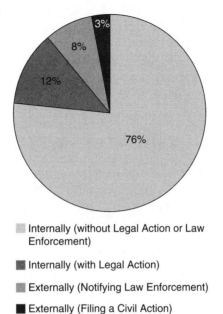

Internally (without Legal Action or Law Enforcement)

Internally (with Legal Action)

Externally (Notifying Law Enforcement)

Externally (Filing a Civil Action)

**Figure C-4**  *How insider intrusions are handled (Source: 2011 CyberSecurity Watch Survey, CSO Magazine, U.S. Secret Service, Software Engineering Institute CERT Program at Carnegie Mellon University, and Deloitte, January 2011.)*

for the crime. Our goal in this book is to help you with these reasons so that you can identify the perpetrator, and you have sufficient evidence to prosecute if you choose to do so.

# Appendix D

# Insider Threat Database Structure

Since 2001, we have been collecting incidents of malicious insider activity that occurred in U.S. organizations. In each of those incidents, the insider was found guilty in a U.S. court of law. To date, we have collected more than 700 cases of insider IT sabotage, fraud, theft of intellectual property, and national security espionage. This data provides the foundation for all of our insider threat research, work in our lab, assessments, workshops, and exercises.

We record actual insider incidents, providing a behavioral and technical framework for characterizing insider activity and analyzing incidents in a meaningful way that can be used to prevent, detect, and respond to insider threats. The recording of the details of an insider incident is commonly referred to as "coding." This appendix describes the structure of the insider threat database, as well as our data collection and coding process. This appendix will most likely be useful to other researchers, as it addresses questions we have received from the research community over the years.

## Data Collection

Incidents are usually identified from media reports, although some are provided to the CERT Program by a collaborative partner or affected organization. We then research the case to collect as much source material as we can find. The majority of our cases come from public sources of information, although more than 200 cases have been obtained through law enforcement partners and victim organizations; those cases include confidential information regarding the insider or the victim organization.

The sources of information we gather and use to **code**[1] insider threat cases are

- Public sources of information
  - Media reports, including Department of Justice and U.S. Attorney's Office press releases
  - Court documents obtained using LexisNexis, from law enforcement, or directly from the courts
  - Other publications, including books, news outlets, police reports, and organization press releases
- Nonpublic sources of information
  - Law enforcement investigations
  - Victim organization investigations
  - Interviews with victim organizations
  - Interviews with convicted insiders
  - Interviews with investigators and prosecutors

Recently, we received feedback from practitioners on the front line of computer network defense that while malicious insider activity is of great concern, of equal concern is nonmalicious (accidental) activity, for which controls also need to be put in place. In addition, we have received feedback from individuals outside the United States, and from global organizations that have branches located outside the United States. They would like to know if the insider activity exhibited in U.S. cases is similar to or different from activity in incidents in organizations outside the United States. In addition, they need to know if the same countermeasures we recommend are legal in various other countries, due to stringent employee privacy laws. Based on this feedback, we have begun collecting incidents from outside the United States, as well as unintentional insider threats, such as accidental data disclosure or clicking on infected email attachments.

---

1. **Code:** in the context of insider threat case research, entering the details of a case in a database according to a set of well-defined criteria.

# Coding Process

Information about three entities is needed when coding insider threat cases: the organization(s) involved, the insider (subject), and the details of the incident. Figure D-1 shows the primary relationships among these three entities.

## Organization Data

Multiple organizations can be involved in a single incident. An organization that is negatively impacted by an incident is designated as a **victim organization.** Incidents may also involve another organization—the victim organization's trusted business partner. In these incidents, the malicious insider is not directly employed by the victim organization, but is able to attack the organization because of authorized access granted to him through a contractual relationship with his or her employer. Chapter 9, Conclusion and Miscellaneous Issues, contains a section devoted to insider threats from trusted business partners.

Incidents, particularly those involving theft of IP, may also have a **beneficiary organization,** an organization that knowingly or unknowingly gains an advantage from the incident to the detriment of the victim organization. We identify the organization and any organizational issues that were relevant to the case, as shown in Table D-1. The tables in this appendix are not the data dictionary for the insider threat database; they are provided to give you insight into the type of information collected for each incident and a few sample values for each type of data.

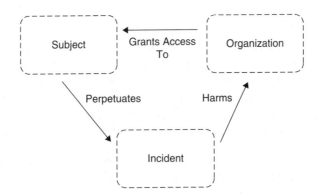

**Figure D-1** *Entities needed when coding insider threat cases*

**Table D-1** *Organization Information Collected*

| Organization Subcategory | Information Collected in the Database |
| --- | --- |
| Organization Descriptors | Name, address, relation to insider |
| Organization Type | Victim, beneficiary, trusted business partner, other |
| Organization Description | Description of the organization |
| Industry Sector | Critical infrastructure sector of the organization |
| Based in the United States? | Location of the organization; based in the United States? |
| Organization Issues | Work environment such as hostile work environment or culture of mistrust; layoffs, mergers and acquisitions, reorganizations, and other workplace events that may have contributed to an insider's decision to act |
| Opportunity Provided to Insider | Actions taken by organization that may have contributed to the insider's decision to take action (such as demotions or transfers of employees); failure on the part of the organization to take action based on concerning behaviors or other events, actions, or conditions; or vulnerabilities—for example, insufficient monitoring of external access |

## Subject Data

We collect any details we can find about the insider, including details regarding planning activities. These details are generally discovered after an incident has already occurred, but are essential to preventing future insider threats. We also collect information about the insider's accomplices, including demographic data, the accomplice's relationship to the insider and the victim organization, and the accomplice's role in the incident.

We do not make any judgments about the insider or attempt to diagnose his or her behavior; we code exactly what we find in the source materials.

Table D-2 describes the subject attributes in more detail.

**Table D-2** *Subject Information Collected*

| Subject Subcategory | Information Collected in the Database |
| --- | --- |
| Descriptors | Name, gender, age, citizenship, residence, education, employee title/type/status, departure date, tenure, access, position |
| Motives and Unmet Expectations | Motives (financial, curiosity, ideology, recognition, external benefit), unmet expectation (promotion, workload, financial, usage) |
| Concerning Behaviors | Tardiness, insubordination, absences, complaints, drug/alcohol abuse, disgruntlement, coworker/supervisor conflict, violence, harassment, poor performance, poor hygiene, etc. |
| Violation History | Security violations, resource misuse, complaints, deception about background |
| Consequences | Reprimands, transfers, demotion, HR report, termination, suspension, access revocation, counseling |
| Substance Abuse | Alcohol, hallucinogens, marijuana, amphetamines, cocaine, sedatives, heroin, inhalants |
| Planning and Deception | Prior planning activities, explicit deceptions |

## Incident Data

Information about the incident includes individual actions taken to set up the attack, vulnerabilities exploited during the attack, steps taken to conceal it, how the incident was detected, and the impact to the victim organization. In addition, when available, data is collected on actions taken by the organization in response to the incident, and events and conditions that may have contributed to an insider's decision to carry out an attack. Table D-3 describes the incident attributes in more detail.

**Table D-3**  *Incident Information Collected*

| Incident Subcategory | Information Collected in the Database |
| --- | --- |
| Case Summary | Incident dates, duration, prosecution |
| Conspirators | Accomplices, type of collusion, relationships to insider |
| Information Sources | Origination, type |
| Incident Chronology | Sequence, date, place, event |
| Investigation and Capture | How identified and caught |
| Prosecution Result | Indictment, subject's story, sentence, case outcome |
| Recruitment | Outside/competitor induced, insider collusion, outsider collusion, acted alone, reasons for collusion |
| IT Accounts Used | Subject's, organization's, system administrator's, database administrator's, coworker's, authorized third party, shared, backdoor |
| Outcome | Data copied/deleted/read/modified/created/disclosed, used in identity theft, unauthorized document created, denial of service |
| Impact | Description, financial |
| How Detected | Software, information system, audit, nontechnical, system failure |
| Who Detected | Self-reported, IT staff, other internal; customer, law enforcement, competitor, other external |
| Log Files Used | System files, email, remote access, ISP |
| Who Responded | Incident response team, management, other internal |
| Vulnerabilities Exploited | Sequence of exploit, description, vulnerability grouping |

| | |
|---|---|
| Technical Methods | Technical methods used to set up and/or carry out the attack (e.g., hardware device, malicious code, modified logs, compromised account, sabotaged backups, modified backups) |
| Concealment Methods | Concealment methods used to hide technical and nontechnical methods |

# Appendix E

# Insider Threat Training Simulation: MERIT *InterActive*

While it has long been understood that quality training is imperative to organizational success, traditional training techniques do not necessarily result in significant job-performance improvement because of the difficulty of effectively capturing the reality of complex challenges and changing priorities that organizations face. Training on subjects in such complex domains as insider threat is often difficult to design because it requires a balance of people, processes, and technology. We have faced the difficulty of transitioning complex lessons about insider threat to an audience that might prefer to focus on individual aspects of the problem, rather than the "big picture." The danger in this narrow focus is that unintended consequences of decisions are felt throughout the organization.

Training games and simulations in complex domains immerse the trainee in a team-oriented, role-playing experience that models important aspects of daily, mission-critical operations in a realistic organizational context. Research evidence suggests such immersion can increase credibility, retention, and job performance, particularly in complex task environments—environments characterized by limited information, complex feedback relationships, conflicting goals, and uncertain causal relationships. Gaming and simulation are becoming increasingly important for providing training in complex socio-technical domains efficiently and effectively.

This appendix describes our development of a training simulation, called MERIT *InterActive,* for the complex socio-technical domain of insider threat [Greitzer 2008]. The first section is geared more toward a research audience, providing background on the effectiveness of various training mechanisms. The second section describes the MERIT *InterActive* prototype, and will be of more interest to practitioners.

As we describe in [Greitzer 2008], MERIT *InterActive* "immerses players in a realistic business setting from which they make decisions about how to prevent, detect, and respond to insider actions and see how their decisions impact key performance metrics. It provides a team-oriented, role-playing experience using model-based simulation of critical aspects of insider threat risk management in a realistic organizational context. Team orientation is critical because organizations typically identify these problems at an organizational enterprise level rather than an individual manager or department level. Role playing is also crucial because solutions generally require collaboration among multiple stakeholders; role playing helps players understand and acquire the necessary skills."

## Background on Effectiveness of Various Training Mechanisms

Our research began with collection and analysis of empirical data from actual cases of insider fraud, theft of intellectual property, and IT sabotage. We soon realized the danger in training practitioners using statistical data. They were not grasping the "big picture" of the insider threat problem. Because of this issue, we created system dynamics models representing the patterns, trends, and evolution of insider incidents, to provide a fuller understanding of indicators, precursors, and effective proactive and reactive countermeasures in the face of a possible attack. Some of those models are outlined in this book.

We were quite satisfied with the reaction to our models, as we seemed to be coming closer to our goal of raising awareness of the people, process, and technology issues surrounding insider threat. At that point in time, one of our U.S. Department of Defense (DOD) sponsors remarked that our material was critical to the military commanders in Iraq, but unfortunately we had no method for widespread delivery of the training, as our only training mechanism was a face-to-face workshop. As a result, Carnegie Mellon's CyLab funded development of MERIT *InterActive*—a proof of concept for an insider threat training simulation. We have discussed and demonstrated our MERIT *InterActive* prototype at several government and industry meetings and conferences, and have received positive feedback [Cappelli 2006, Moore 2007].

The MERIT *InterActive* prototype is based on system dynamics [Sterman 2000, Forrester 1994]. Refer to Appendix F, System Dynamics Background, for more information. The combination of system dynamics to characterize the complex, feedback-rich domain of insider threat, and a remotely playable game-like environment for learner immersion, seems to be a match made in heaven. In the domain of information security, the positive effects of training on performance have been demonstrated [Phelps 2006]. Training simulation techniques can facilitate an organization's difficult transition from a reactive to a proactive management culture [Moore 2006]. Lane [1995] and Groessler [2004] review the history of training simulation and describe the value of and requirements for using these simulations to provide managers with an intellectually and emotionally rich and engaging educational experience. Business management training simulation promotes more effective learning by developing critical attitudes and both the skill and confidence needed to transition lessons learned to an operational environment.

> The combination of system dynamics to characterize the complex, feedback-rich domain of insider threat, and a remotely playable game-like environment for learner immersion, seems to be a match made in heaven.

The benefits of including interactive content in training can be seen in many areas. For example, a test of learning in introductory physics classes called the Force Concept Inventory (FCI) found that learning was approximately double for those classes with an interactive component compared to lecture alone [Mayo 2007]. In addition, empirical evidence suggests specifically that computer games and simulations can be used to enhance learning and understanding in complex domains [Cordova 1996, Ricci 1996]. One simulator, called the Manufacturing Game, has been used with great success at a number of organizations. The Manufacturing Game allows participants to see firsthand the benefits of moving a low-performing organization stuck in reactive maintenance to a more proactive stance in which planned work eliminates the manufacturing-defect generators. The challenge for participants is to resist short-term pressures to eliminate costs directly and focus on eliminating the work that drives the costs. Probably the most prominent application was at the British Petroleum Refinery in Lima, Ohio [Repenning 2001]. The refinery put around 80% of its personnel through the Manufacturing Game workshops over the course of about nine months. The Manufacturing Game workshops helped build a common culture and vision around creating a more reliable operation. The workshops improved the refinery's bottom line by more than $10 million annually by improving output, eliminating waste, and cutting costs.

Another simulation game related to information security, called CyberCIEGE, teaches network security concepts through a Sim City–styled simulation, and has garnered positive feedback [Cone 2006].

## The MERIT *InterActive* Prototype

CyLab funded us to work jointly with a student-led team at Carnegie Mellon's Entertainment Technology Center (ETC) to develop a proof-of-concept, multimedia training simulation for insider threat. This joint effort used an evolutionary prototyping development methodology that involved an iterative process of prototyping and requirements refinement. As shown along the left and bottom sides of Figure E-1, the development of the insider threat models from our analysis of cases in the CERT insider threat database allowed us to identify critical learning objectives and metrics for the training. The insider IT sabotage cases also helped identify fictional scenarios representative of a preponderance of the actual cases as a basis for the story line for the game. This is shown along the right side of the figure. Research in the first semester involved developing the story line for the training as an expansion of the fictional scenario that would be especially suited to teaching

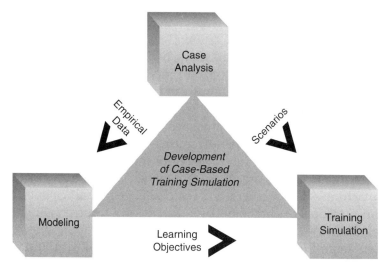

**Figure E-1** *Development of case-based training simulation*

the learning objectives. The second semester focused on the development of the system engine and a user interface that uses state-of-the-art graphics, video, and audio technologies to bring the scenario to life.

You, as a player of Merit *InterActive*, serve as a new team manager for a company that hosts Web sites and stores information for clients. As the manager, your team must migrate the customer database to a Web-based online service providing clients the ability to customize their service faster and more easily. Your mission is to meet the deadline established for migrating the database while adequately managing the team through a set of business and information technology processes. What you don't realize is that one of your team members is disgruntled with the new management situation and covertly plans to execute a logic bomb to destroy the team's work.

The core struggle you face, which makes the game challenging and fun, is to ensure the team's progress toward project completion while mitigating the risk of insider attack.

As in any organization, you work with the human resources (HR) department to manage people and with the information technology (IT) department to manage IT. The game also engages you in regular (video) meetings with your boss to get feedback on how well you are doing and to get advice on future directions in terms of both execution of the migration and mitigation of the risk of insider attack. Figure E-2 shows the interface for the game.

**Figure E-2** *MERIT* InterActive *interface—information technology floor*

As the game is played, a scenario evolves as an interleaving of the events generated by the game and the moves you generate (acting as new manager of the team). The *events* include the following:

- Actions of the malicious insider
- Actions of others within the organization
- Decoy events and other office happenings

The *moves* include your actions to do the following:

- Establish and maintain good relations with employees
- Address disruptive events
- Address malicious events
- Implement proactive IT policies, practices, and technology
- Implement HR policies and practices

The game has a broad range of potential outcomes, as shown in Figure E-3. On the left end of the range, you fail completely: The attack is successful and the project is devastated. On the right end, you succeed: The insider's disgruntlement is assuaged and the project meets the deadlines established. In the more typical situation, your actions achieve mixed success in which the attack is successful and partially recovered from, the attack execution is blocked, or the insider is disgruntled but the attack is deterred. As the game proceeds you may have to make decisions that force you to miss the project deadline to some extent in order to prevent insider attack or mitigate insider threat risk.

The goal of the game is to balance two game measures: the Progress Measure and the Risk Measure. In fact, the core struggle you face is balancing these two measures. The moves you choose, as manager for the organization,

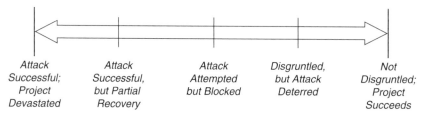

**Figure E-3** *Range of game-playing results*

should affect the game measures in well-defined ways. For example, IT policies, practices, and technologies put in place affect the amount of team resources devoted to product development, in both positive and negative ways. HR policies and practices may affect the team's morale, which in turn affects the team's productivity. Addressing disruptive or malicious actions may take resources directly away from project completion. The events generated by the game are going to have similar effects on the game measures.

The key thread through the game scenario is the interaction between the malicious insider and you, the team manager. Of course, there are other happenings within the workplace, including events that do the following:

- Contribute to completing the team's project
- Contribute to making the office a nice place to work, and thus improving morale
- Disrupt or inhibit progress on the project, or reduce morale, but are not directly tied to the insider attack
- Have no impact on game execution, but improve the realism of the characters and situation

These other events are interleaved with the key (insider threat) thread and provide the realism of the overall player experience. One additional thread concerns progress on the team project—the database migration—that will reflect achieving key milestones on that project (e.g., product requirements, design, and implementation).

The key thread is, of course, crucial to teaching the primary insider threat lessons. The key thread is broken into four stages:

- Stage 1: Expectation Escalation/Management
- Stage 2: Disgruntlement Escalation/Management
- Stage 3: Attack Setup/Monitoring
- Stage 4: Attack Execution/Recovery

The end of each stage can be viewed as a game checkpoint. These stages are based on the MERIT model of insider IT sabotage, and therefore form a direct tie from the game to our research and provide a clear connection for "coaching" you by explaining important model concepts at the checkpoints. The pre- and post-conditions of each stage as well as example properties and lessons of each stage are described in the sidebars. After you go through each stage, the checkpoint provides video-supported player feedback, evaluation, and scoring. Our general strategy is that players should learn by failing, and improving, in a safe environment. So, even perfect performance on your part in our initial prototype still leads to entering Stage 3 (i.e., an insider starting to set up the attack), but good performance could prevent the insider from entering Stage 4 (i.e., attack execution). Table E-1 provides an overview of each stage.

**Table E-1** *Overview of MERIT InterActive Stages*

| Stage | Pre-condition | Post-conditions | Example Properties of the Scenario | Example Key Lessons |
|---|---|---|---|---|
| *Stage 1: Expectation Escalation and Management* | An insider is predisposed to malicious action. | Worst case: an insider whose expectations have been allowed to grow way beyond what can be supported<br><br>Best case: an insider whose expectations were constrained to a level consistent with a clearly defined organizational policy | Expectation escalation is exhibited by the insider's heightened freedom or recognition within the organization, e.g., the more the insider gets, the more he wants, and the more the organization gives in return (up to a point). | Management's communication with its employees concerning organizational policies, appropriate expectations in light of those policies, and management's consistent enforcement of organizational policies can keep insiders' expectations from growing beyond that which can practically be fulfilled. |
| *Stage 2: Disgruntlement Escalation and Management* | The insider's unmet expectations cause disgruntlement to an extent that he starts disrupting the workplace (behaviorally). | Worst case: a seriously disgruntled insider who is motivated to set up a technical attack<br><br>Best case: an insider who is given an appropriate mechanism for dealing with his disgruntlement (e.g., employee-assistance program referral) | Disgruntlement escalation is exhibited by the insider's increased behavioral disruption within the workplace in response to management action (or inaction). | Managers need to handle the initial grievance appropriately. They can also play a key role in providing the insider with a mechanism to reduce his disgruntlement level. |

*Continues*

**Table E-1** *Overview of MERIT InterActive Stages (Continued)*

| Stage | Pre-condition | Post-conditions | Example Properties of the Scenario | Example Key Lessons |
|---|---|---|---|---|
| *Stage 3: Attack Setup and Monitoring* | An insider is disgruntled to an extent that he starts setting up a technical attack. | Worst case: an insider who is ready and willing to execute his technical attack<br><br>Best case: an organization that is aware when the insider takes technical steps to set up the attack, perhaps even preventing the attack from occurring | Attack setup is exhibited by the insider's move toward greater concealment of his disgruntlement and increased technical actions to set up and amplify the impacts of the impending attack. | Given an insider's desire to attack, management's knowledge of access paths available to the insider is essential for beingable to prevent an attack. Auditing can help discover previously unknown paths, but it takes time to work. This delay may be all the insider needs to attack. |
| *Stage 4: Attack Execution and Recovery* | An insider has a technical attack set up and ready to execute. | Worst case: an insider who has attacked the organization's systems and a manager whose project is destroyed<br><br>Best case: an organization that is able to recover quickly from the attack, minimizing the operational and financial impact, because of a proven disaster recovery plan | If the insider's desire to attack upon termination is moderate or if risk aversion is high, discussions post-termination that emphasize the organization's vigilance may result in reducing the insider's desire to attack. | Strong backup and recovery plans and procedures can lessen the impact due to attack. |

# Conclusion

The current prototype provides a coherent, well-grounded, and engaging environment for teaching primary lessons for mitigating risk of insider IT sabotage. Our future research will investigate the effectiveness of training simulation for teaching insider threat concepts. We hypothesize that those experiences that engage the student with direct, mastery experiences, such as would be the case with a gaming or simulation environment, would increase the individual's domain self-efficacy to an extent greater than would be the case with just a vicarious training situation, such as often occurs with a lecture or workshop environment. A hybrid approach that utilizes both direct and vicarious experience, however, should produce even greater increases in domain self-efficacy than either approach individually.

While the particular media used has generally shown not to significantly affect the quality of learning [Russell 2001], the instructional design strategy can play a large role in participant learning and performance improvement. Utilizing Bandura's Social Cognitive Theory, we will examine the nature of the relationship between insider threat training and effectiveness of insider threat management as measured by pre- and post-training assessments of domain self-efficacy. We will also evaluate the individual and relative effectiveness of alternative traditional training modalities, both with and without training simulation. Finally, we will evaluate the individual and comparative effectiveness of differing interactive content within the training simulation.

While the focus so far has been on insider IT sabotage, the design is, to some extent, data-driven allowing the implementation of additional scenarios without necessitating changes to the code. Using this approach, the initial release of MERIT *InterActive* would include the IT sabotage scenario, but subsequent effort would implement additional scenarios for insider fraud and insider theft of intellectual property, based on the models described in this book. Future work in this area will require experiments to determine how well game players are learning important insider threat domain lessons. We believe continued research will produce training simulations for insider threat that will help decision makers make more informed decisions about insider threat risk mitigation.

# Appendix F

# System Dynamics Background

This appendix describes the system dynamics modeling method for those of you who might be interested in more information than we provided in the chapters describing our models.

System dynamics is a method for modeling and analyzing the holistic behavior of complex problems as they evolve over time. It has been used to gain insight into some of the most challenging strategy questions facing businesses and government for several decades. System dynamics provides particularly useful insight into difficult management situations in which the best efforts to solve a problem actually make the problem worse. Examples of these apparently paradoxical effects include the following [Sterman 2000]:

- Low-nicotine cigarettes, supposedly introduced to the benefit of smokers' health, that only result in people smoking more cigarettes and taking longer, deeper drags to meet their nicotine needs
- Levees and dams constructed to control floods that only produce more severe flooding because they disrupt the natural dispersion and dissipation of water

We found in our insider threat research that intuitive solutions to problems with employees often reduce the problem in the short term but make it much worse in the long term. For example, employee termination might solve an immediate problem, but it may also lead to long-term problems for the organization if the insider has the technical means to attack the system following termination. System dynamics is a valuable analysis tool for gaining insight into long-term solutions and for demonstrating their benefits.

A powerful tenet of system dynamics is that the dynamic complexity of problematic behavior is captured by the underlying feedback structure of that behavior. We decompose the causal structure of the problematic behavior into its feedback loops to understand which loop is strongest (i.e., which loop's influence on behavior dominates all others) at particular points through time. We can then thoroughly understand and communicate the nature of the problematic behavior and the benefits of alternative mitigations.

System dynamics model boundaries are drawn so that all the enterprise elements necessary to generate and understand problematic behavior are contained within them. This approach encourages the inclusion of soft (as well as hard) factors in the model, such as policy-related, procedural, administrative, or cultural factors. The exclusion of soft factors in other modeling techniques essentially treats their influence as negligible, which is often not the case. This endogenous viewpoint helps show the benefits of mitigations to the problematic behavior that are often overlooked, partly due to a narrow focus in resolving problems.

In our work we rely on system dynamics as a tool to help understand and communicate contributing factors to insider threats and implications for various mitigation strategies and tactics. It is tempting to use the simulation of the model to help predict the occurrence of insider attacks or the effect of mitigation strategies, but what is the nature of the types of predictions that system dynamics facilitates? Dennis Meadows offers a concise answer by categorizing outputs from models as follows [Meadows et al. 1974]:

- Absolute and precise predictions (e.g., exactly when and where will the next cyberattack take place?)
- Conditional precise predictions (e.g., how much will it cost my organization if a cyberattack occurs?)
- Conditional imprecise projections of dynamic behavior modes (e.g., if a bank mandates background checks for all new employees, will its damages from insider fraud be less than they would have been otherwise?)
- Current trends that may influence future behavior (e.g., what effect will current trends in espionage have on national security in five years?)

- Philosophical explorations of the consequences of a set of assumptions, without regard for the real-world accuracy or usefulness of those assumptions (e.g., if another country succeeds in human cloning, how would this affect the risk of espionage for the United States?)

Our models—and system dynamics models in general—provide information of the third sort. Meadows explains further that "this level of knowledge is less satisfactory than a perfect, precise prediction would be, but it is still a significant advance over the level of understanding permitted by current mental models."

In the models in this book, we have modified the system dynamics causal loop diagram notation to be more suitable for our readers. Arrows still represent the pair-wise influence of the variable at the source of the arrow on the variable at the target of the arrow, but their look indicates how they should be interpreted.

- Roughly, a *solid* arrow indicates a positive influence—that the value of the source and target variables moves in the *same* direction.[1]
- Roughly, a *dashed* arrow indicates a negative influence—that the value of the source and target variables moves in the *opposite* direction.[2]

As mentioned, dynamically complex problems can often be best understood in terms of the feedback loops underlying those problems. There are two types of feedback loops: *balancing* and *reinforcing*.

- Balancing loops describe the system aspects that oppose change, tending to drive organizational variables to some goal state. In other words, balancing loops tend to move the system to an equilibrium state even in the face of change. The behavior of a thermostat is an example of a balancing loop. It continually changes the air flow into a room based on the temperature of the room, with the goal of maintaining an equilibrium temperature.

---

1. More formally, a *solid* arrow indicates that if the value of the source variable increases, the value of the target variable increases above what it would otherwise have been, all other things being equal. And if the value of the source variable decreases, the value of the target variable decreases below what it would otherwise have been, all other things being equal.

2. More formally, a *dashed* arrow indicates that if the value of the source variable increases, the value of the target variable decreases below what it would otherwise have been, all other things being equal. And if the value of the source variable decreases, the value of the target variable increases above what it would otherwise have been, all other things being equal.

- Reinforcing loops describe the system aspects that tend to drive variable values consistently upward or consistently downward. In other words, reinforcing loops can "spiral out of control." A flu epidemic is an example of a reinforcing loop. It spirals out of control as more and more people contract the flu.

System dynamics models are described as a sequence of feedback loops that characterize how the problem unfolds over time. Each feedback loop describes a single aspect of the problem. Multiple feedback loops interact to capture the complexities of the problem domain.

You can determine the type of a feedback loop by counting the number of negative influences along the path of the loop. An odd number of negative influences indicates a balancing loop, and an even (or zero) number of negative influences indicates a reinforcing loop.

## The Security Dynamics Network

The Security Dynamics Network (SDN) is a largely unfunded and loosely coordinated group of national laboratories and universities applying system dynamics to explore issues of cybersecurity, with a specific focus on insider threat.[3] The SDN has gathered five times at the member institutions since 2003 and has met frequently at the annual Conference of the System Dynamics Society. The group has focused on the malicious insider threat and has been a source of expertise, information, and inspiration for many of the insider threat models developed in this book. The SDN is currently being merged into a larger SIG of the System Dynamics Society on Conflict, Defense, & Security.[4]

The SDN has convened three group modeling workshops at member institutions, under the collective (and somewhat retrospective) title of System Dynamics Modeling for Information Security (SDMIS). Group modeling brings together experts from a variety of areas to build models together in a way that achieves consensus for the models developed.

---

3. SDN members include University at Albany; Agder University College; TECNUN, University of Navarra; Worcester Polytechnic Institute; Sandia National Labs; Argonne National Labs; and the CERT Program at the Software Engineering Institute.

4. At the time of this writing, the Web site for the Conflict, Defense, & Security SIG at www.ConflictSIG .org was under construction.

We bring technical security experts together with insider threat experts and behavioral scientists to build models that cover the broad spectrum of behavioral and technical aspects of the problem.

*First SDMIS Workshop:* The first workshop, in February 2003, was attended by a small number of organizations and held at Agder University College in Grimstad, Norway. Group modeling conducted there focused on a particular insider who planted a logic bomb in an organization's systems that he helped engineer because he felt that a new system administrator hired above him in the organization was incompetent. The group published a number of papers in the 2003 System Dynamics Society Conference [Melara 2003] and in a book titled *From Modeling to Managing Security: A System Dynamics Approach*, edited by Jose Gonzalez [Gonzalez 2003].

*Second SDMIS Workshop:* The SDN grew nearly to its present size in convening the second workshop held in February 2004 at the CERT Program at the Software Engineering Institute in Pittsburgh. Group modeling focused on identifying patterns across a set of six actual cases of insider compromise: Two insiders stole for financial gain, two created and detonated a logic bomb, and two stole software critical to the company. The cases varied widely in terms of their technical sophistication and primary motivation. The work established the "dynamic trigger" hypothesis to explain that the dynamic behaviors leading up to and triggering attacks can enable the design of more effective defense strategies. Results were documented at a public Web site, www.cert.org/research/sdmis/, and in a conference paper [Andersen 2004]. Our follow-on work, in collaboration with one SDN member, Dr. Elise Weaver, then from Worcester Polytecnic Institute, led to the development of the insider IT sabotage model [Cappelli 2006].

*Third SDMIS Workshop:* The SDN decided to focus on a particular class of insider crimes—insider fraud—in the third workshop held in November 2004, again at the Software Engineering Institute in Pittsburgh. While the group model developed was based on real cases of insider fraud from the CERT insider threat database, the model was set in the context of a representative (instructional) case that exhibited many of the properties of the real cases. As insider fraud cases typically progress over longer periods of time than other types of insider attacks, signal detection theory and judgment analysis was incorporated into the model and the result used in classroom settings. In addition to a paper at the Society's 2005 conference [Rich 2005], a number of journal papers were published [Martinez-Moyano 2006, Martinez-Moyano 2008].

The SDN had limited success in getting funding for collaboration across all member institutions, but we've gotten together to share information and progress in Grimstad and Albany, with NATO support. In addition, individual member organizations have continued to use system dynamics effectively for their own bodies of work. We have continued to develop models of insider threat based on the CERT database of insider crimes, as described in this book [Moore 2011a, Moore 2011c, Moore 2008, Moore 2007]. Sandia has also recently published an employee life-cycle model of the evolution of insiders within an organization based on cases of insider compromise that it has identified [Duran 2009]. Of course, others outside the SDN have recognized the value of system dynamics modeling for this domain [Foroughi 2008] and we look forward to expanding the network and the domain of modeling as we integrate with the Conflict, Defense, & Security SIG of the System Dynamics Society.

# Glossary of Terms

**access path:**   A sequence of one or more access points that lead to a critical system.

**Ambitious Leader:**   A leader of an insider crime who recruits insiders to steal information for some larger purpose.

**anonymous remailer:**   A server that receives email messages containing embedded instructions on where to forward them. The server then forwards the messages while also masking their originating location.

**anti-spam blacklists:**   A system designed to block spam messages through a system of IP address filtering. Often functions in tandem with a content-recognition system.

**backdoor account:**   An unauthorized account created for gaining access to a system or network known only to the person who created it.

**behavioral precursor:**   An individual action, event, or condition that involves personal or interpersonal behaviors and that precedes and is associated with malicious insider activity.

**beneficiary organization:**   An organization that knowingly or unknowingly gains an advantage from the incident to the detriment of the victim organization.

**change controls:**   Formal processes used to ensure that changes to a product or system are introduced in a controlled and coordinated manner.[1]

---

1. Wikipedia

**code reviews:**   A process to examine source code, typically by someone other than the original coder, with the purpose of identifying and addressing mistakes.

**coded:**   In the context of insider threat case research, the details of a case entered in a database according to a set of well-defined criteria.

**data leakage tools:**   *See* **data loss prevention (DLP) systems.**

**data loss prevention (DLP) systems:**   Refers to systems designed to detect and prevent unauthorized use and transmission of confidential information.[2] Also commonly called **data leakage tools.**

**denial-of-service attack:**   A type of cyberattack in which a large amount of traffic is directed at a server in an attempt to disable it.

**digital rights management (DRM):**   A term for access control technologies that are used by hardware manufacturers, publishers, copyright holders, and individuals to limit the use of digital content and devices.

**digital watermarking:**   The process of embedding information into a digital signal, which may be used to verify its authenticity or the identity of its owners, in the same manner as paper bearing a watermark for visible identification.[3]

**domain names:**   Host names tied to IP resources such as Web sites (adapted from ICANN/Wikipedia).

**economic espionage:**   The conscious and willful misappropriation of trade secrets with the knowledge or intent that the offense will benefit a foreign government, foreign instrumentality, or foreign agent.[4]

**Entitled Independent:**   An insider, usually with some expectation of ownership or entitlement to organization property, acting primarily alone to steal information to take to a new job or to his own side business.

**event correlation:**   A technique for making sense of a large number of events and pinpointing the few events that are really important in that mass of information.[5]

---

2. Wikipedia

3. Wikipedia

4. See www.ncix.gov/publications/reports/fecie_all/fecie_2007/FECIE_2007.pdf.

5. Wikipedia

**file integrity checker:**  A tool that partially automates the process of identifying changes to system files or the addition of malicious code and flagging them for investigation.[6]

**File Transfer Protocol (FTP):**  A communication standard used to transfer files from one host to another over a network, such as the Internet.[7]

**fraud:**  *See* **insider fraud.**

**HTTPS traffic:**  Network traffic that is encrypted via the Secure Sockets Layer protocol.

**identity crime:**  The misuse of personal or financial identifiers in order to gain something of value and/or facilitate some other criminal activity.[8]

**identity management system:**  A system or technology that supports the management of identities. It is generally accepted that an IMS will establish identities, describe identities through one or more attributes, follow identity activity, and be capable of removing an identity from the system it manages (adapted from FIDIS).

**industrial espionage:**  The conscious and willful misappropriation of trade secrets related to, or included in, a product that is produced for, or placed in, interstate or foreign commerce to the economic benefit of anyone other than the owner, with the knowledge or intent that the offense will injure the owner of that trade secret.[9]

**insider fraud:**  An insider's use of IT for the unauthorized modification, addition, or deletion of an organization's data (not programs or systems) for personal gain, or theft of information that leads to an identity crime (e.g., identity theft, credit card fraud).

**insider IT sabotage:**  An insider's use of information technology (IT) to direct specific harm at an organization or an individual.

**insider theft of intellectual property:**  An insider's use of IT to steal proprietary information from the organization. This category includes industrial espionage involving insiders.

---

6. See www.sans.org/resources/idfaq/integrity_checker.php for a discussion of file integrity checkers.

7. Wikipedia

8. This definition comes from the Secret Service Web site: www.secretservice.gov/criminal.shtml.

9. See www.ncix.gov/publications/reports/fecie_all/fecie_2007/FECIE_2007.pdf.

**insider trading:**   The trading of a corporation's stock or other securities (e.g., bonds or stock options) by individuals with potential access to nonpublic information about the company.[10]

**intellectual property:**   Intangible assets created and owned by an organization that are critical to achieving its mission.[11]

**Internet relay chat (IRC) channel:**   Functionally similar to a multiuser chat instance.

**Internet underground:**   A collection of individuals with shared goals where there is some degree of hierarchical structure and the primary communication mechanism or agent of electronic crime involves the Internet. Further, it may demonstrate some degree of pseudoanonymity and/or secrecy, which may be useful for organizing and carrying out electronic crimes.

**IT sabotage:**   *See* **insider IT sabotage.**

**keystroke logger (or key logger):**   A hardware or software device that records the exact keystrokes entered into a computer system.

**least privilege:**   Authorizing people only for the resources needed to do their job.

**logic bomb:**   Malicious code implanted on a target system and configured to execute after a designated period of time or on the occurrence of a specified system action.

**malicious code:**   *See* **malware.**

**malicious insider threat:**   A current or former employee, contractor, or business partner who has or had authorized access to an organization's network, system, or data and intentionally exceeded or misused that access in a manner that negatively affected the confidentiality, integrity, or availability of the organization's information or information systems.

**malware:**   Code intended to execute a malicious function. Also commonly referred to as **malicious code.**

**national security espionage:**   The act of obtaining, delivering, transmitting, communicating, or receiving information about the national defense with an intent, or reason to believe, that the information

10. Wikipedia

11. While IP does not generally include individuals' Personally Identifiable Information (PII), which an organization does not own, it could include a database that the organization developed that contains PII.

may be used to the injury of the United States or to the advantage of any foreign nation. Espionage is a violation of 18 United States Code sections 792–798 and Article 106, Uniform Code of Military Justice.[12]

**network probing:**   Any number of practices in which a particular network is either passively surveilled or actively scanned.

**network sniffer (also known as a sniffer):**   A computer program or a piece of hardware that can intercept and log traffic passing through a network.

**nonrepudiation:**   Ability to verify a particular user is accessing a system or performing a particular action; the goal being to make it more difficult for a user to hide illicit activity.

**password cracker:**   A program used to identify passwords to a computer or network resource; used to obtain passwords for other employee accounts.

**personal predisposition:**   A characteristic historically linked to a propensity to exhibit malicious insider behavior.

**privileged users:**   Users who have an elevated level of access to a network, computer system, or application that is short of full system administrator access. For example, database administrators (DBAs) are privileged users because they have the ability to create new user accounts and control the access rights of users within their domain.

**proxies:**   A proxy server, more commonly known as a proxy, is a server that routes network traffic through itself, thereby masking the origins of the network traffic.

**remote network administration tools:**   Tools to allow the administration of a computer from a location other than the computer being administered.

**removable media:**   Computer storage media that is designed to be removed from the computer without powering the computer off. Examples include CDs, USB flash drives, and external hard disk drives.

**role-based access:**   Access required by a person's duties. Typically, a person's access to data/systems should be no greater than what is required of the person's role.

**rootkit:**   Software that enables continued privileged access to a computer while actively hiding its presence from administrators by subverting standard operating system functionality or other applications.

---

12. Dictionary of Military and Associated Terms. U.S. Department of Defense, 2005.

**separation of duties:**   The separation of tasks among various individuals.

**shared account:**   An account used by two or more people.

**social engineering:**   A nontechnical form of intrusion that relies heavily on human interaction and often involves tricking other people to break normal security procedures.[13]

**Software Development Life Cycle (SDLC):**   Synonymous with "software process" as well as "software engineering," it is a structured methodology used in the development of software products and packages. This methodology is used from the conception phase through to the delivery and end of life of a final software product.[14]

**software keystroke logger:**   A software-based method of recording keystrokes entered from a keyboard.

**stressful events:**   Events that may cause concerning behaviors in individuals predisposed to malicious acts.

**system dynamics:**   An approach to understanding the behavior of complex systems over time. It deals with internal feedback loops and time delays that affect the behavior of the entire system.[15]

**technical precursor:**   An individual action, event, or condition that involves computer or electronic media and that precedes and is associated with malicious insider activity.

**theft of intellectual property:**   *See* **insider theft of intellectual property.**

**thin client:**   A computer that does not run programs or store data itself, but accesses programs and data over a network from a central computer server.

**TIFF images:**   Tagged Image File Format (or .tif) is a file type often used in image-manipulation programs.

**trusted business partner (TBP):**   Any external organization or individual an organization has contracted to perform a service for the organization. The nature of this service requires the organization to provide the TBP authorized access to proprietary data, critical files, and/or internal infrastructure. For example, if an organization contracts with a company to perform billing services, it would have to provide access

---

13. Whatis.com

14. Webopedia

15. MIT System Dynamics in Education Project (SDEP)

to its customer data, thereby establishing a trusted business partnership. However, the TBP concept does not include cases in which the organization is simply a customer of another company. For example, when an organization uses a bank, it is simply a client of the bank. This customer–vendor relationship would not be considered a TBP relationship.

**two-person rule:**  A control mechanism that requires the involvement of two persons for a particular operation (adapted from Wikipedia).

**unintentional insider threat:**  An insider who accidently affects the confidentiality, availability, or integrity of an organization's information or information systems, possibly by being tricked by an outsider's use of social engineering.

**unmet expectation:**  An unsatisfied assumption by an individual that an organization action or event will (or will not) happen, or a condition will (or will not) exist.

**victim organization:**  An organization that is negatively impacted by an incident.

**virtual private network (VPN):**  A virtual network, built on top of existing physical networks, that provides a secure communications tunnel for data and other information transmitted between networks (NIST SP 800-46).

**VPN token:**  A device, possibly physical, that an authorized user of the VPN is given to ease authentication.

**watermarking:**  *See* **Digital Watermarking**.

# References

[1] URLs are valid as of the publication date of this book.

[2] **AICPA 2002** American Institute for CPA. *Consideration of Fraud in a Financial Statement Audit (AU 316.02).* American Institute for CPA, 2002; www.aicpa.org/Research/Standards/AuditAttest/Download ableDocuments/AU-00316.pdf.

[3] **Alberts 2003** C. Alberts and A. Dorofee. *Managing Information Security Risks: The OCTAVE® Approach* (Boston: Addison-Wesley, 2003).

[4] **Andersen 2004** D.F. Andersen, D.M. Cappelli, J.J. Gonzalez, M. Mojtahedzadeh, A.P. Moore, E. Rich, J.M. Sarriegui, T.J. Shimeall, J.M. Stanton, E. Weaver, and A. Zagonel. "Preliminary System Dynamics Maps of the Insider Cyber-Threat Problem." In *Proceedings of the 22nd International Conference of the System Dynamics Society,* July 2004.

[5] **Band 2006** S.R. Band, D.M. Cappelli, L.F. Fischer, A.P. Moore, E.D. Shaw, and R.F. Trzeciak. "Comparing Insider IT Sabotage and Espionage: A Model-Based Analysis." *Software Engineering Institute Technical Report CMU/SEI-2006-TR-026,* Carnegie Mellon University, December 2006; www.cert.org/archive/pdf/06tr026.pdf.

[6] **Cappelli 2006** D.M. Cappelli, A.G. Desai, A.P. Moore, T.J. Shimeall, E.A. Weaver, and B.J. Willke. "Management and Education of the Risk of Insider Threat (MERIT): System Dynamics Modeling of Computer System Sabotage." In *Proceedings of the 24th International Conference of the System Dynamics Society,* July 2006.

[7] **Cappelli 2007** D.M. Cappelli, A.G. Desai, A.P. Moore, T.J. Shimeall, E.A. Weaver, and B.J. Willke. "Management and Education of the Risk of Insider Threat (MERIT): Mitigating the Risk of Sabotage to Employers' Information, Systems, or Networks." *Software Engineering Institute Technical Note CMU/SEI-2006-TN-041*, March 2007; www.sei .cmu.edu/reports/06tn041.pdf.

[8] **Cappelli 2008a** D.M. Cappelli, T. Caron, R.F. Trzeciak, and A.P. Moore. "Spotlight On: Programming Techniques Used as an Insider Attack Tool." *Joint CyLab (CMU) and CERT (SEI) Report*, December 2008; www .cert.org/archive/pdf/insiderthreat_programmers_1208.pdf.

[9] **Cappelli 2008b** D.M. Cappelli, A.P. Moore, R.F. Trzeciak, and T.J. Shimeall. "Common Sense Guide to Prevention and Detection of Insider Threats: 3rd Edition." *Joint CyLab (CMU) and CERT (SEI) Report*, September 2008 (updated from July 2006 and April 2005); www.cert.org/archive/pdf/CSG-V3.pdf.

[10] **Cone 2006** B.D. Cone, M.F. Thompson, C.E. Irvine, and T.D. Nguyen. "Cyber Security Training and Awareness Through Game Play." In *IFIP International Federation for Information Processing*, Volume 201, Security and Privacy in Dynamic Environments; S. Fischer-Hubner, K. Rannenberg, L. Yngstrom, and S. Lindskog, Eds. (Boston: Springer, 2006), pp. 431–436.

[11] **Cordova 1996** D.I. Cordova and M.R. Lepper. "Intrinsic Motivation and the Process of Learning: Beneficial Effects of Contextualization, Personalization, and Choice." *Journal of Education Psychology* 88: pp. 715–730, 1996.

[12] **Cressey 1974** D.R. Cressey. *Other People's Money: A Study in the Social Psychology of Embezzlement* (Montclair, NJ: Patterson Smith, 1972).

[13] **CSO 2011a** *CSO* Magazine, Secret Service, Software Engineering Institute CERT Program at Carnegie Mellon University, and Deloitte. *2011 CyberSecurity Watch Survey: Press Release*, January 2011; www .cert.org/archive/pdf/CyberSecuritySurvey2011.pdf.

[14] **CSO 2011b** *CSO* Magazine, Secret Service, Software Engineering Institute CERT Program at Carnegie Mellon University, and Deloitte. *2011 CyberSecurity Watch Survey: Data*, January 2011; www.cert.org/ archive/pdf/CyberSecuritySurvey2011Data.pdf.

[15] **Duran 2009** F.A. Duran, S.H. Conrad, G.N. Conrad, D.P. Duggan, and E.B. Held. "Building a System for Insider Security." *IEEE Security and Privacy*, pp. 30–38, November/December 2009.

[16] **Foroughi 2008** F. Foroughi. "The Application of System Dynamics for Managing Information Security Insider-Threats of IT Organization." In *Proceedings of the World Congress on Engineering 2008*, Vol. I, WCE 2008, July 2–4, 2008, London, U.K.

[17] **Forrester 1994** J.W. Forrester. "Learning through System Dynamics as Preparation for the 21st Century." Keynote address for Systems Thinking and Dynamic Modeling Conference for K–12 Education, 1994.

[18] **Gonzalez 2003** J.J. Gonzalez, Ed. *From Modeling to Managing Security: A System Dynamics Approach.* Vol. 35, Research Series (Kristiansand, Norway: Norwegian Academic Press, 2003).

[19] **Greitzer 2008** F.L. Greitzer, A.P. Moore, D.M. Cappelli, D.H. Andrews, L.A. Carroll, and T.D. Hull. "Combating the Insider Cyber Threat." *IEEE Security and Privacy* 6(1): January/February 2008.

[20] **Groessler 2004** A. Groessler. "Don't Let History Repeat Itself – Methodological Issues Concerning the Use of Simulators in Teaching and Experimentation." *System Dynamics Review* 20(3): pp. 263–274, 2004.

[21] **Hanley 2009** M. Hanley, A.P. Moore, D.M. Cappelli, and R.F. Trzeciak. "Spotlight On: Malicious Insiders with Ties to the Internet Underground Community." *Joint CyLab (CMU) and CERT (SEI) Report*, March 2009; www.cert.org/archive/pdf/CyLab%20Insider%20Threat%20Quarterly%20on%20Internet%20Underground%20-%20March%202009P.pdf.

[22] **Hanley 2010** M. Hanley. "Candidate Technical Controls and Indicators of Insider Attack from Socio-Technical Models and Data." In *Proceedings of the 2010 NSA Center of Academic Excellence (CAE) Workshop on Insider Threat*, November 2010 (also published as *SEI Technical Note CMU/SEI-2011-TN-003*, January 2011).

[23] **Hanley 2011a** M. Hanley, J. Montelibano. "Insider Threat Control: Using Centralized Logging to Detect Data Exfiltration Near Insider Termination." *SEI Technical Note CMU/SEI-2011-TN-024*, Software Engineering Institute, Carnegie Mellon University, October 2011.

[24] **Hanley 2011b** M. Hanley, T. Dean, W. Schroeder, M. Houy, R. F. Trzeciak, and J. Montelibano. "An Analysis of Technical Observations in Insider Theft of Intellectual Property Cases." *SEI Technical Note CMU/SEI-2011-TN-006*, Software Engineering Institute, Carnegie Mellon University, 2011.

[25] **Keeney 2005** M.M. Keeney, E.F. Kowalski, D.M. Cappelli, A.P. Moore, T.J. Shimeall, and S.N. Rogers. "Insider Threat Study: Computer System Sabotage in Critical Infrastructure Sectors." *Joint SEI and U.S. Secret Service Report*, May 2005; www.cert.org/archive/pdf/insidercross051105.pdf.

[26] **King 2011** C. King. "Spotlight On: Malicious Insiders and Organized Crime Activity." *SEI Technical Note CMU/SEI-2011-TN-025*, September 2011.

[27] **Kowalski 2008a** E.F. Kowalski, M.M. Keeney, D.M. Cappelli, and A.P. Moore. "Insider Threat Study: Illicit Cyber Activity in the Information Technology and Telecommunications Sector." *Joint SEI and U.S. Secret Service Report*, January 2008; www.cert.org/archive/pdf/insiderthreat_it2008.pdf.

[28] **Kowalski 2008b** E.F. Kowalski, T. Conway, S. Keverline, M. Williams, D. McCauley, D.M. Cappelli, B.W. Willke, and A.P. Moore. "Insider Threat Study: Illicit Cyber Activity in the Government Sector." *Joint SEI and U.S. Secret Service Report*, January 2008; www.cert.org/archive/pdf/insiderthreat_gov2008.pdf.

[29] **Lane 1995** D. Lane. "On a Resurgence of Management Simulations and Games." *The Journal of the Operational Research Society* 46(5): pp. 604–625, 1995.

[30] **Martinez-Moyano 2006** I. Martinez-Moyano, E. Rich, S.H. Conrad, and D. Andersen. "Modeling the Emergence of Insider Threat Vulnerabilities." Informs Winter Simulation Conference, Monterey, CA, 2006.

[31] **Martinez-Moyano 2008** I. Martinez-Moyano, E. Rich, S.H. Conrad, D. Andersen, and T. Stewart. "A Behavioral Theory of Insider-Threat Risks: A System Dynamics Approach." *ACM Transactions on Modeling and Computer Simulation* 18(2): 2008. Abstract.

[32] **Mayo 2007** M.J. Mayo. "Games for Science and Engineering Education." *Communications of the ACM* 50(7): pp. 31–35, July 2007.

[33] **Meadows 1974** D.L. Meadows, W.W. Behrens, D.H. Meadows, R.F. Naill, J. Randers, and E.K.O. Zahn. *Dynamics of Growth in a Finite World* (Cambridge, MA: Wright-Allen Press, Inc., 1974).

[34] **Melara 2003** C. Melara, J.M. Sarriegui, J.J. Gonzalez, A. Sawicka, and D.L. Cooke. "A system dynamics model of an insider attack on an

information system." In *Proceedings of the 21st International Conference of the System Dynamics Society*, New York City, July 20–24, 2003.

[35] **Montelibano 2011** J. Montelibano. "Insider Threat Control: Using a SIEM Signature to Detect Potential Precursors to IT Sabotage." *CERT Program Technical Report, SEI Technical Note CMU/SEI-2011-TN-021*, Software Engineering Institute, Carnegie Mellon University, April 2011.

[36] **Moore 2006** A.P. Moore and R.S. Antao. "Improving Management of Information Technology: System Dynamics Analysis of IT Controls in Context." In *Proceedings of the 24th International System Dynamics Conference*, July 2006.

[37] **Moore 2007** A.P. Moore, D.M. Cappelli, H. Joseph, and R.F. Trzeciak. "An Experience Using System Dynamics to Facilitate an Insider Threat Workshop." In *Proceedings of the 25th International Conference of the System Dynamics Society*, July 2007; www.cert.org/archive/pdf/ISDC2007.pdf.

[38] **Moore 2008** A.P. Moore, D.M. Cappelli, and R.F. Trzeciak. "The 'Big Picture' of Insider IT Sabotage Across U.S. Critical Infrastructures." In *Insider Attack and Cyber Security: Beyond the Hacker*. S.J. Stolfo et al., Eds., Springer Science + Business Media, LLC, 2008 (also published in *SEI Technical Report - CMU/SEI-2008-TR-009*); www.cert.org/archive/pdf/08tr009.pdf).

[39] **Moore 2009** A.P. Moore, D.M. Cappelli, T. Caron, E. Shaw, and R.F. Trzeciak. "Insider Theft of Intellectual Property for Business Advantage: A Preliminary Model." In *Proceedings of the 1st International Workshop on Managing Insider Security Threats (MIST2009)*, Purdue University, West Lafayette, IN, June 16, 2009; www.cert.org/insider_threat/docs/Insider_Theft_of_IP_Model_MIST09.pdf.

[40] **Moore 2011a** A.P. Moore, D.M. Cappelli, T. Caron, E. Shaw, and R.F. Trzeciak. "A Preliminary Model of Insider Theft of Intellectual Property." *Journal of Wireless Mobile Networks, Ubiquitous Computing, and Dependable Applications* 2(1), Special Issue: Addressing Insider Threats and Information Leakage, 2011, pp. 28–49 (also published as *SEI Technical Note CMU/SEI-2011-TN-013*).

[41] **Moore 2011b** A.P. Moore, A. Cummings, and D. Spooner. "Modeling and Analysis of Insider Fraud." In *2010 CERT Research Annual Report*, 2011.

[42] **Phelps 2006** D. Phelps and J. Gathegi. "Information Security Self-Efficacy." In *Proceedings of the 2006 Americas Conference on Information Systems* (AMCIS 2006), Acapulco, Mexico, August 2006.

[43] **Randazzo 2004** M.R. Randazzo, M.M. Keeney, E.F. Kowalski, D.M. Cappelli, and A.P. Moore. "Insider Threat Study: Illicit Cyber Activity in the Banking and Finance Sector." *Joint SEI and U.S. Secret Service Report,* August 2004; www.secretservice.gov/ntac/its_report_040820.pdf.

[44] **Repenning 2001** N. Repenning and J.D. Sterman. "Nobody Ever Gets Credit for Fixing Problems That Never Happened: Creating and Sustaining Process Improvement." *California Management Review* 43(4): pp. 64–88, 2001.

[45] **Ricci 1996** K. Ricci, E. Salas, and J.A. Cannon-Bowers. "Do computer based games facilitate knowledge acquisition and retention?" *Military Psychology* 8(4): pp. 295–307, 1996.

[46] **Rich 2005** E. Rich, I.J. Martinez-Moyano, S. Conrad, D.M. Cappelli, A.P. Moore, T.J. Shimeall, D.F. Andersen, J.J. Gonzalez, R.J. Ellison, H.F. Lipson, D.A. Mundie, J.M. Sarriegui, A. Sawicka, T.R. Stewart, J.M. Torres, E.A. Weaver, and J. Wiik. "Simulating Insider Cyber-Threat Risks: A Model-Based Case and a Case-Based Model." In *Proceedings of the 23rd International Conference of the System Dynamics Society,* July 2005; www.cert.org/insider_threat/docs/insider_threatISDC2005.pdf.

[47] **Spooner 2008** D. Spooner, D.M. Cappelli, A.P. Moore, and R.F. Trzeciak. "Spotlight On: Insider Theft of Intellectual Property inside the U.S. Involving Foreign Governments or Organizations." *Joint CyLab (CMU) and CERT (SEI) Report,* December 2008; www.cert.org/archive/pdf/insiderthreat_programmers_1208.pdf.

[48] **Sterman 2000** J.D. Sterman. *Business Dynamics: Systems Thinking and Modeling for a Complex World* (McGraw-Hill, 2000).

[49] **Weiland 2010** R.M. Weiland, A.P. Moore, D.M. Cappelli, R.F. Trzeciak, and D. Spooner. "Spotlight On: Insider Threat from Trusted Business Partners." *Joint CyLab (CMU) and CERT (SEI) Report,* February 2010; www.cert.org/archive/pdf/TrustedBusinessPartners0210.pdf.

# About the Authors

 **Dawn Cappelli,** CISSP, is technical manager of the CERT Insider Threat Center and the Enterprise Threat and Vulnerability Management Team at Carnegie Mellon University's Software Engineering Institute. She has devoted the past ten years of her career to helping organizations in government and industry to protect themselves from the ultimate betrayal of trust: insider threats. She works with the Secret Service, U.S. Department of Homeland Security, U.S. Department of Defense, and other government agencies and private organizations. She leads a team of more than 30 security analysts who address real-world problems by performing modeling and analysis, creating practical solutions, and disseminating solutions broadly to government and industry. Dawn has more than 30 years of experience in software engineering, technical project management, information security, and research. She is often an invited speaker at national and international venues, is adjunct professor in Carnegie Mellon's Heinz College of Public Policy and Management, and is vice-chair for the CERT Computer Security Incident Handler Certification Advisory Board. She is on the program committee for several prominent security conferences, and was recently awarded the Software Engineering Institute Director's Office Award of Excellence. Before joining CMU in 1988 she worked for Westinghouse as a software engineer developing nuclear power systems. She spends every spare moment she can at her cabin in the mountains with her family, and volunteers her time for the Friends of Flight 93.

**Andrew P. Moore** is a lead researcher in the CERT Insider Threat Center and senior member of the technical staff at Carnegie Mellon University's Software Engineering Institute. He explores ways to improve the security, survivability, and resiliency of enterprise systems through insider threat and defense modeling, incident management, and architecture engineering and analysis. Andy also works with teams across the SEI applying modeling and simulation techniques to hard system and software engineering problems. Before joining the SEI in 2000, he worked for the Naval Research Laboratory (NRL) investigating high-assurance system development methods for the U.S. Navy. He has more than 20 years of experience developing and applying mission-critical system analysis methods and tools, leading to the transfer of critical technology to both industry and the military. Andy has served as principal investigator on numerous projects sponsored by NSA and DARPA; has served on numerous computer assurance and security conference program committees and working groups; and has published two book chapters and a wide variety of technical journal and conference papers. His research interests include computer and network attack modeling and analysis, IT management control analysis, survivable systems engineering, formal assurance techniques, and security risk management. Andy received a master's degree in computer science from Duke University, a bachelor's degree in mathematics from the College of Wooster, and a graduate certificate in system dynamics from Worcester Polytechnic Institute.

**Randall F. Trzeciak** is currently the technical team lead for the Insider Threat Research Group in the CERT Insider Threat Center and senior member of the technical staff at Carnegie Mellon University's Software Engineering Institute. The team focuses on insider threat research, exploring both the technical and nontechnical ways in which insiders have harmed organizations; threat analysis and modeling; and incident management. Prior to joining Carnegie Mellon University in 1999, he worked for nine years at Software Technology Incorporated in Alexandria, Virginia, supporting multiple contracts primarily at the Naval Research Laboratory (NRL), building and supporting large-scale information systems. Randy has more than 20 years of experience in software engineering; project management; information security; and database design, development, and maintenance. For more than ten years, Randy has been an adjunct faculty member at Carnegie Mellon's Heinz College of Information Systems and Management. He was invited to chair the Security and Risk track at the 2012 SEPG Conference. Randy regularly represents the Insider Threat Center by speaking at security conferences around the United States and has also spoken internationally. Randy holds a master's degree in management from the University of Maryland, and bachelor's degrees in management information systems and business administration from Geneva College.

# Index

S.R. Band, D.M. Cappelli, L.F. Fischer, A.P. Moore, E.D. Shaw, and R.F. Trzeciak, "Comparing Insider IT Sabotage and Espionage: A Model-Based Analysis," *Software Engineering Institute Technical Report CMU/SEI-2006-TR-026*, Carnegie Mellon University, December 2006. http://www.cert.org/archive/pdf/06tr026.pdf.

D.M. Cappelli, T. Caron, R.F. Trzeciak, and A.P. Moore, "Spotlight On: Programming Techniques Used as an Insider Attack Tool," Joint CyLab (CMU) and CERT (SEI) Report, December 2008. http://www.cert.org/archive/pdf/insiderthreat_programmers_1208.pdf

D.M. Cappelli, Moore, A.P., Trzeciak, R.F. and Shimeall, T.J., "Common Sense Guide to Prevention and Detection of Insider Threats: 3rd Edition," Joint CyLab (CMU) and CERT (SEI) Report, September 2008 (updated from July 2006 and April 2005). http://www.cert.org/archive/pdf/CSGV3.pdf

D.M. Cappelli, A.G. Desai, A.P. Moore, T.J. Shimeall, E.A. Weaver, B.J. Willke, "Management and Education of the Risk of Insider Threat (MERIT): Mitigating the Risk of Sabotage to Employers' Information, Systems, or Networks," *Software Engineering Institute Technical Note CMU/SEI-2006-TN-041*, March 2007. http://www.sei.cmu.edu/reports/06tn041.pdf

M. Hanley, J. Montelibano, "Insider Threat Control: Using Centralized Logging to Detect Data Exfiltration Near Insider Termination," *SEI Technical Note SEI-TN-024*, Software Engineering Institute, Carnegie Mellon University, October 2011.

M. Hanley, T. Dean, W. Schroeder, M. Houy, R.F. Trzeciak and J. Montelibano, "An Analysis of Technical Observations in Insider Theft of Intellectual Property Cases," *SEI Technical Note CMU/SEI-2011-TN-006*, Software Engineering Institute, Carnegie Mellon University, 2011.

M. Hanley, A.P. Moore, D.M. Cappelli, and R.F. Trzeciak, "Spotlight On: Malicious Insiders with Ties to the Internet Underground Community," Joint CyLab (CMU) and CERT (SEI) Report, March 2009. http://www.cert.org/archive/pdf/CyLab%20Insider%20Threat%20Quarterly%20on%20Internet%20Underground%20-%20March%202009P.pdf

C. King, "Spotlight On: Malicious Insiders and Organized Crime Activity," *SEI Technical Note CMU/SEI-2011-TN-025*, September 2011.

J. Montelibano, "Insider Threat Control: Using a SIEM Signature to Detect Potential Precursors to IT Sabotage," *SEI Technical Note SEI-TN-021*, Software Engineering Institute, Carnegie Mellon University, April 2011.

A.P. Moore, A. Cummings, and D. Spooner, "Modeling and Analysis of Insider Fraud," in 2010 CERT Research Annual Report, 2011.

D. Spooner, D.M. Cappelli, A.P. Moore, and R.F. Trzeciak, "Spotlight On: Insider Theft of Intellectual Property inside the U.S. Involving Foreign Governments or Organizations," Joint CyLab (CMU) and CERT (SEI) Report, December 2008. http://www.cert.org/archive/pdf/insiderthreat_programmers_1208.pdf

R.M. Weiland, A.P. Moore, D.M. Cappelli, R.F. Trzeciak, D. Spooner "Spotlight On: Insider Threat from Trusted Business Partners," Joint CyLab (CMU) and CERT (SEI) Report, February 2010. http://www.cert.org/archive/pdf/TrustedBusinessPartners0210.pdf

A.P. Moore, D.M. Cappelli, T. Caron, E. Shaw, and R.F. Trzeciak, "A Preliminary Model of Insider Theft of Intellectual Property." *SEI Technical Note CMU/SEI-2011-TN-013*.

A.P. Moore, D.M. Cappelli, and R.F. Trzeciak, "The 'Big Picture' of Insider IT Sabotage Across U.S. Critical Infrastructures," *SEI Technical Report CMU/SEI-2008-TR-009* http://www.cert.org/archive/pdf/08tr009.pdf)

M. Hanley, "Candidate Technical Controls and Indicators of Insider Attack from Socio-Technical Models and Data," in Proceedings of the 2010 NSA Center of Academic Excellence (CAE) Workshop on Insider Threat, November 2010 (also published as *SEI Technical Note CMU/SEI-2011-TN-003*, January 2011).

A.P. Moore, D.M. Cappelli, T. Caron, E. Shaw, and R.F. Trzeciak, "A Preliminary Model of Insider Theft of Intellectual Property." Journal of Wireless Mobile Networks, Ubiquitous Computing, and Dependable

Applications 2, 1 (Special Issue Addressing Insider Threats and Information Leakage, 2011): 28–49 (also published as *SEI Technical Note CMU/SEI-2011-TN-013*).

A.P. Moore, D.M. Cappelli, T. Caron, E. Shaw, and R.F. Trzeciak, "Insider Theft of Intellectual Property for Business Advantage: A Preliminary Model," in Proceedings of the 1st International Workshop on Managing Insider Security Threats (MIST2009), Purdue University, West Lafayette, USA, June 16, 2009. http://www.cert.org/insider_threat/docs/Insider_Theft_of_IP_Model_MIST09.pdf

A.P. Moore, D.M. Cappelli, and R.F. Trzeciak, "The 'Big Picture' of Insider IT Sabotage Across U.S. Critical Infrastructures," in *Insider Attack and Cyber Security: Beyond the Hacker*, eds. Stolfo, S.J., et. al., Springer Science + Business Media, LLC, 2008 (also published in SEI Technical Report - CMU/SEI-2008-TR-009 http://www.cert.org/archive/pdf/08tr009.pdf)

A.P. Moore, D.M. Cappelli, H. Joseph, R.F. Trzeciak, "An Experience Using System Dynamics to Facilitate an Insider Threat Workshop," in Proceedings 25th International Conference of the System Dynamics Society, July 2007. http://www.cert.org/archive/pdf/ISDC2007.pdf

*CSO* Magazine, Secret Service, Software Engineering Institute CERT Program at Carnegie Mellon University and Deloitte, 2011 CyberSecurity Watch Survey: Press Release, January 2011. http://www.cert.org/archive/pdf/CyberSecuritySurvey2011.pdf

*CSO* Magazine, Secret Service, Software Engineering Institute CERT Program at Carnegie Mellon University and Deloitte, 2011 CyberSecurity Watch Survey: Data, January 2011. http://www.cert.org/archive/pdf/CyberSecuritySurvey2011Data.pdf

M.M. Keeney, E.F. Kowalski, D.M. Cappelli, A.P. Moore, T.J. Shimeall, and S.N. Rogers, "Insider Threat Study: Computer System Sabotage in Critical Infrastructure Sectors," Joint SEI and U.S. Secret Service Report, May 2005. http://www.cert.org/archive/pdf/insidercross051105.pdf

E.F. Kowalski, M.M. Keeney, D.M. Cappelli, and A.P. Moore, "Insider Threat Study: Illicit Cyber Activity in the Information Technology and Telecommunications Sector," Joint SEI and U.S. Secret Service Report, January 2008. http://www.cert.org/archive/pdf/insiderthreat_it2008.pdf

E.F. Kowalski, T. Conway, S. Keverline, M. Williams, D. McCauley, D.M. Cappelli, B.W. Willke, and A.P. Moore, "Insider Threat Study: Illicit Cyber Activity in the Government Sector," Joint SEI and U.S. Secret Service Report, January 2008. http://www.cert.org/archive/pdf/insiderthreat_gov2008.pdf

M.R. Randazzo, M.M. Keeney, E.F. Kowalski, D.M. Cappelli, A.P. Moore, "Insider Threat Study: Illicit Cyber Activity in the Banking and Finance Sector," Joint SEI and U.S. Secret Service Report, 2004, August, available at http://www.secretservice.gov/ntac/its_report_040820.pdf.

## The CERT® Insider Threat Vulnerability Assessment: *Identify vulnerabilities and remediation strategies from the inside out.*

Do you know how vulnerable your organization is to its own insiders? Employees, contractors, or business partners can exploit their knowledge to attack your organization.

The CERT Insider Threat Center, part of Carnegie Mellon University's Software Engineering Institute, studies the technical and behavioral aspects of real insider compromises. Our Insider Threat Vulnerability Assessment for government, private, public, for-profit, and not-for-profit organizations is a confidential, on-site evaluation of your entire organization's ability to prevent, detect, and respond to insider threats. The results are incorporated into an actionable framework for managing your organization's vulnerability.

**To learn more about the Insider Threat Center, visit the CERT website: *http://www.cert.org/insider_threat*.**

**To learn more about the Insider Threat Assessment or to schedule one, email the Insider Threat Center staff: *insider-threat-feedback@cert.org*.**

# Safari Books Online

## FREE Online Edition

Your purchase of **The CERT® Guide to Insider Threats** includes access to a free online edition for 45 days through the **Safari Books Online** subscription service. Nearly every Addison-Wesley Professional book is available online through **Safari Books Online**, along with thousands of books and videos from publishers such as Cisco Press, Exam Cram, IBM Press, O'Reilly Media, Prentice Hall, Que, Sams, and VMware Press.

**Safari Books Online** is a digital library providing searchable, on-demand access to thousands of technology, digital media, and professional development books and videos from leading publishers. With one monthly or yearly subscription price, you get unlimited access to learning tools and information on topics including mobile app and software development, tips and tricks on using your favorite gadgets, networking, project management, graphic design, and much more.

## Activate your FREE Online Edition at informit.com/safarifree

**STEP 1:** Enter the coupon code: PRIVHFH.

**STEP 2:** New Safari users, complete the brief registration form. Safari subscribers, just log in.

If you have difficulty registering on Safari or accessing the online edition, please e-mail customer-service@safaribooksonline.com